THREE RIVERS COOK

The Good Taste of Pittsburgh

Cover Design and Illustrations by Susan Gaca.

CHILD HEALTH ASSOCIATION OF SEWICKLEY, INC.

Sewickley, Pennsylvania

1990

1994 Update

Since its introduction in April of 1990, THREE RIVERS COOKBOOK III, published by the Child Health Association of Sewickley, has become a favorite of cooks all over the United States. Although our primary market is Western Pennsylvania, our books are sold in bookstores all over the country, as well as by direct sale from our volunteer run office. Eighty thousand copies have already been sold. This newest printing will bring the number of copies in print to 100,000, quite a milestone for any publication. When you add this to the over 600,000 copies of THREE RIVERS COOKBOOK I and THREE RIVERS COOKBOOK II already in print, the numbers really get impressive.

Running an all volunteer business is quite a challenge, but when you have a membership which is committed to a common goal, improving the lives of children, it can be a genuine pleasure. Cookbooks are our primary, but by no means only, source of funding. Our annual ball, biannual house tour, special events such as golf tournaments, concerts, dramatic productions, and our used sporting good sale, have all contributed to our funding. Our newest event is the Sewickley Country Carnival, two days of games, entertainment, and delicious THREE RIVERS COOKBOOK food to delight the whole family. Through the hard work of the 70 active members who make up the Child Health Association of Sewickley, over $1,900,000 have been granted to child related charities throughout Western Pennsylvania. The help and support of our 200 associate members is essential to our success. Their past efforts have laid the groundwork for everything we do.

"Quality recipes for better quality life for children" is the goal of THREE RIVERS COOKBOOKS. Libraries, women's shelters, performing arts groups, a special school for troubled teens, and various social service agencies are but a few of the recipients who have benefited from our efforts to aid the physically or mentally handicapped child, the abused child and the well child. We are proud of the variety of help our cookbooks have enabled us to provide. We thank you for supporting our efforts by purchasing our cookbooks. We hope you will enjoy using THREE RIVERS COOKBOOK III as much as we have enjoyed bringing it to you.

Mary Lee Parrington

June, 1994

Mary Lee Parrington
President

Our grateful appreciation to the following companies and foundations for their generosity in helping to underwrite the first printing of THREE RIVERS COOKBOOK III.

Acacia Group, Inc.
The All American Gourmet
Allegheny Ludlum Steel, Inc.
Dollar Bank
H.J. Heinz Company Foundation
Larson Sales Company
IBM
Johnson and Higgins of PA
Marsh & McLennan, Inc.
Metaltech
Mulach Steel Corporation
O/P/U/S/, Inc. - Ann Connelly
S.P. Kinney Engineers, Inc.
Steelmet, Inc.
WEEP/WDSY

First Printing	50,000 April, 1990
Second Printing	30,000 December, 1990
Third Printing	20,000 June, 1994

For additional copies, use the order blanks
in the back of the book or write directly to:

THREE RIVERS COOKBOOKS
Child Health Association of Sewickley, Inc.
1108 Ohio River Boulevard
Sewickley, Pennsylvania 15143
(412) 741-3221 or (800) 624-8753

Printed by
Geyer Printing Company, Inc.
Pittsburgh, Pennsylvania

Founded in 1923, the Child Health Association of Sewickley is a non-profit organization dedicated to promoting the welfare of children. For nearly 67 years, its volunteer and financial commitment to the greater Pittsburgh community has been extraordinary. Since incorporation in 1946, the Association has given grants to 174 child-related agencies totalling $1,521,086. The membership has volunteered over 75,000 hours to local community projects. Child Health maintains a dental hygiene program in four schools and offers vision screening at ten pre-school sites.

Child Health is unique in its giving record. While most other funding organizations allocate to projects in a single service area, Child Health applies funds in the arts, health-related, and educational fields. Child Health supports fledgling organizations and new program start-ups as well as established groups. Recent recipients include Pittsburgh Children's and Carnegie Museums, numerous libraries, St. Peter's Child Development Centers, Parent and Child Guidance Center, summer camps for handicapped youth, the Association of Retarded Citizens, D.T. Watson Rehabilitative Hospital, the Children's Festival, and the Pittsburgh Ballet Theatre School.

The outstanding success of THREE RIVERS COOKBOOK I, introduced in 1973, and THREE RIVERS COOKBOOK II, in 1981, accounts for the majority of these disbursements. In all, an active membership of up to 70 women over the past sixteen years have processed and promoted 554,000 copies through twenty-four printings of these two popular cookbooks. In addition, a loyal associate membership has supported Child Health's other fund raising endeavors. House tours, golf tournaments, jazz and dramatic productions, and an annual charity ball are examples of this teamwork.

It is a privilege to present the third volume in Child Health's THREE RIVERS COOKBOOK trilogy. We are confident that you will find as equally fine a selection of recipes in THREE RIVERS COOKBOOK III as you found in Volumes I and II. These volumes have consistently ranked among the top ten community cookbooks. We would expect nothing less from Volume III. We appreciate you, our customers, for your enthusiasm and look forward to serving you for years to come. Thank you for helping us to continue our commitment to the children of southwestern Pennsylvania.

Susan D. Craig

May, 1990

Susan D. Craig
President

Pittsburghers and other fans of THREE RIVERS COOKBOOKS I and II have continued their reputation for generosity. In the tradition of our first two volumes, thousands of recipes were received and carefully tested in order to select more than 450 top-rated recipes to fill this, our third volume.

Cooking methods and culinary preferences do change over the years, so in order to keep pace with these changes, we have included microwave and health-conscious selections, as well as regional and ethnic recipes. However, you told us by the types of recipes you submitted, that you wanted Three Rivers Cookbooks to continue to be general cookbooks containing recipes that are not only dependably good, but are quick and easy to prepare.

Once again we extend our sincere thanks to all of you who so generously submitted your favorite recipes. We do not claim that all recipes included are original, only that they are tried and true favorites of the contributors as well as the testers. Due to space limitations, we were unable to include all of the outstanding recipes which were received and tested. Editorial adjustments have been made in order to standardize measurements and procedures, and to provide you with appropriate guidelines in preparation. We trust that liberties taken will meet with the approval of our contributors. Finally, we extend our special thanks to our families, fellow Child Health members and associate members, and friends. Without their unfailing support during the past two years, this book would not have been possible.

Jane A. Birnie . . . . Chairman
Marilyn J. Sittig . . . . Co-Chairman
Susan Gaca . . . . Artist
Karen C. Rossin . . . . Testing-Chairman
Lynn B. Popovich . . . . Testing-Chairman
Christine D. Morrison . . . . Recipe-Chairman
Anne F. Dithrich . . . . Commentaries

6

CONTENTS

INDEX OF ILLUSTRATIONS

©**GALS SEWICKLEY CALENDAR**

OPENERS

PENNSYLVANIA BREWING COMPANY

The home of Penn Pilsner, a microbrewery, stands on the site of the former Eberhardt and Ober Brewery (1852). At the foot of Troy Hill in the North Side, this stunning 4 million dollar renovation as a business complex provides Pittsburghers with an authentic beer hall and Penn Pilsner on tap.

Additional illustrations in this section:

These hand painted mugs are from the dining room of the rectory of St. Anthony's Chapel on Harpster Street in Troy Hill. Here, in 1876, Father Mollinger, a wealthy nobleman who took his holy orders, recreated the elegance of his native Belgium.

The Byers-Lyon house on the North Side is an Alden and Harlow design. It has 90 rooms and 14 baths and served as a double house for two familes.

A stained glass window of William Penn graces the entrance of the Byers-Lyon house. The house now serves as a student union for Allegheny Community College.

Beulah Church is Pittsburgh's oldest church (1837). Located in Churchill Borough, it stands in perfect preservation. Thirty-four revolutionary war veterans are buried here.

The Pirate Parrot, the Pittsburgh Pirates' mascot.

The Majestic is a 4 million dollar, 1,000 passenger Mississippi-style side wheeler and is the latest addition to the Gateway Clipper Fleet.

This "water babies" fountain is the work of Edith Parsons. It was designed for the garden of Mr. and Mrs. George Clapp of Edgeworth in 1903.

The Sarah Heinz house stands near Heinz-USA providing a recreation club for boys and girls ages 7 through 18.

BEVERAGES

BOURBON SLUSH

"A lot different from Bourbon and branch"

2 cups sugar
9 cups water
12 oz. frozen orange juice, concentrate
12 oz. frozen lemonade, concentrate
2 cups Bourbon
soda - Squirt, Wink, etc.

Bring the sugar and water to a boil and simmer for 15 minutes. Let this syrup cool. Then add frozen juices and Bourbon and put in the freezer for a few days. When serving, fill a glass ½ full of slush and ½ full of soda.

Preparation: 5 min.	Easy	Yield: 2½ qts.
Cooking: 15-20 min.	Must do ahead	Must freeze

Jane Birnie

IRISH CREME

1 fifth Scotch (cheapest)
1 12-oz. can evaporated milk
1 14-oz. can Eagle Brand milk
1 pint Half & Half cream
2 eggs, well beaten
1 tsp. vanilla
¼ cup chocolate syrup

Blend all ingredients together in large container. Put into bottles and store in refrigerator for 3 months, if possible.

Preparation: 15 min.	Easy	Yield: 3 fifths
	Must do ahead	

Ruth P. Truckey

SLUSHY BRANDY

"Don't leave this until the last minute"

9 cups water
2 cups Brandy
1 12-oz. can frozen lemonade
  concentrate, thawed
1 12-oz. can frozen orange
  juice concentrate, thawed
fresh mint sprigs (garnish)

Combine first 4 ingredients in 4 quart container. Cover and freeze at least 8 hours, preferably overnight (mixture will remain slushy). Spoon into individual glasses and garnish with mint.

Preparation: 5 min.   Easy   Yield: 3½ qts.
    Must do ahead   Must freeze

Tina Morrison

CAROLYN'S COMFORT PUNCH

"This is cold comfort"

1 fifth Southern Comfort
6 oz. fresh lemon juice
6 oz. frozen orange juice,
  concentrate
6 oz. frozen lemonade,
  concentrate
3 quarts 7-Up
ice
lemon slices

Pre-chill 7-Up and Southern Comfort separately. Mix the first 4 ingredients. Add the 7-Up last. Add ice and lemon slices.

Preparation: 10 min.   Easy   Serves: 32
    Can do ahead

The Committee

CHAMPAGNE PUNCH

"A bridesmaid's favorite"

6 lemons
1 cup sugar
1 qt. water
1 6-oz. can frozen orange juice,
  concentrate
1 46-oz. can pineapple juice
1 bottle Champagne, well-chilled
8 oz. bottle ginger ale

Thinly peel rind from lemons. Combine rinds with sugar and water; bring to a boil. Stir until sugar is dissolved. Cover. Simmer 5 minutes. Strain. Squeeze lemons and add orange juice concentrate, pineapple juice, and hot lemon syrup. Stir until well blended. Chill thoroughly. Just before serving, pour over a ring mold of ice; add Champagne and ginger ale. Serve at once.

Preparation: 20 min.   Easy   Yield: 3½ qts.
Cooking: 5 min.   Must do ahead   Must freeze

Karen Rossin

MAKE-AHEAD WINE COOLERS
"A happy summertime drink"

1 6-oz. can frozen cranberry juice cocktail concentrate, thawed
1 6-oz. can frozen orange juice concentrate, thawed
1 6-oz. can frozen pineapple juice concentrate, thawed
4 cups dry white wine
4 cups carbonated water

Garnish:
orange wedges
skewered cranberries OR
pineapple chunks

In a small air-tight container (or jar with screwtop lid), stir together all concentrates. Cover and chill (stays good up to 2 weeks). Before serving, put fruit concentrate in a 3-quart pitcher; add wine and water and mix well. Serve over ice in tall glasses. Garnish.

FOR SINGLE SERVING:
Add ⅓ cup wine and ⅓ cup of carbonated water to 3 Tbsp. of concentrate.

Preparation: 10 min.   Easy   Serves: 12
                          Must do ahead   Can freeze

Tina Morrison

SPICED HOT TOMATO BOUILLON

1 large can V-8 juice
2½ cups boiling water with 3 beef broth cubes (OR 2 cans beef broth)
sugar and salt, to taste
dash Tabasco sauce
½ cup orange juice
peel of a whole orange

In a cheesecloth bag, place:
½ stick cinnamon
4-5 whole cloves
¼ tsp. fresh grated nutmeg
4-5 whole allspice berries

½ tsp. instant Constant Comment Tea
sour cream and chives for garnish

Simmer all ingredients, except tea, for an hour or two. Add the tea at the very end. Serve hot with garnish of sour cream and chives.

Preparation: 15 min.   Easy   Serves: 6-8
Cooking: 1 hr. +   Can do ahead   Can freeze

Mary Anne Riley

SPICY AUTUMN CIDER

"For spooks and goblins, large and small"

1 gallon apple cider
1 orange
4 tsp. whole cloves
1 lemon, halved
6 cinnamon sticks
1 cup orange juice (preferably fresh-squeezed)
2 cups dry white wine (optional)
1 cup fresh lemon juice

Place cider in large saucepan. Pierce orange with cloves and add to cider. Add lemon halves and cinnamon sticks. Boil 5 minutes; reduce heat and simmer for 10 minutes. Add remaining ingredients. Simmer for 1 hour, skimming top as needed. Can be prepared ahead. Store in refrigerator in non-aluminum container. Reheat to serve.

Preparation: 5 min.   Easy   Serves: a crowd
Cooking: 1 hr. 15 min.   Can do ahead

Clee McBee

MULLED CIDER

2 quarts apple cider or juice
1 orange, sliced
1 lemon, sliced
2 Tbsp. maple syrup or honey
4 sticks cinnamon
6 whole cloves
¼ tsp. nutmeg
¼ tsp. powdered ginger

In large saucepan, combine all of the ingredients. Bring mixture to a boil. Reduce the heat to low and simmer the cider for 30-40 minutes. Strain and serve hot.

Preparation: 10 min.   Easy   Serves: 16
Cooking: 35-45 min.   Can do ahead

Diane Abell

HOT CRANBERRY TEA

"Serve this at a Holiday Ladies' Tea"

32 oz. jar Ocean Spray cranberry juice
½ cup sugar
2 cups brewed hot tea
2 cinnamon sticks
10 cloves

Combine all ingredients in pan and heat gently. Strain and heat when ready to serve.

Preparation: 10 min.   Easy   Yield: 1 qt. +
Cooking: 30 min.   Can do ahead

Catherine Clarke Johnson

APPETIZERS

SPINACH FETA STRUDEL SLICES
"Fun with Phyllo"

2 lbs. spinach
¼ cup butter
12 green onions, minced
6 oz. Feta cheese, chilled and
   crumbled (1½ cups)
½ cup parsley, minced
4 egg whites
4 tsp. dillweed
salt and pepper, to taste
1 cup unsalted butter
¾ lb. Phyllo leaves
½ cup Italian bread crumbs

Cook spinach until tender, cut off any hard stems. Rinse with cool water and drain. Melt ¼ cup butter in skillet and sauté onions. Place all ingredients in processor, except Phyllo, unsalted butter and bread crumbs. Blend well. Melt unsalted butter in saucepan. Place first sheet of Phyllo on wax paper and brush with butter; then sprinkle with bread crumbs. Continue using all sheets and butter and bread crumbs - on last sheet, spread spinach mixture. Roll like a jelly roll. Place on cookie sheet. Brush with butter. Bake at 375° for 30-35 minutes. Slice before serving.

Preparation:	20 min.	Easy
Cooking:	30-35 min.	Can do ahead

Yield: 20-24 slices
Can freeze before baking

Carol Klauss

STUFFED GRAPE LEAVES

"Use your youngest grape leaves"

40 grape leaves
cold water
6 oz. ground veal
6 oz. ground beef
⅓ cup chopped dill
6 mint leaves, chopped
3 Tbsp. grated firm Goat cheese
2 medium onions, chopped
⅔ cup cooked rice
salt and pepper
2 carrots
1 medium onion, sliced
2 cups chicken bouillon

Blanch grape leaves for 5 minutes. Drain and rinse in cold water. Combine veal, beef, dill, mint leaves, Goat cheese, 2 onions chopped, rice, salt and pepper. Divide this mixture into 36 parts. Place 1 part on each leaf and roll to enclose. Slice carrots, the other onion, and place on bottom of roasting pan. Cover with the 4 remaining grape leaves. Arrange stuffed leaves on top. Pour bouillon over all. Bring to a boil; reduce heat and simmer for 35 minutes. Drain and keep warm.

Preparation:	1 hour	Moderately difficult	Yield: 36
Cooking:	40 min.	Can do ahead	Can freeze

Paula A. Doebler

CRANBERRY MEATBALLS

2 lbs. ground beef
1 cup corn flakes
½ cup parsley
2 Tbsp. soy sauce
¼ tsp. pepper
½ tsp. garlic salt
⅓ cup ketchup
2 Tbsp. onion
1 16-oz. can cranberry sauce
1 12-oz. jar chili sauce
2 Tbsp. brown sugar
1 tsp. lemon juice

Mix beef, corn flakes, parsley, soy sauce, pepper, garlic salt, ketchup and onion together; then roll into little meatballs. Mix the cranberry sauce, chili sauce, brown sugar and lemon juice together and pour over meatballs. Bake at 350° for 30 minutes in a shallow baking dish, uncovered.

Preparation:	20 min.	Easy	Yield: 60 meatballs
Cooking:	30 min.	Can do ahead	

Lisa C. Young
Holy Family Institute

16

SPICED MEATBALLS IN WINE

"Featuring cinnamon and allspice"

3¼ cups Concord grape wine
½ cup sugar
1 tsp. cinnamon
1 tsp. allspice
2 lbs. lean ground round of beef
⅛ tsp. allspice
⅛ tsp. cinnamon
3 Tbsp. grated onion
2 tsp. salt
¼ tsp. black pepper
dash of cayenne

Put 2½ cups wine in a saucepan. Add ½ cup sugar, 1 tsp. cinnamon and 1 tsp. allspice. Simmer until slightly thickened. Put beef in a bowl. Add ⅛ tsp. allspice, ⅛ teaspoon cinnamon, 3 Tbsp. grated onion, 2 tsp. salt, ¼ tsp. black pepper, dash of cayenne and rest of wine. Form into balls the size of a small walnut. Heat sauce to boiling. Drop in about 20 balls or less at a time. Cook five minutes.

Drain. Serve on cocktail picks. When making ahead, cool in the sauce. Refrigerate or freeze until ready to use. Remove from sauce and heat gently.

Preparation: 1 hour   Easy   Yield: 50-60 appetizers
Cooking: 5 min.   Can do ahead   Freeze after cooking

Gertrude N. Marsh

GREEK APPETIZER PIZZAS

"Get out your sharpest chopping knife"

4 pita rounds
3-4 Tbsp. olive oil
1 clove garlic, finely minced
2 tomatoes, chopped
1 bunch scallions, chopped
¾ cup chopped Greek olives
1½ tsp. oregano
1 cup crumbled Feta cheese
1 cup shredded Kasseri or
    Provolone cheese

Split and brush pita rounds with 2 Tbsp. olive oil. Sprinkle rounds with garlic, tomatoes, scallions and olives. Then sprinkle with oregano. Add Feta and then Kasseri or Provolone cheese. Drizzle with remaining olive oil. Bake at 350° for 10-12 minutes. Place briefly under broiler to brown lightly. Cut each round in fourths and serve warm.

HINT: Chop, mince and shred all ingredients ahead of time, then assemble and bake shortly before guests arrive.

Preparation: 45 min.   Easy   Yield: 32 appetizers
Cooking: 15-18 min.   Serve immediately

Susan Mull

BASIL CHEESE TORTE
"Attention basil lovers"

2-3 cups fresh basil, loosely
  packed
1 cup fresh parsley, loosely
  packed
¾ cup freshly grated Parmesan
  cheese
1½ Tbsp. olive oil
3 Tbsp. pine nuts (optional)
11 oz. cream cheese, softened
½ cup soft butter
½ Tbsp. lemon juice
dash salt
⅛ tsp. red pepper sauce

In food processor, combine basil, parsley, Parmesan cheese and olive oil; process until smooth. Transfer to small bowl and stir in nuts. In processor, combine remaining ingredients; blend until smooth. Dampen enough cheesecloth to line an empty ice-cube tray or favorite 3 cup mold. Divide each mixture in half and alternate layers in mold, beginning with basil and ending with cheese. Fold cheesecloth over and press to smooth top. Refrigerate 1 hour. Unmold and serve with crackers.

Preparation: 35 min.   Moderately difficult   Serves: 20
                         Must do ahead

Dee Delaney

CREAM CHEESE TWISTS
"Start these yesterday"

½ cup margarine
4 cups flour
1 pkg. dry yeast
¼ cup warm water
2 eggs
1 cup sour cream
powdered sugar and flour for
  rolling

Filling:
1 8-oz. pkg. cream cheese
1 egg yolk
1 tsp. grated lemon rind
sugar, to taste

Cut margarine into flour like pie dough. Dissolve yeast in warm water. Mix with dough. Beat eggs; add sour cream. Add to mixture. Refrigerate overnight. Place a mixture of powdered sugar and flour on a pastry board. Roll half of dough into a rectangle ⅛" thick and spread with half of filling. Fold in half. Cut into 1" strips and twist. Repeat with other half of dough and filling. Bake on greased cookie sheet at 350° for 20 minutes or until done.

Filling:
Blend together cream cheese, egg yolk, lemon rind and sugar to taste.

Preparation: 1 hr.   Easy   Yield: 4-5 doz.
Cooking: 20 min.   Must do ahead   Can freeze

Nellie Lampich

BATTER FRIED TURKEY STRIPS

"Can also be a main dish"

1 4-lb. frozen turkey breast,
  thawed
¼ cup lemon juice
1½ tsp. rosemary
½ cup salad oil
1 tsp. salt

Batter:
1½ cups all-purpose flour
1½ cups water
2 tsp. double-action baking
  powder
1½ tsp. paprika
2 tsp. salt
salad oil

Sauce:
2 11-oz. cans drained apricot
  halves
¼ bottle chili relish sauce
1 Tbsp. brown sugar
1½ tsp. salt

lemon slices for garnish

On cutting board, with sharp knife, remove and discard skin and bone from turkey. Cut turkey breast into 5″ x 1″ strips. Place in a 9x13″ baking dish. Mix lemon juice, rosemary, oil and salt and pour over turkey strips. Toss gently, then cover and refrigerate 2 hours, turning pieces once.

Batter: In medium bowl, combine flour, water, baking powder, paprika and salt. In 12″ skillet over medium heat, heat 1″ of salad oil to 370°. Dip turkey strips in batter and fry for 3-5 minutes. Drain on paper towels. Arrange on large platter. Garnish with lemon slices. Serve with apricot sauce.

Apricot sauce: In blender or mixer, beat apricot halves, chili relish sauce, brown sugar and salt until smooth.

Preparation: 1 hour   Moderately difficult   Serves: A crowd
Cooking: 3-5 min.

Ruth E. Baric

BLEU CHEESE 'N ONIONS

"Very unusual"

2 cups sweet onion, quartered
  and thinly sliced (Vidalia is
  best)
½ cup oil
1 tsp. salt
2 Tbsp. fresh lemon juice
fresh ground pepper
dash of paprika
dash of pepper sauce
½ tsp. sugar
⅓ cup crumbled good Bleu
  cheese

Put onion on bottom of 9 x 13"
glass dish. Mix oil, salt, lemon
juice, pepper, paprika, pepper
sauce, sugar. Stir in cheese.
Pour mixture over onions. Cover
and chill for 2-5 days, stirring
occasionally. Serve as appetizer
with thin, buttered slices of
pumpernickel.

Preparation: 20 min.   Easy   Serves: 12-14
                        Must do ahead

Clee McBee

EASY BOURSIN CHEESE SPREAD

"A marvelous simple blend"

2 8-oz. pkgs. cream cheese,
  softened
¼ cup mayonnaise
2 tsp. Dijon mustard
2 Tbsp. finely chopped chives
2 Tbsp. finely chopped fresh
  dillweed or 1 Tbsp. dry dillweed
1 large clove garlic, minced

Beat all ingredients together.
Chill. Serve with crackers or
bagel chips.

Preparation: 10 min.   Easy   Serves: 12
                        Can do ahead

Catherine Clarke Johnson

BRIGHT GREEN DIP

"Serve in a hollow red cabbage for the holidays"

2 cups mayonnaise
⅓ cup chopped parsley
⅓ cup chopped green onions
⅓ cup spinach, chopped with
  stems removed
¼ cup sour cream
¼ cup fresh lemon juice
2 Tbsp. grated onion
salt, pepper and dark
  Worcestershire sauce, to taste

Put all ingredients in food processor or blender. Process until
smooth. Chill.

NOTE: Good served with cold
shrimp, chicken chunks,
vegetables.

Preparation: 10 min.   Easy   Serves: 12-15
                        Can do ahead

Anne F. Dithrich

CHEESE BAKE
"Best to use a plate and fork with this"

6 whole eggs
⅛ tsp. salt
¾ cup sugar
½ cup flour
½ cup milk
2 lbs. small curd cottage cheese
1 lb. Brick cheese, grated
¼ cup butter, melted

Beat eggs well; add salt, sugar, flour and milk. Beat well. Fold in cottage cheese and Brick cheese. Pour batter in a well-greased 9 x 13" glass dish. Dribble melted butter, with spoon, on top of cheese mixture. Bake at 350° for 1 hour. Cut in small squares and serve warm.

| Preparation: | 10 min. | Easy | Yield: 20-25 squares |
| Baking: | 1 hour | Can do ahead | Can Freeze before baking |

Lynn Popovich

VEGETABLE DIP
"Pink and pretty"

1 8-oz. pkg. cream cheese
⅓ cup chopped onion
⅓ cup chili sauce
3 Tbsp. mayonnaise
¼ tsp. Worcestershire sauce

Blend ingredients together. Serve with favorite raw vegetables.

| Preparation: | 5 min. | Easy | Serves: 10 |
| | | Can do ahead | |

Paula A. Doebler

SWISS ARTICHOKE PUFFS
"A hearty appetizer"

1 loaf dark cocktail rye bread
¾ cup mayonnaise
⅓ cup grated Parmesan cheese
1 tsp. chopped parsley
¼ tsp. onion powder
¼ tsp. Worcestershire sauce
1 14-oz. can artichoke hearts, quartered
Swiss cheese, thinly sliced and cut to fit top of bread

Toast bread. Combine mayonnaise and Parmesan cheese. Add parsley, onion powder, and Worcestershire sauce. Put one piece of artichoke on rye round and spread cheese mixture on top. Cover with pieces of Swiss cheese. Arrange on cookie sheet and broil until cheese melts or is lightly browned.

| Preparation: | 10 min. | Easy | Yield: 18 appetizers |
| Cooking: | 2-3 min. or microwave for 1 minute on high | Can do ahead | |

Susi S. Mark

SWEET-SOUR SAUSAGE BALLS

"This is a crowd pleaser"

4 lbs. bulk pork sausage
4 eggs, slightly beaten
1½ cups soft bread crumbs
3 cups ketchup
¾ cup brown sugar, firmly
   packed
½ cup white wine vinegar
½ cup soy sauce

Mix together sausage, eggs, and bread crumbs. Using palms of hands, shape mixture into balls the size of small walnuts. Sauté in frying pan until browned on all sides; drain. Combine ketchup, brown sugar, vinegar, and soy sauce; pour over sausage balls and simmer for 30 minutes. Stir occasionally. Serve hot.

NOTE: If made ahead, refrigerate or freeze sausage balls in their sauce. To serve: reheat in a 350° oven for 20 minutes.

Preparation: 30 min.   Easy   Yield: 150 appetizers
Cooking: 30 min.   Can do ahead   Can freeze

Mary Ann Nichi

CHEDDAR CHUTNEY PUFFS

"Something different in a puff"

Puffs:
1 cup water
½ cup butter
½ tsp. salt
1 cup flour
4-5 whole eggs, room
   temperature

Filling:
½ cup mango chutney,
   chopped
1 cup grated Cheddar cheese
2-3 Tbsp. condensed cheese
   soup

Preheat oven to 400°. Lightly grease baking sheets. Place water, butter and salt in pan and heat. When mixture boils, add flour all at once. Stir rapidly until mixture leaves sides of pan and forms a ball. Remove from heat and cool 2-3 minutes. Add eggs, one at a time, and beat briskly after each. Decide whether or not to add the fifth egg, based on how stiff the paste is. It is ready if a teaspoonful can be dropped on a baking sheet and made to form a small "peak". Drop by teaspoonsful about 1" apart. Shape into rounded mounds. Bake 10 minutes at 400°. Reduce the temperature and bake 15-20 minutes longer at 325°. Cool before filling.

NOTE: Unfilled puffs can be frozen for a couple of months.

Filling: Mix ingredients together; fill puffs and heat at 325° for about 10 minutes.

Preparation: 30-40 min.   Moderately difficult   Yield: 50-60 appetizers
Cooking: 40 min.   Can do ahead

Clee McBee

CHEESE PUFFS

3 slices thick bacon
8 oz. whipped cream cheese
½ cup shredded Cheddar
  cheese
1 Tbsp. grated Parmesan cheese
1 small white onion, minced
3 sprigs fresh parsley, chopped
2 sheets Pepperidge Farm puff
  pastry

Cook bacon until crisp; crumble. Add bacon to all other ingredients, except puff pastry. Mix thoroughly. Roll each pastry sheet to a 15" square. Cut into 3" squares (25 each sheet). Put ½-1 tsp. of mixture on each square. Brush tips of square with water and pinch opposite corners. Freeze on cookie sheet

for 30 minutes, then transfer to freezer bag. (These are always done ahead!) To serve, put on cookie sheet and bake at 400° for 12-15 minutes or until golden brown. Serve immediately.

Preparation: 30 min.   Easy   Yield: 50
Cooking: 15 min.   Must do ahead   Can freeze

Diana Morrow

SALMON SPREAD

"Also good with fresh veggies"

1 7¾-oz. can red salmon
  (or 8 oz. fresh, poached)
1 3-oz. pkg. cream cheese,
  softened
¼ cup mayonnaise
2 tsp. lemon juice
4 drops hot sauce (more if you
  like it spicy)
1 Tbsp. finely minced onions
¼ tsp. dry mustard
¼ tsp. curry powder
salt and pepper, to taste

Place salmon in strainer and drain thoroughly (only if using canned salmon). Flake salmon with fork. Combine all ingredients and mix until smooth. Chill overnight before using. Spread on toast points or fill rosette cups.

Preparation: 15 min.   Easy   Yield: 30-35 toast points
                         Must do ahead

Lynn Popovich

SUPERB STUFFED MUSHROOMS

"Good microwave recipe"

1½ lbs. medium mushrooms
   (about 30)
½ lb. Italian "hot" sausage
½ cup shredded Mozzarella
   cheese
¼ cup seasoned bread crumbs
parsley for garnish

Using a melon ball scoop, remove stems from cleaned mushrooms. Chop stems and set both mushrooms and finely chopped stems aside. In microwave dish, cook sausage in microwave on HIGH for 3 minutes. Stir and cook for additional 1 minute increments until fully cooked. Remove sausage from dish, set aside. Spoon off all but 1 Tbsp. sausage grease. Stir chopped mushroom stems into dish. Microwave on HIGH for 2-3 minutes until soft. Remove from microwave. Stir in sausage, cheese and breadcrumbs. Again, using melon ball scoop, fill each cap with mixture. Arrange on microwave dish (can refrigerate for 1-2 hours at this stage). Cook in microwave on HIGH for 3-4 minutes until mushroom caps are cooked. Garnish with parsley and serve.

NOTE: Even though this recipe used "hot" sausage, these appetizers are not very spicy.

Preparation: 45 min.   Easy   Yield: 30 appetizers
Cooking: 8-12 min.   Can do ahead

Joyce Scalercio

MUSHROOM CANAPÉS

"Yumm - well worth the time"

Shells:
1 loaf thin sliced Pepperidge
   Farm bread
2 Tbsp. butter or margarine

Filling:
4 Tbsp. butter
3 Tbsp. finely chopped shallots
½ lb. mushrooms, finely
   chopped
2 Tbsp. flour
1 cup whipping cream
¼ tsp. cayenne pepper
1 Tbsp. chopped parsley
1½ Tbsp. chopped chives
½ tsp. lemon juice

Shells: Cut each slice into a 2¼" round. Roll flat with a rolling pin, butter and mold into a mini-muffin tin. Bake at 350° for 8-10 minutes.

Filling: Sauté shallots in butter for about 4 minutes. Add mushrooms. Cook until liquid has evaporated. Sprinkle with flour and stir. Add cream. Bring to a boil. Cook for about 1 minute. Remove from heat. Add seasoning, herbs, and lemon juice. Fill baked shells. Bake at 400° for 10-12 minutes.

Preparation: 1 hour   Moderately difficult   Yield: 24 + canapés
Cooking: 10-12 min.   Can do ahead   Can freeze

Lorraine Trice

CHEESY/BACON STUFFED MUSHROOMS

"Use your food processor for the tasty filling"

7 slices bacon
¼ cup chopped onion
1 clove garlic, finely chopped
1 cup cottage cheese
⅔ cup shredded Swiss cheese
2 tsp. chicken broth
1 cup herb-seasoned stuffing
   mix, crushed
30 fresh mushrooms, medium
   size, stems removed
melted margarine

Cut bacon into small pieces and fry. Drain. Cook onion and garlic in bacon drippings. Drain. Mix onion, garlic, and bacon with remaining ingredients (except mushrooms and margarine). Brush mushrooms with melted margarine. Fill with stuffing. Place in shallow baking dish and bake for 10-12 minutes at 350°. Refrigerate leftovers.

Preparation: 20 min.   Easy   Yield: 30 appetizers
Cooking: 10-12 min.   Can do ahead

Nancy L. Farris

HANKY-PANKY'S

"Use hot sausage and Velveeta/Jalepeño for a little more zip"

1 lb. Bob Evans Bulk sausage
1 lb. ground beef
½ tsp. Worcestershire sauce
½ tsp. garlic powder
¼ tsp. oregano
1 lb. Velveeta cheese
2 loaves party rye bread
olives for garnish, sliced

Brown sausage and ground beef; drain. Add Worcestershire sauce, garlic powder and oregano. Cube the cheese; add to mixture and stir until melted. Place 1 Tbsp. of the mixture on a slice of party rye. Continue until all of the mixture is used up. Garnish with olives. Bake at 350° on cookie sheet for 10 min.

Preparation: 30 min.   Easy   Yield: 36 appetizers
Cooking: 10-12 min.   Can do ahead   Freeze before baking

Diane C. Letizo

MUSTARD-PRETZEL DIP

"This will make plenty for all your friends"

2 small cans McCormick's dry
   mustard (1⅛ oz. each)
1 cup vinegar
1 cup sugar
2 eggs, beaten
½ pint sour cream

Soak dry mustard in vinegar overnight. Add sugar and eggs. Cook in double boiler until thick (about 30 minutes). When cool, add the sour cream.

Preparation: 35 min.   Easy   Serves: A large crowd
                     Must do ahead

Karen G. Smith

VEGETABLE PIZZA APPETIZERS
"This pizza crust is a snap"

2 pkgs. crescent dinner rolls
¾ cup mayonnaise
2 8-oz. pkgs. cream cheese,
  softened
1 pkg. Hidden Valley Ranch
  Dressing Mix
3 cups chopped vegetables:
  carrots
  broccoli
  cauliflower
  green pepper
  green onion
  tomatoes
1 cup grated sharp Cheddar
  cheese

Unfold rolls flat onto large cookie sheet. Seal seams and press out as necessary to completely cover pan. Bake at 350° for 8-10 minutes. Cool. Mix next 3 ingredients; spread on crust. Chop vegetables in blender or food processor. Drain well and spread over cream cheese mixture. Sprinkle cheese over all. Chill. Cut into small pieces if used as an appetizer OR can be served for a family dinner.

Preparation: 1 hour   Easy   Serves: 20 as appetizer
Cooking: 8-10 min.   Can do ahead

Suzi Fair

RANCHERETTES

1 1-oz. envelope of ranch salad
  dressing mix
1 tsp. dried savory
½ tsp. garlic powder
½ tsp. dried dill
½ cup vegetable oil
2 7-oz. boxes oyster crackers
lemon, to taste
salt, to taste
peper, to taste

Mix first five ingredients in bowl. Stir in oil and crackers. Place in a 9x13″ glass baking dish. Bake about 20 minutes at 200°, stirring frequently, until golden. Store in tin container. This can be frozen, but is better fresh.

Preparation: 10 min.   Easy   Yield: 2 cups
Cooking: 20 min.   Can do ahead   Can freeze

Carolyn Hultman

BONNIE'S EASY HORS D'OEUVRE

1 12-oz. jar pineapple preserves
1 12-oz. jar apple jelly
1 5-oz. jar horseradish
1¼ tsp. dry mustard
¼ tsp. cracked pepper
1-3 large pkgs. cream cheese

Mix all ingredients, except cream cheese, in blender until mostly smooth. Serve over a large cream cheese.

NOTE: This recipe makes enough sauce to spread over 2-3 large cream cheese rectangles.

Preparation: 5 min.   Easy   Serves: A crowd
                          Must do ahead

Bonnie Rees

ZUCCHINI PIZZA

3 cups grated zucchini
½ cup green pepper, finely
   chopped
½ cup onion, finely chopped
4 eggs, beaten well
½ cup grated Mozzarella cheese
½ cup grated Parmesan cheese
1 cup pepperoni, finely cut
½ tsp. oregano
2 tsp. parsley
½ cup oil
1 cup Bisquick baking mix
garlic powder (dash)
salt (dash)

Mix ingredients well. Place in a
well-greased 9x13″ baking dish.
Bake at 350° for 40-45 minutes.

NOTE: Best if made ahead and
cooled a little before cutting into
squares.

Preparation: 25 min.   Easy   Yield: 32 squares
Cooking: 40-45 min.   Can do ahead   Can freeze

Berneta A. Gebhardt

RIPE AND RYE APPETIZERS

"Olives and bacon add wonderful flavor"

4 slices crisp bacon, crumbled
1 cup shredded sharp Cheddar
   cheese
½ 3-oz. can pitted ripe olives,
   sliced
1 cup Hellmann's mayonnaise
¼ cup grated onion
party rye

Mix the first five ingredients
together and spread on party rye
bread. Bake in 375° oven for
about 8 minutes. Serve hot.

Preparation: 10 min.   Easy   Serves: 24 appetizers
Cooking: 8 min.   Can do ahead   Can freeze

Mrs. G. William Coyle

QUICK CRAB SPREAD

1 lb. blue crabmeat, fresh or
   pasteurized
1 pkg. Italian salad dressing
   mix
1 cup sour cream
½ cup mayonnaise or salad
   dressing
1 Tbsp. horseradish mustard
chopped parsley for garnish

Remove shell and cartilage from
crabmeat. Combine all ingredients. Chill if desired. Garnish
with parsley.

Preparation: 30 min.   Easy   Yield: 3 cups
                             Can do ahead   Can freeze

Judy B. Scioscia

SIX LAYER MEXICAN DIP

"No beans in this dip"

2 large avocados
⅛ tsp. garlic powder
⅛ tsp. salt
1 Tbsp. lemon juice
2 Tbsp. mayonnaise
8 oz. sour cream
2 8-oz. jars Picante sauce,
  well-drained
¾ cup black olives, chopped
3 cups tomatoes, peeled and
  chopped
1½ cups shredded Cheddar
  cheese

Mix first 5 ingredients together with a pastry blender and spread in bottom of a 12 x 8" dish or platter. Spread sour cream over first layer. Spread Picante sauce over cream. Sprinkle chopped olives evenly over above. Sprinkle tomatoes over olives. Distribute cheese evenly to cover. Cover with plastic wrap and refrigerate.

NOTE: Best if made 1 day ahead for flavors to develop fully. Good served with corn chips.

Preparation: 20 min.   Easy   Serves: A crowd
                         Can do ahead

Judy Jones

TACO APPETIZER

"Olé amigos"

1 large can refried beans
1 cup sour cream
1 8-oz. jar medium taco sauce
Cheddar cheese, shredded
chopped tomato
sliced ripe olives
tortilla chips

Mix beans, sour cream and taco sauce together. Garnish with shredded cheese, tomato, and olives. Serve with tortilla chips.

Preparation: 5 min.   Easy   Serves: A crowd
                        Can do ahead

Wanda Wolf

BONNIE'S HUMMUS

"Use over toasted pita bread brushed with oil"

1¾ cups chickpeas
5 Tbsp. chicken broth
  (Campbell's condensed)
¾ cup tahini (ground sesame
  seeds)
½ cup lemon juice
2 Tbsp. garlic, minced
salt and pepper, to taste

Blend all ingredients in blender or food processor until smooth.

Preparation: 10 min.   Easy   Serves: A crowd
                         Can do ahead

Jane VanKirk

SUPER NACHOS

½ lb. lean ground beef
½ lb. Chorizo, casing removed*
1 large yellow onion, chopped
salt, to taste
Tabasco sauce, to taste
2 lbs. refried beans
1 cup green bottled taco sauce
3 cups shredded Monterey
   Jack and/or Cheddar cheese
2 4-oz. cans chopped chilies

Garnishes:
¼ cup chopped green onion
1 cup sliced olives
3 very ripe avocados, mashed
2 cups sour cream
¼ cup fresh cilantro, chopped
8-10 cups tortilla chips

*Can substitute ½ lb. hot sau-
sage + ½ tsp. ground cumin
+ ½ tsp. crushed Mexican
oregano for the Chorizo.

Brown beef, Chorizo, and onion; drain excess fat. Season with salt and Tabasco sauce to taste. Spread beans in large casserole dish. Top beans evenly with meat mixture. Drizzle taco sauce over all. Cover evenly with cheese and green chilies. Cover and chill if making ahead. Bake at 400°, uncovered, for 20-25 minutes. Garnish with green onions and olives. Make a mound in the center with avocado. Top avocado with sour cream and cilantro. Serve with tortilla chips.

Preparation: 20 min.   Easy   Serves: 8-10
Cooking: 20-25 min.   Can do ahead

Susan Gibson

SHRIMP BREAD WEDGES

1 lb. loaf round bread
3 cloves garlic, minced
½ cup parsley, minced
1 stick butter, softened
½ tsp. pepper
½ lb. shrimp, peeled

Remove top from bread and hollow it, then process bread in food processor until finely ground; set aside. Add garlic and parsley to butter and pepper and blend until smooth. Arrange half of shrimp in bottom of bread. Spread one-third of butter mixture on top, then sprinkle with half of the bread crumbs. Arrange remaining shrimp over crumbs and spread with another third of butter mixture and remaining crumbs. Dot top with remaining butter. Bake at 400° for 25 minutes. Place lid of bread on top and bake for 5 minutes more. Cut into wedges to serve.

NOTE: This can also be done in small individual hard rolls.

Preparation: 15 min.　　Easy　　　　Serves: 6-8
Cooking:　　25-30 min.

Carolyn S. Hammer

SHRIMP WITH BACON

1 cup ketchup
1 cup chili sauce
1 Tbsp. Worcestershire sauce
1 clove garlic, crushed
½ cup chopped onion
½ cup chopped celery
½ cup chopped green pepper
several drops of Tabasco sauce
2 lbs. shrimp, boiled and shelled
sliced bacon, cut in half

Mix all ingredients for marinade, except the bacon and shrimp. Marinate shrimp at least 24 hours. Wrap each shrimp in 1/2 piece of bacon. Fasten with a toothpick and broil.

Preparation: 30 min. +　　Easy　　　　Yield: 3-4 dozen
Cooking:　　5 min.　　Must do ahead

Francye Kinney

SHRIMP DIP

"Nice and crunchy"

1 4¼-oz. can baby shrimp,
　rinsed and well-drained
1 8-oz. pkg. cream cheese
5 Tbsp. ketchup
1 tsp. Dijon mustard
2 tsp. chopped onion
4 tsp. chopped celery
1 dash garlic
1 dash salt

Mix all ingredients together with an electric mixer. Cover and refrigerate for 8 hours. Serve with Triscuits or Ritz crackers.

Preparation: 15 min.　　Easy　　　　Serves: 8
　　　　　　　　　　　Must do ahead

Debra Pushic Gibbs

30

KING CRAB CANAPÉS
"Looks great - tastes great"

6 oz. cream cheese
6 oz. King crab, thawed and
  drained
1 Tbsp. mayonnaise
¼ tsp. celery salt
¼ tsp. Worcestershire sauce
paprika
36 bread rounds, toasted on
  one side

Beat cream cheese until soft. Add crabmeat, mayonnaise, salt and Worcestershire sauce. Mix thoroughly. Cover and chill until ready to serve. Toast bread rounds on one side under broiler. Cover toasted side with crab mix, sprinkle with paprika. Broil for a few seconds. Serve hot.

Preparation: 10 min.   Easy   Yield: 36 canapés
Cooking: A few min. Can do ahead

Linda D. Orsini

SHRIMP AND CRABMEAT DIP
"A ritzy dip"

2 Tbsp. butter
4 stalks celery, chopped
1 green pepper, chopped
2 Tbsp. Worcestershire sauce
1½ cups Hellmann's mayonnaise
2 Tbsp. lemon juice
2 6½-oz. cans shrimp, drained
2 6½-oz. cans crabmeat, picked
  and drained
½ tsp. salt
¼ tsp. pepper
12-15 crushed Ritz crackers
½ cup fresh Parmesan cheese,
  grated

Sauté chopped celery and green pepper in butter and Worcestershire sauce. Cool. Add mayonnaise. Add lemon juice, shrimp and crabmeat. Season with salt and pepper. Transfer to buttered casserole. Cover with layer of crushed Ritz crackers. Top with grated Parmesan cheese. Heat at 350° for 40 minutes. Cover with foil. Can be kept in warm oven for an hour. Transfer to chafing dish for serving. Serve with Ritz crackers.

NOTE: "Doubles" easily - can be reheated.

Preparation: 20 min.   Easy   Serves: 8-12
Cooking: 40 min.

Cynthia Pierce Liefeld

BLANCHE'S SALMON SPREAD

1 small can red salmon
1 8-oz. pkg. cream cheese, at
  room temperature
2 Tbsp. Half & Half
¼ cup pickle relish
2 green onions
1 Tbsp. Nature's Season salt
2 Tbsp. lemon juice

Drain salmon. In a food processor, blend all ingredients well. Chill. Serve with crackers.

Preparation: 10 min.   Easy   Yield: 2 cups
                         Can do ahead

Blanche Lovelace

SOUPS

NEW ORLEANS STYLE SHRIMP SOUP
"Authentic New Orleans hot stuff"

1 Tbsp. butter or margarine
1 clove garlic, minced
4 oz. fresh carrot, cut in 1½"
   thin strips
3 oz. green pepper, chopped
3 oz. celery, cut in crescents
2 oz. green onions, cut in slices
2 Tbsp. fresh basil, chopped
24 oz. clam juice
24 oz. vegetable juice
1 oz. wild rice
1 cup water
1 tsp. red peppercorns, crushed
1 tsp. hot sauce
1 lb. shrimp, raw, peeled and
   deveined

Melt butter in a stock pot. Add next six ingredients. Sauté lightly for 5 minutes. Add clam and vegetable juices, water, wild rice, red peppercorns, and hot sauce. Bring to a boil. Simmer for 15 minutes. Add raw shrimp and continue to simmer until done (about 5 minutes).

| Preparation: | 25 min. | Moderately difficult | Serves: 6-8 |
| Cooking: | 30 min. | Can do ahead | Can freeze |

Catherine Connell
D. T. Watson Hospital

GUMBO WITH SEAFOOD

"Will make 6-8 people happy"

1 medium carrot, finely chopped
¼ cup butter
3 Tbsp. flour
2 Tbsp. tomato paste
1 24-oz. can whole tomatoes in juice, undrained and chopped
4 cups water
1 10-oz. pkg. frozen cut okra
1 small onion, finely chopped
¼ green pepper, chopped
1 Tbsp. Worcestershire sauce
⅛ tsp. thyme
⅛ tsp. basil
6 drops Tabasco sauce
⅛ tsp. cayenne pepper
dash salt and pepper
1 Tbsp. Gravy Master
¼ cup fresh parsley, chopped
1 pkg. frozen cod fillets, cubed
½ lb. cleaned, cooked frozen shrimp
croutons

Cook carrot in melted butter for 3-5 minutes, until soft. Stir in flour. Cook, stirring for 1 minute. Stir in tomato paste, tomatoes, juice and water. Boil, stirring until smooth. Add okra, onion, green pepper and seasonings. Decrease heat and simmer for 15 minutes. Add cubed fish and simmer 5-8 minutes, until tender. Add shrimp and parsley. Remove from heat. Let stand, covered, for 10 minutes. Serve in bowl and sprinkle with croutons.

NOTE: Approximately 160 calories per serving.

Preparation: 30 min.	Moderately difficult	Serves: 6-8
Cooking: 20 min.	Can do ahead	

Joyce Scalercio

SHRIMP BISQUE

"A special soup for special guests"

¼ cup butter
1 large onion, chopped
½ cup celery, chopped
2 cloves (1 tsp.) garlic, minced
2 Tbsp. flour
2 Tbsp. tomato paste
3 cups milk
2 cups broth (chicken, clam or fish)
1 bay leaf
½ tsp. basil
½ tsp. Tabasco sauce
1½ lbs. raw shrimp, shelled and deveined
¼ cup sliced scallions

In a large pot melt butter; sauté onion, celery, garlic until tender (about 5 minutes). Stir in flour and tomato paste; cook 1 minute. Gradually stir in milk, broth, bay leaf, basil and Tabasco sauce. Bring to a boil. Reduce heat and simmer for 10 minutes. Add shrimp, scallions and simmer for 5 minutes longer. Remove bay leaf and serve.

Preparation: 10 min.	Easy	Serves: 6-8
Cooking: 25 min.	Serve immediately	

Karen Z. Petley

MEDITERRANEAN FISH CHOWDER

"Great the next day, too!"

1 medium onion, chopped
2 cloves garlic, minced
3 Tbsp. olive oil
1 29-oz. can stewed tomatoes
2 Tbsp. tomato paste
½ cup dry white wine
1 bay leaf
oregano and basil, to taste
1-2 lbs. monkfish, pollock, or
   hake, cut into 2" squares

Sauté onion and garlic in olive oil; add tomatoes, paste, wine and seasonings. Stir well and correct the consistency with more paste or wine as needed. Lay fish squares on top of other ingredients; cover and simmer gently for 15-20 minutes.

Preparation: 20 min.   Easy
Cooking: 15-20 min. Can do ahead

Serves: 4-6

Janice L. Wendt

SEAFOOD BISQUE

"Fast and tasty"

1 can each: tomato soup
   mushroom soup
   cream of celery soup
   green pea soup
1 pint Half & Half
1 soup can of milk
1 lb. crabmeat, (fresh is best)
1½ lbs. shrimp, cooked and
   peeled
Sherry, to taste
salt and pepper, to taste
parsley for garnish

Mix all ingredients, except parsley, and heat slowly for 25-30 minutes.

NOTE: Best if completely cooled, then refrigerated and reheated second day to serve.

Preparation: 5 min.   Easy
Cooking: 25-30 min. Can do ahead

Serves: 6-8

Bev Kelley

BROCCOLI SOUP

"So easy, anyone can make this"

½ stick butter
½ cup flour
2 cans chicken stock
1 10-oz. pkg. frozen chopped
   broccoli
1 pint Half & Half

Melt butter. Stir in flour and cook until bubbling (about 1-2 minutes). Slowly stir in stock, whisking constantly. Heat to a near boil until soup thickens. Add broccoli and Half & Half and heat slowly. Serve.

NOTE: May be cooled and reheated second day.

Preparation: 10-15 min. Easy
Cooking: 20 min.   Can do ahead

Serves: 4-6

Bev Kelley

SKIP JACK CHOWDER

"A hearty oyster stew"

2 medium red onions, chopped
  (1 cup)
¼ cup snipped fresh parsley
2 Tbsp. butter
1 Tbsp. soy sauce
1 tsp. dried thyme, crushed
½ tsp. salt
1 bay leaf
dash hot pepper sauce
1 pint fresh oysters
2 cups milk
½ cup light cream
2 cups shredded sharp Cheddar cheese
½ cup dry white wine

In a large saucepan, cook onion and parsley in butter until tender, but not brown. Stir in soy sauce, thyme, salt, bay leaf and pepper sauce. Add oysters; cook and stir over low heat about 5 minutes until edges curl. Stir in milk and cream. Heat through. Add cheese, taking care not to boil. Remove from heat; stir in wine.

Preparation:	20 min.	Easy	Serves: 6
Cooking:	12 min.	Serve immediately	

Patricia A. Morrison

MONDAVIE SHRIMP SOUP

"Enjoyed by 400 people at the Child Health Ball"

2 qts. heavy cream
8 cloves garlic
3 oz. fresh chopped ginger
4 oz. peeled, sliced potato
12 oz. shrimp in shell
salt, to taste
white pepper, to taste
fresh chopped parsley

Bring cream, garlic, ginger and potato to a boil; reduce heat, simmer slowly until potato is cooked (approx. 30 minutes). Add shrimp in shell to cream mixture, and cook approx. 5 minutes or until the shrimp are done. Remove shrimp, peel, devein and chop into medium-size pieces.

Purée cream mixture and strain; add salt and white pepper to taste. Add chopped shrimp and serve topped with parsley.

Preparation:	20 min.	Easy	Serves: 10
Cooking:	40 min.	Can do ahead	

Jack Rittelmann, Chef
Edgeworth Club

GERMAN POTATO SOUP
"A soothing comfort soup"

7-8 medium white potatoes
1 carrot, diced
1 small onion, diced
4 Tbsp. butter
2 Tbsp. flour
4 cups milk (can use skim)
1 chicken bouillon cube
3 hard-boiled eggs, chopped
2 Tbsp. parsley flakes
1 tsp. salt
1/8 tsp. pepper
1/2 tsp. seasoned salt

Cook potatoes* in water until tender. Drain and peel. Dice half of potatoes, mash other half with fork. Set aside. Sauté carrot and onion in butter until tender in 2½-quart saucepan or Dutch oven. Add flour and cook until bubbly, stirring constantly over medium heat. Slowly add milk. Add bouillon cube. Stir until mixture thickens. When thickened, add potatoes and eggs. Add parsley, salt, pepper and seasoned salt.

*Potatoes may be cooked in microwave on HIGH for 15 minutes.

Preparation: 30 min.   Moderately difficult   Serves: 4-6
Cooking: 30 min.   Can do ahead

Barbara Ann Martz

SPLIT PEA SOUP
"A classic favorite"

1 lb. dried split peas, well rinsed
2 qts. water
1 meaty ham bone, or ham
  hock (approx. 2 lbs.)
1 28-oz. can tomatoes, drained
  and cut in chunks; reserve
  liquid
1 large onion, chopped (1 cup)
3 ribs celery, chopped (1 cup)
2 medium carrots, diced
  (1 cup)
3 large cloves garlic, crushed
1-1½ tsp. salt
½ tsp. pepper

In large kettle of water, bring to a boil, the peas, ham bone, tomato liquid, onion, celery, carrots, and garlic. Cover and simmer about 2 hours, or until the peas are tender, stirring occasionally. Remove the bone and cut off the meat. Return ham to soup. Add tomato chunks, salt and pepper. Simmer 1 hour longer until the peas are very soft, stirring occasionally. Thin with water if necessary.

NOTE: May substitute 6 large fresh tomatoes for the canned, if desired.

Preparation: 20 min.   Easy   Serves: 6
Cooking: 3 hours   Must do ahead   Can freeze

Cindy Wright

TANGY BROCCOLI-CHEDDAR SOUP

"Your food processor will make this easy"

¼ cup butter
1 cup chopped onions
1 tsp. garlic
2 Tbsp. flour
2 cups Half & Half
3 cups chicken broth
¾ lb. sharp Cheddar cheese,
  grated
½ tsp. nutmeg
¾ tsp. salt
½ tsp. pepper
⅛ to ¼ tsp. cayenne pepper
2 Tbsp. Dijon mustard
3 cups broccoli, diced (parboil
  or not, depending on desired
  tenderness)

Melt butter in large saucepan, add onions and sauté until tender. Add garlic and sauté 30 seconds. Add flour, stir for 2 minutes. Whisk in the Half & Half and chicken broth. Bring to boil, reduce to simmer, add grated cheese. Add seasonings and mustard. Add broccoli. Do not let soup boil after cheese has been added. Garnish with additional shredded Cheddar or diced red pepper.

Preparation: 20 min.	Moderately difficult	Yield: 2 qts.
Cooking: 25 min.	Can do ahead	

Bonnie Casper

MINESTRONE

"Nice to cook on a winter afternoon"

½ lb. Italian sweet sausage
1 Tbsp. olive oil
1 cup diced onion
1 clove garlic, crushed
1 cup diced carrots
1 tsp. basil
2 small zucchini, sliced
1 1-lb. can Italian tomatoes, undrained
2 10-oz. cans beef bouillon
2 cups finely shredded cabbage
salt and pepper
1 1-lb. can kidney beans, undrained
½ cup rice
½ cup red wine (optional)
freshly grated Parmesan cheese

Slice sausage into ½" pieces; brown in olive oil in a deep pot. Add onion, garlic, carrots, and basil; then cook for 5 minutes. Add zucchini, tomatoes with liquid, bouillon, cabbage, salt and pepper. Bring to a boil. Reduce heat and simmer for 1 hour. Add beans and their liquid, rice and wine; cook for 25 minutes. Cool and refrigerate. The next day, reheat. Soup should be thick. If you want it thinner, add more beef bouillon. Serve in a bowl topped with freshly grated Parmesan cheese.

Preparation: 50 min.	Easy	Serves: 6
Cooking: 1½ hrs.	Must do ahead	

Emilie Szakach

HODGE-PODGE LENTIL SOUP

"Everyone, kids included, likes this"

First Step:
¼ cup salad oil
3 cups diced cooked ham
**½ lb. Polish or Italian sausage,
   cut in ½" slices**
1 cup chopped onion
1 clove garlic, thinly sliced

Second Step:
**2 cups thinly sliced celery with
   leaves**
1 cup chopped canned tomatoes
2½-3 qts. cold water
1 lb. (2⅓ cups) lentils, washed
1½ tsp. salt

Third Step:
**1 10-oz. pkg. frozen chopped
   spinach, thawed**
½ tsp. hot red pepper sauce
salt, to taste
Parmesan or Romano Cheese

First Step:
Cook ingredients of first step over medium heat for about 4 minutes, stirring frequently.

Second Step:
Combine all with the meat mixture in a heavy kettle or Dutch oven. Use beef or chicken stock and/or water if desired, cutting salt if stock is used. Cover tightly and cook over low heat for 2 hours — more time won't hurt it!

Third Step:
About 15 minutes before serving, add spinach and hot red pepper sauce. Add salt if needed. Cook over low heat. Serve with grated Parmesan cheese or Romano cheese to top individual servings. Refrigerate or freeze left-overs.

FOR SLOW COOKER: Use frying pan for first step. Combine all ingredients except spinach and hot red pepper sauce in slow cooker. Cook on low for about 10 hours. Quickly add spinach and pepper sauce; finish cooking on HIGH for about 1 hour.

Preparation: 30 min.	**Moderately difficult**	**Serves: 14-16**
Cooking: 2½-3 hours	**Can do ahead**	**Can freeze**

Janet L. Mackey

KARWENDEL SOUP

"Very thick, almost a stew"

¼ lb. diced lean bacon
¾ lb. smoked Polish sausage,
    sliced in ½" pieces
1 cup finely chopped onion
½ cup chopped carrots
½ cup chopped celery
1 lb. can peeled tomatoes,
    broken up
2½ cups water
1 cup lentils, rinsed
½ tsp. basil
¼ tsp. marjoram
⅛ tsp. sugar
1 large bay leaf
salt and pepper, to taste
2 Tbsp. chopped parsley
2 Tbsp. Dijon or German-style
    mustard
grated cheese (optional)

Cook bacon in soup pot or Dutch oven. Remove bacon and set aside. Pour out excess fat from pot and add sausage. Slightly brown, then drain and set aside. Sauté onions, carrots and celery until onions are tender. Add tomatoes, lentils and water. Add bacon, sausage and remaining ingredients. Simmer about 1 hour, salt and pepper to taste. Sprinkle with parsley and a dab of mustard on each bowlful. (Also grated cheese is good).

| Preparation: | 30 min. | Easy | Serves: 4 |
| Cooking: | 1 hour | Can do ahead | Can freeze |

Sue Harvey

TORTELLINI MINESTRONE

1½ lbs. bulk Italian sausage
6 cups beef broth
1 cup chopped onions
½ cup dry or semi-dry red wine
1 lb. can undrained tomatoes
2 cups thinly sliced carrots
1 cup thinly sliced celery
1 cup ketchup
1 tsp. Italian seasoning
2 cloves garlic, minced
2 cups sliced zucchini
½ lb. cheese-filled tortellini,
    uncooked
1 medium green pepper, diced
¼ cup chopped fresh parsley
grated Parmesan cheese

In 5-quart Dutch oven, brown sausage; drain excess fat. Add broth and next 8 ingredients. Bring to a boil; simmer, uncovered, for 30 minutes. Skim any fat from soup. Stir in zucchini, tortellini, green pepper and parsley. Simmer, covered, until pasta is tender, about 35-40 minutes. Sprinkle with Parmesan cheese before serving.

| Preparation: | 40 min. | Easy | Serves: 8-10 |
| Cooking: | 1 hr. 20 min. | Can do ahead | Can freeze |

Ruth E. Baric

CARROT AND WALNUT SOUP

"Not soup to nuts—its soup and nuts"

2 Tbsp. butter
1 lb. carrots
2 oz. walnuts, chopped
2 oz. onions, chopped
28 oz. chicken stock
8 oz. light cream
salt
pepper, freshly ground
chives and walnuts, garnish

Melt the butter and sauté the carrots and onions briefly. Add the walnuts and 20 oz. of the chicken stock. Bring to a full boil, reduce heat and simmer for 30 minutes. Place in a food processor and purée mix until creamy. Add 8 oz. boiling chicken stock and the cream. Adjust seasoning. Serve hot, garnished with chopped chives and grated walnuts.

Preparation:	30 min.	Easy	Serves: 6
Cooking:	30 min.	Can do ahead	Can freeze

Norbert Bomm, Executive Chef
Orchard Cafe
Vista International Hotel

CARROT BISQUE

"This will go chop chop with a food processor"

3-5 slices bacon, chopped
1¼ lbs. carrots, pared and
  coarsely chopped
5 oz. fresh mushrooms, wiped
  clean, and chopped
½ cup coarsely chopped scallions
1 cup coarsely chopped celery
  with leaves
5 cups chicken broth
1 tsp. fresh thyme or ¼ tsp.
  dried thyme
1 bay leaf
1½ cups Half & Half
freshly ground pepper

Sauté bacon in Dutch oven over medium heat until crisp. Stir in carrots, mushrooms, scallions, and celery and coat thoroughly with bacon drippings; sauté, stirring thoroughly, about 5 minutes. Cover, reduce heat to low, and simmer for about 10 minutes. Stir in chicken broth, thyme, and bay leaf. Increase heat to high until boiling, then cover and simmer 50 minutes. Remove from heat and let cool slightly. Remove and discard bay leaf. Purée soup in blender or food processor in two batches. Return soup to pan and stir in Half & Half. Heat, stirring frequently, until hot; but do not boil. Add pepper to taste.

Preparation:	30-40 min.	Easy	Serves: 8
Cooking:	1 hr.	Can do ahead	Can freeze

Missy Zimmerman

SWEET POTATO VICHYSSOISE

"Now this is different"

1 lb. sweet potatoes or yams
2 large leeks
3 Tbsp. butter
4 cups chicken broth
½ - ¾ cup whipping cream
juice of 1 lime
nutmeg
salt
pepper
minced chives

Peel and slice sweet potatoes. Slice white part of leeks. Melt butter in large saucepan and cook vegetables over medium-low heat for 5 minutes until leeks are softened. Stir in chicken broth. Simmer over medium heat 15 minutes until potatoes are soft. Purée and stir in whipping cream and lime juice. Season with nutmeg, salt and pepper to taste. Serve warm or chilled, sprinkled with chives.

Preparation:	40 min.	Easy	Serves: 6-8
Cooking:	20 min.	Can do ahead	Can freeze

Ann H. Garrett

SALAD SOUP

"A totally unique soup"

1 cup chicken broth
1½ tsp. flour
2 cups leftover green salad
  with dressing*
garlic croutons or freshly
  grated Parmesan cheese

***NOTE: Do not use with Ranch
or cream-style dressing**

Put chicken broth and flour in blender. Add salad and purée until smooth. Cook soup on low for about 1 hour; stir fairly often, it should be thick. Serve with croutons or sprinkled with Parmesan cheese.

Preparation:	5 min.	Easy	Serves: 4
Cooking:	1 hour	Can do ahead	

Clee McBee

ART COUNCIL CHOWDER

"A cup of this, a can of that = soup"

2 cups water
¼ cup long grain rice
1 pkg. Mrs. Weiss Kluski
  soup mix
1 onion, chopped
1 8-oz. can creamed corn
1 5-oz. can chicken
2 cups milk
bacon, cooked and crumbled
  (optional)

Mix water, rice, soup mix and onion in a 2-quart saucepan. Bring to a boil. Cover and simmer on low for 20-25 minutes until rice is tender. Add creamed corn, chicken and milk. Heat until hot. Pour into bowls; sprinkle with bacon.

Preparation:	20 min.	Easy	Serves: 6
Cooking:	30-40 min.	Can do ahead	Can freeze

Betsy McCloskey

CREAM OF PARISIAN VEGETABLE SOUP

"C'est si bon"

2 cups water
1 20-oz. pkg. broccoli, cauliflower
  and carrots
½ cup butter
½ cup margarine
½ cup chopped onion
½ cup chopped celery
1 cup flour
6 cups milk
4 chicken bouillon cubes,
  crushed
1 cup chopped ham

Cook vegetables in water until tender. DO NOT DRAIN. Set aside. Melt butter and margarine in Dutch oven or soup pot. Add onion and celery and cook until clear. Mix flour and milk with butter mixture. Cook until mixture thickens. Add bouillon cubes and ham to soup. Add vegetables to soup. Season to taste.

Preparation: 30 min. Easy Serve: 6-8
Cooking: 45 min. Can do ahead

Gae C. Bradley

BRIE SOUP

"A sophisticated soup"

2½ lbs. Brie cheese (about ½
  of large wheel)
1 quart hot chicken stock or
  broth
2 Tbsp. butter
1¼ cups fresh sliced mushrooms
1 cup carrots, julienne
1 cup green onions, sliced
¼ cup dry Sherry
2 cups heavy cream

After removing the crust from Brie, dissolve in hot chicken stock in large saucepan. Strain. Melt butter in Dutch oven over low heat. Add mushrooms, carrots, green onions and sauté until tender. Add cheese mixture. Stir in Sherry and cream. Serve hot.

Preparation: 30 min. Easy Serves: 6
  Can do ahead

Anne S. Courneen

SPRING ASPARAGUS SOUP

"Asparagus means Spring"

1½ lbs. fresh asparagus
2 Tbsp. butter
3 Tbsp. chopped chives
1 can condensed chicken broth
2 cups milk or light cream
salt and pepper, to taste

To prepare asparagus, break off end of each stalk as far down as it snaps easily. Discard ends. Wash tips and cut into 1" pieces. In medium saucepan, melt butter over medium heat. Add asparagus and chives and sauté 3 minutes, stirring frequently. Add broth and bring to a boil. Cover and cook over low heat until asparagus is tender. Remove from heat and add milk. Pour all into blender and blend until smooth. Return to heat and add salt and pepper. Do not boil. Serve hot, garnished with additional chives.

Preparation: 10 min. Easy Serves: 4
Cooking: 20 min. Can freeze

Missy Zimmerman

CHLODNIK

4 cups buttermilk
1 cup sour cream
1½ cups beets, diced, peeled
   and cooked
1½ cups diced, seeded
   cucumbers
3 Tbsp. dill
2 Tbsp. minced scallions
salt and pepper, to taste
¼ cup red wine vinegar
½ cup sugar
1 tsp. prepared mustard
3 hard-boiled eggs, chopped

Mix the buttermilk and sour cream together. Add the beets, cucumbers, dill, scallions, and salt and pepper to taste. Blend the wine vinegar, sugar and mustard together. Add to mixture and blend. Chill for 5 hours before serving. Add chopped eggs for garnish.

Preparation: 20-25 min.   Easy   Serves: 6
Cooking: 45-60 min.   Must do ahead

Hannah Wedeen

CHILLED RED RASPBERRY SOUP

3½ pints fresh raspberries OR
   3 cans frozen raspberries
6 oz. granulated sugar
7 oz. honey
1½ oz. Chambord liqueur
23 oz. apple juice
32 oz. heavy whipping cream
sour cream to garnish
mint leaves to garnish

Purée raspberries, sugar and honey in food processor until smooth; strain. Add apple juice and Chambord; blend well. Stir in heavy cream. Garnish with dollop of sour cream and fresh mint leaves.

Preparation: 20 min.   Easy   Serves: 12
                  Can do ahead

Gregory Powell, Chef
Wooden Angel Restaurant

TOMATO SOUP

"Has a surprising flavor"

2 cups tomato juice
1 Tbsp. tomato paste
2 scallions, minced
salt and pepper, to taste
pinch of thyme
½ tsp. curry powder
1 tsp. lemon juice
½ cup sour cream
sugar, to taste
chopped parsley

Mix all ingredients together. Serve cold or hot. If served hot, do not boil. Sprinkle with chopped parsley.

NOTE: If freezing, freeze before adding sour cream.

Preparation: 5 min.   Easy   Serves: 4
Cooking: 5 min.   Can do ahead   Can freeze

Mrs. Robinson F. Barker

CHILLED AVOCADO SOUP

"Perfect for a hot summer day"

1 avocado, peeled and pitted
1 can Cross and Blackwell
  consommé madrilene
1 cup sour cream
⅛ tsp. salt
⅛ tsp. chili powder (scant)
⅛ tsp. cayenne (scant)
⅛ tsp. grated onion
chives, for garnish

Put avocado pulp, consommé and sour cream in blender and liquify. Season with salt, chili powder, cayenne and grated onions. Mix in and chill. Adjust spices to suit. Garnish with chives.

Preparation: 5 min.   Easy   Serves: 4
                       Must do ahead

Reba Page

CANTALOUPE SOUP

2 medium cantaloupes, cut in
  1" pieces (seeds and rind
  removed)
juice of 1 lemon
juice of 1 lime
1 cup simple syrup (recipe
  follows)
¼ cup Midori Melon liqueur,
  optional
1 cinnamon stick
1 lime, thinly sliced

Place all ingredients, except cinnamon stick, in blender and purée. Add cinnamon and refrigerate overnight. Serve cold garnished with thin lime slices.

Simple Syrup:
Place water and sugar in a small saucepan, stir, and bring to a boil. Reduce heat and simmer for 3 minutes. Remove from heat and refrigerate.

Simple Syrup:
1 cup water
1¼ cups sugar

Preparation: 20 min.   Easy   Serves: 6
Cooking: 3 min.   Must do ahead

Cathy Armburger
Alphorn Restaurant

QUICK PEACHY SOUP

"Delicious warm or cold"

1 21-oz. can peach pie filling
2 cups apricot nectar
2-3 Tbsp. orange liqueur
dash nutmeg
sour cream and orange peel as
  garnish, if desired

In medium saucepan, combine all ingredients and heat through. DO NOT BOIL. Serve warm. If desired, garnish with sour cream and orange peel.

NOTE: Fruit soup may be served cold. Combine all ingredients; chill before serving. Serve it warm or cold as an appetizer for dinner, as dessert or as fruit cup for brunch.

Preparation: 2 min.   Easy   Serves: 4-6
Cooking: 5 min.   Can do ahead   Can freeze

Mary Elizabeth Eckman

BREADS

BENEDUM CENTER

The performing arts complex is the 42 million dollar home of the Pittsburgh Ballet Theatre, the Pittsburgh Opera, the Pittsburgh Dance Council and the Civic Light Opera. The Center emerged from a meticulous historic restoration and expansion of the former Stanley Theatre.

Additional illustrations in this section:

Dancers from the International Folk Theatre performed their debut at the Benedum Center this year.

This chandelier hangs in the office where the late Mayor Richard S. Caliguiri spent a decade laying the foundation for Renaissance II.

The Fork Sculpture at the North Shore Center. The Center features an art park in conjunction with newly constructed buildings.

Pittsburgh's new skyline as viewed from the Veterans Bridge and the East Street Expressway.

The Chief - the late Art Rooney, owner of the Pittsburgh Steelers.

BREADS

GLORIOUS MORNING MUFFINS

2 cups flour
1 cup sugar
2 tsp. baking soda
2 tsp. cinnamon
½ tsp. salt
2 cups grated carrots
½ cup raisins
½ cup chopped pecans
½ cup sweetened shredded
  coconut
1 apple, peeled, cored and
  grated
3 large eggs
1 cup vegetable oil
2 tsp. vanilla

Sift together flour, sugar, baking soda, cinnamon and salt. Stir in carrots, raisins, pecans, coconut and apple. In another bowl, beat eggs with vegetable oil and vanilla and stir the mixture into the flour mixture until the batter is just combined. Spoon batter into well-greased muffin pan cups, filling them to the top, and bake muffins in oven at 350° for 35 minutes or until springy to the touch. Let muffins cool in the tins on a rack for 5 minutes, turn out and let cool completely.

*Note: Pan size will determine quantity and cooking time.

Preparation: 15 min.	Easy	Yield: 12-18 muffins
Cooking: 25-35 min.	Can do ahead	Can freeze

Martha D. Smith

APPLE CARROT MUFFINS

3 eggs
⅔ cup sugar
½ cup oil
3 medium apples, shredded
2 large carrots, shredded
1 tsp. vanilla
1 cup graham flour
1 cup cake flour
1 Tbsp. baking powder
½ tsp. baking soda
½ tsp. salt
½ tsp. cinnamon
½ cup chopped walnuts or
   pecans

In large bowl, combine eggs, sugar, oil, apples, carrots, vanilla. Mix well. In another bowl, combine flours, baking powder, baking soda, salt, cinnamon, and nuts. Stir with fork to mix. Combine mixtures by folding together gently until just mixed. Do not over mix. Spoon into muffin papers, filling ⅔ full. Combine topping ingredients by stirring with fork. Sprinkle on top of muffins. Bake at 375° for 25-30 minutes.

Topping:
4 Tbsp. sugar
2 Tbsp. flour
¾ tsp. cinnamon
1 Tbsp. soft margarine

Preparation: 20 min.   Easy   Yield: 12-16 muffins
Cooking: 25-30 min. Can do ahead   Can freeze

Mary Jo Johnson

BRAN-CARROT MUFFINS

"High fiber, low fat, so good for you"

¾ cup margarine, melted and
   cooled
3 eggs
1 cup Nabisco 100% Bran
1¾ cups flour
1 cup sugar
2 tsp. baking powder
1 tsp. baking soda
1½ tsp. cinnamon
1½ cups grated carrots (about
   3 medium-sized)
1 Tbsp. molasses
½ cup raisins (optional)

In large bowl, beat margarine and eggs at medium speed until well blended. Stir in bran. Let stand 5 minutes. In small bowl, combine flour, sugar, baking powder, baking soda, and cinnamon. Blend into bran mixture. Add molasses and carrots. (Mixture will be thick.) Bake in greased muffin tin for 20 minutes at 350°.

Preparation: 20 min.   Easy   Yield: 18 muffins
Cooking: 20 min.   Can do ahead   Can freeze

Carol Regan Dickson

LEMON MUFFINS
"A different refreshing taste"

½ cup vegetable oil
½ cup sugar
2 egg yolks
1 cup unsifted flour
1 tsp. baking powder
¼ tsp. salt
4 Tbsp. fresh lemon juice
1 Tbsp. grated fresh lemon peel
2 egg whites

Topping:
2 Tbsp. sugar
¼ tsp. nutmeg

Beat oil and sugar very well. Add egg yolks one at a time, beating well after each addition. Add flour, baking powder, and salt to creamed mixture alternately with lemon juice. Fold grated peel into batter. Beat egg whites until stiff, but not dry. Carefully fold egg whites into batter. Fill muffin papers ¾ full. After mixing sugar and nutmeg, sprinkle on top of muffins. Bake at 375° for 25 minutes—WATCH CAREFULLY TOWARD THE END.

Preparation: 15 min.   Easy   Yield: 1 dozen
Cooking: 25 min.   Can do ahead   Can freeze

Catherine Clarke Johnson

BLUEBERRY MUFFINS
"A perennial favorite"

1¾ cups all-purpose flour
⅔ cup sugar
1 Tbsp. baking powder
¾ tsp. salt
6 Tbsp. butter or margarine
  (¾ stick), softened
1 egg
½ cup milk
1 tsp. grated lemon peel
½ tsp. vanilla extract
1 cup fresh or frozen
  blueberries*

*If frozen blueberries are used,
  do not thaw before adding
  them to batter.

Preheat oven to 400°. Grease muffin-pan cups. In large bowl, mix flour, sugar, baking powder and salt. With pastry blender or two knives used scissor-fashion, cut in butter or margarine until mixture resembles fine crumbs. In small bowl, beat egg, milk, lemon peel and vanilla extract until blended. Stir egg mixture into flour mixture just until flour is moistened. (Batter will be lumpy.) Fold blueberries into batter. Spoon batter into muffin-pan cups. Bake 20-25 minutes until golden and toothpick inserted in center of muffin comes out clean.

Immediately remove muffins from pan. Serve warm. Cool muffins, if desired, on a wire rack. They can be reheated to serve later. 365 calories each.

Preparation: 15 min.   Easy   Yield: 12 muffins
Cooking: 25 min.   Can do ahead   Can freeze

Betsy Spalding

49

ORANGE DATE MUFFINS

1 large orange, rind removed
  and reserved
½ cup fresh orange juice
½ cup chopped dates
1 stick unsalted butter, cut into
  bits and softened
1 large egg, beaten slightly
1½ cups all-purpose flour
¾ cup sugar
1 tsp. baking soda
1 tsp. double-acting baking
  powder
1 tsp. salt

Remove pith from orange, seed and quarter it. In a food processor with steel blades, blend reserved rind, orange juice, dates, butter and egg until mixture is well combined and rind is finely ground. Transfer to a large bowl. In separate bowl, sift together all dry ingredients. Add to orange mixture and stir until just combined. (Batter should be lumpy.) Spoon batter into 18 well-greased muffin tins, filling them ⅔ full. Bake in a preheated oven at 400° for about 15 minutes or until golden brown. Let muffins cool on a rack for 5 minutes before removing from tin. These are very moist and need no extra butter at serving time. Serve warm.

NOTE: This recipe will also make 40-50 petite muffins, should be baked about 10 minutes.

Preparation: 15 min.	Easy	Yield: 18 muffins
Cooking: 15 min.	Can do ahead	Can freeze

Sue Harvey

PUMPKIN BREAD

"Bake this for Halloween or Thanksgiving"

2 cups Crisco oil
2 cups sugar
5 eggs
2 cups pumpkin
3 cups flour
2 tsp. baking soda
2 tsp. baking powder
1 tsp. salt
1 tsp. cinnamon
1 tsp. nutmeg
1 cup chopped nuts
2 pkgs. instant coconut cream
  pie filling

Mix oil, sugar, eggs and pumpkin. Add sifted dry ingredients and the dry pie filling. Grease and flour 2 loaf pans. Bake at 350° for about 1¼ hours. Refrigerate 1 day before serving.

Preparation: 20 min.	Easy	Yield: 2 loaves
Cooking: 1¼ hrs.	Must do ahead	Can freeze

Mrs. Lois Bodnar

GREAT BANANA MUFFINS

"Keep in freezer for a quick breakfast"

½ cup butter, at room
  temperature
1 cup sugar
2 eggs
1½ cups unbleached flour
1 tsp. baking soda
½ cup non-fat, plain yogurt
1 tsp. vanilla
1¼ cups ripe bananas, mashed
½ cup chopped pecans
  (optional)

Preheat oven to 350°. Cream butter and sugar together with electric mixer. Add eggs. Sift dry ingredients together and add to butter mixture alternately with yogurt mixed with bananas and vanilla. Line muffin tins with foil liners. Fill each cup ¾ full. Bake for approximately 25 minutes or until golden brown.

Preparation: 20 min.   Easy   Yield: 18
Cooking: 25 min.   Can do ahead   Can freeze

Jane C. Biggar

BANANA OATMEAL MUFFINS

"Use up those brown bananas"

½ cup sugar
½ cup margarine
2 eggs
3 bananas, mashed
¾ cup honey
1½ cups flour
1 tsp. baking powder
1 tsp. baking soda
¾ tsp. salt
1 cup quick-cooking oatmeal

Cream together sugar and margarine. Beat in eggs, banana and honey. Stir together flour, baking powder, baking soda and salt. Add to creamed mixture, beating just until blended. Stir in oatmeal. Fill 24 greased muffin cups (or use papers) ⅔ full. Bake at 375° for 18-20 minutes.

Preparation: 15 min.   Easy   Yield: 24 muffins
Cooking: 18-20 min.   Can do ahead   Can freeze

Sandra L. Kuriger

OLD SOUTH BANANA NUT BREAD

½ cup butter
1 cup white sugar
½ cup brown sugar
2 eggs
1½ cups flour, sifted
½ tsp. salt
1 tsp. baking soda in ½ cup
  buttermilk
1 cup mashed bananas
½ cup chopped pecans

In a bowl, cream butter and sugars together. Add eggs, flour and salt; mix. Add buttermilk mixture and beat well. Mix in bananas and nuts. Pour into a greased and floured loaf pan. Bake at 350° for 1 hour or until done.

Preparation: 20 min.   Easy   Yield: 1 loaf
Cooking: 1 hr.-1 hr. 15 min.   Can do ahead   Can freeze

Francine A. DeFazio

CREAM SCONES

1 cup buttermilk
1 egg
2 Tbsp. sugar (honey)
3½ cups unbleached flour
2 tsp. baking powder
1 tsp. baking soda
½ tsp. salt
½ cup melted butter
⅓ cup currants

Preheat oven to 400°. Beat buttermilk, egg and sugar together. Sift 3 cups of flour together with the baking powder, soda and salt. Add about two-thirds of the flour mixture to the buttermilk mixture and stir well. Gradually add the melted butter. Mix thoroughly in the mixture. Stir in remaining flour mixture and currants. A little more flour may be necessary to form a stiff dough. Knead dough on a lightly-floured board for several minutes. Separate into 3 equal parts. Shape each part into a thick circle 4"-5" across. Cut circles into quarters. Arrange on buttered cookie sheet. Bake for 20-25 minutes or until lightly browned on top.

Preparation: 20 min.   Moderately difficult   Yield: 1 doz.
Cooking: 20-25 min.

Hyun Hochsmann

FRENCH PEASANT BREAD

"Great appearance with a chewy consistency"

2 cups lukewarm water
1 pkg. dry yeast
1 Tbsp. sugar
2 tsp. salt
4 cups flour (bread or
  all-purpose)
1 Tbsp. cornmeal
melted butter or margarine

In a large bowl, combine water, yeast, sugar and salt. Stir until dissolved. Stir in flour. Turn the dough out on to a floured plate. Clean the bowl and grease with butter. Return the dough to the bowl, cover with a damp towel. Let rise in warm place for 45 minutes or until double in bulk. Grease a baking sheet and sprinkle it with the cornmeal. Flour your hands and divide into 2 parts, shaping each into an oblong loaf but DO NOT KNEAD. Place both loaves on the prepared baking sheet. Let the loaves rise another 45 minutes until almost doubled in size. Preheat oven to 425°. Brush the tops of loaves with melted butter and bake 10 minutes. Reduce temperature to 375° and bake 20 minutes more. While the loaves are still hot, brush with more butter and serve.

Preparation: 30 min.   Moderately difficult   Yield: 2 loaves
Cooking: 30 min.   Must do ahead

Mrs. Howard G. Schutte, Jr.

OAT BRAN DATE MUFFINS

"Get your fiber here"

1½ cups oat bran
1 cup flour
1 cup wheat flour
1 tsp. baking powder
1 tsp. baking soda
½ - ⅔ cup brown sugar
1 cup chopped dates
2 eggs
½ cup oil
1 cup buttermilk or sour milk

Mix all dry ingredients plus dates and set aside. Beat eggs; add oil and buttermilk. Mix egg mixture with dry ingredients until just moistened. Fill greased muffin tins and then bake for 14-16 minutes at 375°.

Preparation:	10 min.	Easy	Yield: 12
Cooking:	14-16 min.	Can do ahead	Can freeze

Margaret Dollar

LEMON EASTER BREAD

"Try it toasted on Easter morning"

2 doz. eggs, beaten
2 1-oz. bottles lemon extract
3 large cakes yeast
2 cups warm water
4 cups milk
3 lbs. sugar
2 Tbsp. salt
3 cups Crisco shortening
11 cups flour
1 egg yolk
2 Tbsp. water

In large mixing bowl, beat eggs. Add lemon extract. Dissolve yeast in warm water and add to eggs. Scald the milk. Add sugar, salt and Crisco to milk. Do not melt the Crisco completely. Cool before adding to eggs and yeast mixture. Add flour. Mix and knead until smooth. Let rise until doubled. Divide dough into seven parts. Braid the dough by dividing each of the seven parts into three strands. Braid the strands and place in greased angel food or bundt cake pans to create round loaves. Round cake pans may also be used. One can place colored eggs throughout the braids for decorations. Allow to rise again until doubled in size. Bake in preheated 350° oven for 40-45 minutes. You may have to use a foil tent if top browns too quickly. Use a toothpick to test inside for doneness. Before removing from oven, gently brush with egg yolk and 2 Tbsp. water mixture to give it a shiny look. Cool on wire racks. You may wish to ice a loaf with a powdered sugar and milk glaze instead of egg yolk glaze.

Preparation:	2-3 hrs.	Moderately difficult	Yield: 7 loaves
Cooking:	40-45 min.	Can do ahead	Can freeze

Linda Chufe

1978 RICHARD S. CALIGUIRI 1988

NABISCO SHREDDED WHEAT BREAD

"Won first place in a bread-baking contest"

2½ cups hot water (120-130°)*
2 reg. shredded wheat biscuits,
   broken into small pieces
⅓ cup sugar
1 Tbsp. salt
⅓ cup molasses
3 Tbsp. shortening
1½ pkg. dry yeast
4 cups all-purpose flour AND
   2 cups whole wheat flour OR
   6-7 cups all-purpose flour.

*For hot water of 120-130°,
use a microwave with a
probe, if you have one. You
will always get an exact
temperature reading with this
method.

Pour hot water over shredded wheat biscuits. Add sugar, salt, molasses and shortening. Combine flours. In a large mixing bowl, thoroughly mix 2½ cups flour mixture with undissolved yeast. Gradually add hot water mixture to dry ingredients and beat for 2 minutes at medium speed of electric mixer, scraping bowl occasionally. Stir in enough additonal flour to make a stiff dough. Turn out onto lightly floured board and knead until smooth and elastic, about 8-10 minutes. Cover with plastic wrap, then a towel. Let rest for 20 minutes. Divide dough in half. Roll each half to 14x9" rectangle.

Roll the short side up to form a loaf. Place in 2 greased 9x5x3" loaf pans. Brush loaves with oil and cover with plastic wrap. Refrigerate 2 to 24 hours. When ready to bake, remove from refrigerator. Uncover dough carefully. Let stand for 10 minutes. If it has not risen enough, let it sit for 1 hour or more to rise in a warm place. Puncture any gas bubbles that may have formed on the top of the bread with a metal skewer or toothpick. Bake at 400° for about 40 minutes or until done. Remove from pans and cool on wire rack. Brush tops of bread with butter while still warm.

Preparation: 30 min.	Moderately difficult	Yield: 2 loaves
Cooking: 40 min.	Can do ahead	Can freeze

Sheree C. Peery

FROZEN POPOVERS

"Wonderful to have on hand"

2 eggs
1 cup flour
1 cup milk
½ tsp. salt
1 Tbsp. melted butter

With whisk, beat eggs slightly. Add remainder of ingredients. DO NOT OVERBEAT, just enough until smooth. Pour into 6 well-greased custard cups. Place in freezer and freeze. To bake, preheat oven to 400°. Place frozen popovers still in cups (as many as desired) onto foil-lined cookie sheet. Bake for 60 minutes. Serve immediately.

Preparation: 10 min.	Easy	Yield: 6 popovers
Cooking: 60 min.	Must do ahead	Must freeze

Betsy McCloskey

CINNAMON RAISIN BREAD

"Take the day off and have fun in the kitchen"

1½ cups milk
¼ cup sugar
2 tsp. salt
½ cup butter
1½ cups raisins
½ cup very warm water
2 pkgs. active dry yeast
3 eggs
7½ cups flour, unsifted
½ cup sugar
4 tsp. cinnamon
¼ cup melted butter

In small saucepan, heat milk until bubbles form around edge of pan; remove from heat. Add ¼ cup sugar and the salt, ½ cup butter and the raisins. Stir until butter melts. Cool to lukewarm. Sprinkle yeast over warm water in large bowl, stirring until dissolved. Stir in milk mixture. Add eggs and 4 cups flour. Beat vigorously with a wooden spoon (about 2 minutes). Gradually add remaining flour. Mix in last by hand until dough is stiff enough to leave side of the bowl. Turn out dough onto lightly floured pastry board. Knead until smooth and elastic (about 10 minutes). Place in lightly greased large bowl; turn dough over to bring up greased side. Cover with a towel. Let rise in a warm place (85°), free from draft, until double in bulk (about 1½ hours). In small bowl mix ½ cup sugar and cinnamon. Turn dough out onto lightly floured pastry board. Divide in half. Roll out ½ of dough into 16x8" rectangle. Sprinkle with sugar and cinnamon mixture and roll up jelly roll fashion, pinching ends and folding them under. Repeat for other half. Place each loaf seam down in a greased loaf pan. Brush with melted butter and cover with a towel. Let rise in warm place, free from draft, until sides come up to top of pan (about 1 hour). Preheat oven to 375°. Place rack in middle of oven. Brush each loaf again with remaining melted butter and sprinkle with the sugar and cinnamon mixture. Bake at 375° for 35-40 minutes. Rap with knuckle to check doneness. (It is done when it sounds hollow.)

Preparation: 4-5 hrs.	Moderately difficult	Yield: 2 loaves
Cooking: 40 min.	Must do ahead	Can freeze

Lori O. Haley

CASSEROLE RYE BREAD

"An easy bread with a cake-like texture"

1 cup milk, scalded
¼ cup brown sugar
2 tsp. salt
¼ cup butter
2 pkgs. dry yeast
1 cup warm water
2 Tbsp. caraway seed
3 cups flour
2 cups rye flour
milk
caraway seed for top

Pour milk over sugar, salt and butter; cool to lukewarm. Dissolve yeast in warm water, add to milk. Add caraway and ½ of each of the flours. Mix for 2 minutes. Add remaining flour and mix for 2 minutes more. Cover and let rise for 1 hour. Stir batter for ½ minute. Put in a well-greased 2 quart casserole dish. Brush with milk and sprinkle with caraway seed. Bake at 350° for 50-55 minutes.

Preparation: 1½ hrs.	Easy	
Cooking: 1 hr.	Must do ahead	Can freeze

Holly B. Worth

BELGIAN WAFFLES

1 cup cottage cheese
3 eggs
½ tsp. salt
1 Tbsp. sugar
¼ cup flour
½ stick butter, melted
1 tsp. vanilla

Mix all ingredients well. (Blender may be used.) Cook on heated waffle iron.

Preparation:	5 min.	Easy	Serves: 4-6
Cooking:	10-12 min.	Serve immediately	

Lucille Lynd Calhoun

CLOUD BISCUITS

2 cups flour
1 Tbsp. sugar
4 tsp. baking powder
½ tsp. salt
½ cup shortening
1 egg, slightly beaten
⅔ cup buttermilk
16 sugar cubes
¼ cup orange juice

Preheat oven to 400°. Mix first 4 ingredients. Cut in the shortening with a pastry blender. Stir in egg and milk. Knead lightly on a floured surface and roll until ¾" thick. Cut into any shape and place on ungreased cookie sheet. Dip sugar cubes in orange juice and press lightly onto top of each biscuit. Bake 12-14 minutes. Serve warm.

Preparation:	20 min.	Easy	Yield: 16 biscuits
Cooking:	12-14 min.		

Linda D. Orsini

BUTTERSCOTCH COFFEE CAKE

"Cake mix and instant pudding make this easy"

1 box Duncan Hines yellow
   cake mix
1 lg. box instant butterscotch
   pudding
4 eggs
½ cup Puritan oil
1 cup water
2 Tbsp. margarine
¾ cup walnuts
¾ cup brown sugar

Mix all ingredients until well blended. Pour half of cake batter in greased and floured 9x13" pan. Sprinkle half of nut mixture (margarine, walnuts and brown sugar) over batter. Pour remaining batter in pan. Sprinkle remainder of nut mixture over batter. Bake at 350° for 50-60 minutes. Test with toothpick. If it comes out clean, remove from oven.

Preparation:	30 min.	Easy	Serves: 12 +
Cooking:	50-60 min.	Can do ahead	Can freeze

Judie D. Froman

HOBO BREAD

"Baked in coffee cans"

2½ cups coffee
4 tsp. baking soda
2 cups raisins
¾ cup sugar
¾ cup brown sugar
1½ cups broken nut meats
4 cups flour
¼ tsp. salt
cream cheese for spreading

Bring coffee to a boil. Pour coffee over baking soda and raisins. Let stand overnight. Add to this mixture, the sugar, brown sugar, nuts, flour and salt. Mix well. Divide batter into 3 well-greased (1 lb. size) coffee cans. Bake at 325° for 65 minutes. Let cool in cans. Slice and spread with cream cheese between slices.

NOTE: This is low cholesterol (no fat).

Preparation: 15 min.	Easy	Yield: 3 loaves
Cooking: 65 min.	Must do ahead	Can freeze

Margaret M. Dollar

CHOCOLATE ZUCCHINI BREAD

"Moist and tasty"

2 cups flour
½ tsp. baking soda
½ tsp. baking powder
½ tsp. salt
3 eggs, beaten
1 cup oil
2 cups sugar
1 tsp. vanilla
3 squares unsweetened baking
   chocolate, melted
1 cup chopped nuts
2 cups grated zucchini, packed

Sift flour with dry ingredients. Add eggs, oil, sugar, vanilla and chocolate to flour mixture and mix well. Fold in nuts and zucchini. Use 2 regular-sized loaf pans or 5 small ones. Bake at 350° for 45 minutes for small pans or 55 minutes for large pans. (Spray pans with a small amount of PAM first). Leave in pans a few minutes before removing.

Preparation: 30 min.	Easy	Yield: 2-5 loaves
Cooking: 45 min.	Can do ahead	Can freeze

Linda D. Orsini

SWEET BREAKFAST PIZZA
"Allow time for dough to double"

1 1-lb. loaf frozen white bread dough, thawed, cut in half
2 8-oz. pkgs. cream cheese, softened
½ cup sugar
6 Tbsp. flour
2 egg yolks
2 tsp. fresh lemon juice
⅔ cup strawberry jam
4 Tbsp. toasted sliced almonds

Cover dough, let rise in warm, draft-free area until doubled. Place each half on a greased baking sheet or pizza pan. Pat each half into a 12" diameter circle to form crust; set aside. Beat cream cheese, sugar, flour, egg yolks and lemon juice until smooth. Spread each crust with half the cheese mixture to within ½" of edges. Cover lightly; let rise 30 minutes. Bake in a preheated 375° oven for 15-20 minutes or until browned. Spread each half with jam. Sprinkle with almonds. Bake 5 minutes longer. Makes 2 12" pizzas.

Preparation: 15 min.	Easy	Yield: 2 12" pizzas
Cooking: 20-25 min.	Can do ahead	Can freeze

Martha D. Smith

COFFEE RING
"Easy and moist"

1 box any flavor Pillsbury Quick Bread mix
1 stick butter or margarine
½ cup brown sugar
½ tsp. vanilla
½ cup chopped pecans (best with pecans, but other nuts may be used)

Grease bundt pan with shortening. Mix quick bread according to package directions. Set aside. Melt butter in a saucepan. Add sugar and vanilla. Set aside. Spread pecans around bundt pan. Pour brown sugar mixture over nuts. Pour in quick bread mix. Bake at 350° for 35-40 minutes. Invert immediately on serving plate. Serve warm.

Preparation: 15 min.	Easy	Serves: 6-8
Cooking: 35-40 min.	Serve immediately	

Bonnie J. Weber

PENNSYLVANIA GERMAN CORN PONE

"Tastes best when served warm from oven"

¾ cup sugar
¼ cup shortening
1 egg
¾ cup roasted cornmeal*
1¼ cups flour
1 tsp. baking soda
½ tsp. salt
1 cup buttermilk OR milk

*If you cannot find roasted cornmeal, place yellow cornmeal on a cookie sheet in oven at 350° until lightly browned. Roasted cornmeal gives this recipe its unique taste.

Mix sugar, shortening and egg well. Add the cornmeal and mix. Combine flour, soda and salt. Add alternately with milk or buttermilk. Pour into two 8" round pans or one 9x9" square pan. Bake at 350° degrees for 20-25 minutes.

NOTE: May also be used for muffins.

| Preparation: 10 min. | Easy | Serves: 5-6 |
| Cooking: 25 min. | Can do ahead | Can freeze |

Peggy J. Goodman

GOLDEN RAISIN BUNS

"This is a breakfast bread based on the old cream puff."

1 cup water
½ cup margarine
1 tsp. sugar
¼ tsp. salt
1 cup flour
4 eggs
½ cup golden raisins (plump in hot water 15 minutes and drain)

Frosting:
1 Tbsp. margarine, melted
1½ Tbsp. cream or milk
1 cup powdered sugar
½ tsp. lemon juice
½ tsp. vanilla

Combine water, margarine, sugar and salt in saucepan. Bring to a boil. Add flour all at once. Over low heat, beat with a wooden spoon for 1 minute or until mixture leaves side of pan and forms smooth, thick dough. Remove from heat and continue beating for 2 minutes to cool slightly. Add eggs, one at a time, beating after each addition until mixture has a satiny sheen. Stir in raisins. Drop by heaping tablespoonsful, 2" apart, on a greased baking sheet. Bake in a preheated 375° oven for 30-35 minutes. Put on rack and frost while warm.

Frosting:
Melt the margarine, then stir in the cream (or milk). Remove from heat and stir in powdered sugar and lemon juice and vanilla.

| Preparation: 20 min. | Moderately difficult | Serves: 6-8 |
| Cooking: 35 min. | Serve immediately | |

Joanne Taylor

BRAIDED CREAM CHEESE COFFEECAKE

"Start this the day before"

1 cup sour cream
½ cup sugar
1 tsp. salt
½ cup butter, melted
2 pkgs. dry yeast
½ cup warm water (115-120°)
2 eggs, beaten
4 cups flour

Heat sour cream over low heat; stir in sugar, salt and butter. Cool to lukewarm. Sprinkle yeast over warm water in a large mixing bowl, stirring until yeast dissolves well. Add sour cream mixture, eggs and flour; mix well. Cover tightly and refrigerate overnight.

Cream cheese filling:
2 8-oz. pkgs. cream cheese, softened
¾ cup sugar
1 egg, beaten
⅛ tsp. salt
2 tsp. vanilla extract

Glaze:
2 tsp. vanilla
4 Tbsp. milk
2 cups powdered sugar

Filling:
Combine cream cheese and sugar in a small mixing bowl. Add egg, salt, and vanilla; mix well. Divide dough into 4 equal parts. Roll out each part on a well-floured board into a 12x8" rectangle. Spread ¼ of the filling on each rectangle. Roll up jelly roll fashion, beginning at the long sides. Pinch edges together and fold sides under slightly. Place the rolls, seam side down, on greased baking sheets. Slit each roll at 2" intervals about ⅔ of the way through dough so it will resemble a braid. Cover and let rise in a warm place, free from drafts, until double in bulk (about 1 hour). Bake at 375° for 12-15 minutes. Spread with glaze while warm.

Glaze:
Cream sugar and milk with spoon. Add vanilla; mix well. Spread on warm loaves.

Preparation:	1½ hrs.	Moderately difficult	Yield: 4 loaves
Cooking:	15 min.	Must do ahead	Can freeze

Mary Anne Riley

NUT SPIRALS

"Unbaked bread sticks make this a snap"

¾ cup pecan pieces or halves
6 Tbsp. sugar
1 tsp. cinnamon
4-5 Tbsp. unsalted butter
1 11-oz. can refrigerator (unbaked) soft bread sticks

Preheat oven to 375° and spray large baking sheet with PAM. Process the first 3 ingredients in food processor until nuts are evenly chopped (or chop nuts by hand), then blend with sugar and cinnamon. (This is the topping.) Melt the butter. Separate bread sticks. Put the topping in a shallow dish. Put the butter in another shallow dish. Coat each bread stick "rope" with melted butter, then roll in topping. Form bread dough into spirals on baking sheets. Bake until golden at 350° for about 12-14 minutes.

Preparation:	15 min.	Easy	Serves: 8
Cooking:	12-14 min.	Can do ahead	Can freeze

Clee McBee

SWEET POTATO BUNS

"Wonderful change from white buns"

1 cup milk
⅔ cup butter
½ cup sugar
1 tsp. salt
1 cup mashed sweet potatoes,
    drained (canned are easier to
    use)
1 pkg. dry yeast
½ cup warm water (105-115°)
6 cups flour
½ tsp. ground cardamom
2 eggs, beaten
½ cup currants (optional) OR
    ½ cup drained crushed
    pineapple

Scald milk; then add butter, sugar, salt and sweet potatoes. Cool to lukewarm. Dissolve yeast in warm water in a separate bowl. Mix flour and cardamom in a large bowl; add milk mixture, eggs and yeast. Mix in pineapple and/or currants. Knead on floured board until smooth. Place in greased bowl, cover, and let rise until doubled. Punch down and let it rest for 10-12 minutes. Divide in 2 equal parts. Pull off and make 9 buns from each half. Place in 2 round greased 8" or 9" pans. Cover and let rise until doubled (approx. 1 hour). Bake at 375° for 20-25 minutes.

Preparation:	2½ hrs.	Easy	Yield: 18 buns
Cooking:	20-25 min.	Can do ahead	Can freeze

Lynn Popovich

DAD'S PUFFY PANCAKE

"A nice alternative to regular pancakes"

4 strips lean bacon*
3 eggs (or Egg Beaters)
⅓ cup milk
⅓ cup flour
¼ tsp. salt
2 Tbsp. bacon drippings**
cinnamon sugar

*¼ cup thinly sliced apple may
  be substituted for bacon
  strips.

**2 Tbsp. Puritan oil may be
  substituted for bacon
  drippings.

NOTE: Using above substitutions and Egg Beaters instead of eggs will make this a low cholesterol meal.

In a cast iron 10" fry pan, fry bacon* until crisp. Drain bacon on paper towel, then crumble it. Beat eggs slightly. Add milk, flour and salt; beating with rotary beater until smooth. Stir in bacon. Measure 2 Tbsp. bacon drippings into skillet (or Puritan oil); heat skillet. Tilt skillet from side to side to coat all surfaces. Turn egg mixture into hot skillet. Bake, uncovered, in a 400° oven for 20 minutes. Remove from skillet onto a dinner plate. Serve immediately with a sprinkling of sugar (or cinnamon sugar).

*When using apples, sprinkle apple slices over top of egg mixture in hot skillet.

Preparation:	15 min.	Easy	Serves: 2
Cooking:	20 min.	Serve immediately	

Betty Pecore

CORN PONE

"Serve with stew or soup"

1½ cups self-rising cornmeal
3 tsp. baking powder
3 Tbsp. sugar
4 eggs, beaten
1 cup sour cream
1 15½-oz. can cream-style corn
1 cup grated Cheddar cheese
1 cup chopped green pepper
1 cup chopped onion
½ cup Wesson oil
¾ tsp. salt

Mix all ingredients together. Bake in a 9x13″ pan or iron skillet at 450° for 20-30 minutes.

Preparation: 15 min.   Easy   Serves: 12 +
Cooking: 20-30 min.

Patricia I. Berini

CORN BREAD

"A real winner"

1¾ cups flour
¾ cup cornmeal
½ cup sugar
1 tsp. salt
3 tsp. baking powder
¼ cup margarine
1 cup milk
2 eggs

In medium bowl, sift together flour, cornmeal, sugar, salt and baking powder. Add margarine, milk and eggs. Mix all ingredients thoroughly on high speed with electric mixer. Pour into well-greased 8x8″ pan and bake at 400° for 20-30 minutes.

NOTE: This is a moist and high-rising corn bread.

Preparation: 15 min.   Easy   Serves: 6-8
Cooking: 20-30 min.   Can do ahead   Can freeze

Sharon Hays

ENTRÉES

CLAYTON, POINT BREEZE

Henry Frick's home, Clayton, in Point Breeze is now a public museum of his life. It remains today exactly as it was when Frick left. The estate houses the Frick Art Museum with its paintings and decorative arts from the 13th to 18th centuries.

Additional illustrations in this section:

These handpainted Pysanka eggs are sold every Palm Sunday at Sts. Peter and Paul Ukrainian Orthodox Church in Carnegie.

Metropol is a newly renovated entertainment and dance center. The building was a former warehouse in the Strip District.

Children are enjoying their reading room at the Braddock Free Library. This is the oldest Carnegie Library (1889) built for the men of the Edgar Thomson Plant of the Carnegie Steel Company.

Two fine examples of this Romanesque revival-style library, executed in sandstone.

Children having a ball at IKEA, a newly opened outlet in Pittsburgh for Swedish-design furniture and accessories.

A Carnegie Mellon University rowing club approaches Herrs Island in the Allegheny River.

George Segal's "Tightrope Walker" greets visitors to the Carnegie Museum. The building was designed in 1890 by Longfellow, Alden and Harlow.

The Workers Sculpture at North Shore Center honors "the men who made Pittsburgh."

These stone maidens and other sculptural fragments from lost buildings make their home in an exhibit space next to the Old Post office on the North Side. They were a gift of the Hillman Foundation.

Trimont on Mt. Washington provides tower residences with spectacular three-river views of the city.

Large mural paintings by Maximilian Vanka adorn the ceilings of the St. Nickolas Roman Catholic Church of Millvale. Painted in 1937, these vivid scenes of life in Croatia are executed in true Fresco style.

Federated Investors Tower at Liberty Center is headquarters for one of the nation's largest investment management firms.

Mario Lemieux - The Pittsburgh Penguins All-Star hockey player.

Carved in a sandstone fireplace of "La Tourelle," a home in Fox Chapel, these words are translated, "...this splendid fire is for you."

Wholey's Fish Market is located in the popular Strip District, where shoppers may purchase fresh foods directly from wholesalers.

A view of One Mellon Bank Center, USX Tower, the Allegheny Jail and County Courthouse building provides an interesting contrast between old and new.

The New Pittsburgh Sports Garden - a sports-theme entertainment center at Station Square. In the background is the subway station.

"La Tourelle" is the dream house designed for Edgar Kaufmann by Benno Janssen in Fox Chapel.

D'ANGELOS SAUSAGE CHEESE PIE
"Five kinds of cheese"

Filling:
3 lbs. hot Italian sausage, loose
½ cup grated Parmesan or Romano cheese
½ lb. mild Cheddar cheese
½ lb. sharp Cheddar cheese
¼ lb. American cheese
¼ lb. extra-sharp Cheddar cheese
4 eggs, well beaten

Pastry:
4½ cups flour, sifted
½ tsp. salt
⅔ cup cold milk
1 cup + 2 Tbsp. sausage drippings (if short this amount, use salad oil)

Glaze:
1 egg
1 Tbsp. milk

Filling: Fry sausage and break into small pieces. Drain, saving all of the drippings. Cool sausage pieces and mix with other filling ingredients.

Pastry: Preheat oven to 350°. In large bowl, sift flour and salt. Make hole in center and add milk and drippings all at once. Stir with fork until blended. With hands, form a ball and divide in two. Roll out one ball on lightly floured surface to fit in an 11x17" baking sheet. Mold to fit pan with excess pastry hanging over sides. Place filling on pastry, evenly distributing it (not higher than pan). Roll out second pastry ball and place over top. Press edges with fork, trim any excess. Cut four rows of 1" steam vents.

Glaze: Mix ingredients. Brush on top of pastry.

Bake for 45 minutes or until golden.

Preparation: 40 min.	Moderately difficult	Serves: 12
Cooking: 45 min.	Can do ahead	Can freeze

The Cookbook Committee

NANN'S CHEESE STRATA

8 slices Italian bread, ¾" thick
butter
1½ lbs. cheese, grated
  (½ Cheddar, ½ Meunster)
6 eggs
2½ cups Half & Half
1 shallot, finely minced
¼ tsp. paprika
½ tsp. dry mustard
½ tsp. Beau Monde seasoning
½ tsp. salt
⅛ tsp. pepper
½ tsp. Worcestershire sauce
¼ tsp. cayenne pepper

Let the bread air-dry for 24 hours. Preheat oven to 300°. Cut off crusts and butter bread slices well; then cut into ½" pieces. Butter a 9x13" casserole dish. Mix bread with cheese and place in prepared dish. Place the remaining ingredients in a blender and mix until well blended. Pour over bread. Cover and chill for at least 2 hours. Before serving, let sit at room temperature for 30 minutes. Bake 1½ hours or until brown and bubbly.

Preparation: 30 min.   Easy   Serves: 6-8
Cooking: 1½ hrs.   Must do ahead

Francye Kinney

EGGS FLORENTINE-KENZIE

2 10-oz. pkgs. frozen chopped
  spinach
2 Tbsp. minced onion
2 Tbsp. lemon juice
1 cup grated Cheddar cheese
4 sliced hard-boiled eggs

White sauce:
3 Tbsp. butter
3 Tbsp. flour
½ tsp. salt
½ tsp. dry mustard
¼ tsp. pepper
1½ cups milk

Topping:
1 cup bread crumbs
1 Tbsp. melted butter

Preheat oven to 400°. Cook spinach according to package directions. Mix cooked spinach with onion and lemon juice and spread in bottom of an 8x8" baking pan. Sprinkle with cheese and sliced eggs. Top with white sauce and sprinkle topping.

White sauce: Melt butter over low heat. Blend in flour, salt, mustard and pepper. Cook over low heat, stirring until mixture is smooth and bubbly. Remove from heat; add milk. Heat to boiling, stirring constantly. Boil and stir for 1 minute.

Topping: Mix bread crumbs with butter and sprinkle over top of spinach mixture.

Preparation: 45 min.   Easy   Serves: 4
Cooking: 20 min.

Jacqueline L. Deramo

66

CHEESE AND BACON FRITTATA
"Great for the brunch bunch"

6 eggs
1 cup milk
1 green onion, minced
2 Tbsp. butter, melted
½ tsp. salt
freshly ground black pepper,
  to taste
4 oz. Cheddar cheese,
  shredded
½ of 3-oz. can crumbled bacon
  or fresh

Preheat oven to 400°. Grease a 9x9" baking pan. With a whisk, beat the eggs, milk, onion, butter, salt, and pepper until well blended. Pour mixture into the prepared baking dish. Sprinkle the cheese and bacon over the top. Bake 20 minutes until set and golden.

Preparation:	20 min.	Easy	Serves: 4
Cooking:	20 min.	Can do ahead	

Missy Zimmerman

ZIPPY CORNBREAD

1 pkg. or box corn bread mix
4 eggs
1 small onion, grated
1 pkg. frozen chopped spinach,
  thawed
1 cup grated sharp Cheddar
  cheese
½ cup cottage cheese
¾ stick butter or margarine

Mix all ingredients together. Place in 8-9" square pan. Bake at 400° for 30 minutes.

Preparation:	15 min.	Easy	Yield: 9 lg. squares
Cooking:	30 min.	Can do ahead	Can freeze

Lynn Popovich

CHEESE AND SPINACH PIE
"Great for a Sunday night supper"

1 9" unbaked pie shell
2 slices Swiss cheese (7x4")
½ cup cooked chopped frozen
  spinach
½ cup sliced mushrooms
1 can ham, chicken or turkey
3 eggs, beaten
1 cup Half & Half
2 tsp. flour
½ tsp. salt
½ cup shredded Cheddar
  cheese

Place Swiss cheese on bottom of pie crust. Sprinkle with spinach, mushrooms and meat. Mix the next 4 ingredients together. Pour into pie shell. Sprinkle with Cheddar cheese. Bake at 350° for 40-45 minutes.

Preparation:	15 min.	Easy	Serves: 4
Cooking:	45 min.	Can do ahead	

Debra Pushic Gibbs

CRUSTLESS SALMON QUICHE

"If you like salmon, you will love this"

1 15½-oz. can salmon, reserve
liquid
½ cup shredded sharp cheese
1 Tbsp. grated onion
3 eggs, beaten
1 cup sour cream
¼ cup mayonnaise

Flake salmon. Add cheese and onion. In another bowl, blend eggs, sour cream, mayonnaise and salmon liquid. Add water to salmon liquid to make ½ cup. Stir in salmon mixture. Pour into greased quiche pan. Bake at 325° for 45 minutes.

Preparation: 10 min.	Easy	Serves: 8
Cooking: 45 min.	Serve immediately	

Teresa A. Surgeon

SAUSAGE BREAKFAST CASSEROLE

"Great for house guests"

6 slices English Muffin bread
butter
1 lb. bulk sausage
1½ cups cheese, grated (i.e.
Old English sharp Cheddar)
6 eggs, beaten
2 cups Half & Half
1 tsp. salt

Remove crusts from bread. Butter bread and place in a 9x13" baking dish. Cook and crumble sausage until brown. Drain. Spoon over bread slices. Sprinkle with cheese. Combine eggs with Half & Half and salt. Mix well and pour over cheese. Cover and chill overnight. Remove from refrigerator 15 minutes before baking. Bake, uncovered, at 350° for 45 minutes or until set.

Preparation: 20 min.	Easy	Serves: 8
Cooking: 45 min.	Must do ahead	

Geraldine S. Holst

MUSHROOM QUICHE

Pastry:
8 oz. all-purpose flour
2 oz. lard
2 oz. margarine
pinch of salt
cold water
1 egg, beaten

Filling:
2 Tbsp. chopped shallots or
   green onions
1½ oz. butter
1 lb. fresh mushrooms, sliced
1 tsp. salt
1 tsp. lemon juice
2 Tbsp. Madeira or Port wine,
   optional
3 eggs, beaten
⅔ pint whipping cream
1 oz. grated Parmesan cheese

Pastry: Sift flour and salt into a large mixing bowl. Cut fat into small cubes and add to flour. Using fingertips, lightly and gently rub pieces of fat into flour (lifting hands up high to incorporate air and being as quick as possible to keep mixture cool). When mixture looks crumbly, start to sprinkle about 4 Tbsp. of water all over. Use a round-bladed knife to start mixing and bring the mixture together. Carefully add more water, a little at a time, as needed; then finally bring the mixture together with your hands to form a smooth ball. (If there are bits that won't adhere, you need more water.) Rest the pastry, wrapped in foil or plastic wrap, in the refrigerator for 20-30 minutes before rolling out. Preheat oven to 350°. Lightly grease a 9″ container (preferably metal with a loose base). Roll out pastry and line container. Press firmly on base and sides, then prick with a fork all over. Cover inside of pastry shell with foil to prevent it coming away from sides. Bake for 15 minutes; then remove from oven and paint inside with beaten egg (from filling ingredients). Put back in oven for another 5 minutes.

Filling: Preheat oven to 375°. Cook shallots in saucepan with butter for a few moments. Stir in mushrooms, salt, lemon juice and optional wine. Cover and cook on moderately low heat for 8 minutes. Uncover, raise heat and boil until liquid is evaporated and mushrooms are beginning to sauté in their butter. Gradually stir mushrooms into eggs and cream. Pour into pastry shell, sprinkle with cheese, dot with butter and bake for 25-30 minutes.

Preparation: 40 min.	Moderately difficult	Serves: 8-10
Cooking: 45 min.	Can do ahead	Can freeze

Mrs. Maureen P. Green

69

ROQUEFORT SOUFFLÉ
"Blend and bake"

6 eggs
½ cup heavy cream
1 tsp. Worcestershire sauce
dash Tabasco sauce
¼ tsp. pepper
pinch salt
½ lb. Roquefort cheese
11 oz. cream cheese
1 Tbsp. butter

Put ingredients in blender in order given. Beat at high speed for 5 seconds. Pour in buttered pan or 4 cup soufflé dish. Bake at 375° for 40-45 minutes. Do not do ahead!

Preparation:	10 min.	Easy	Serves: 8-12
Cooking:	40-45 min.	Serve immediately	

Marianne Caspary

ORTEGA PEPPER SOUFFLÉ

2 cans Ortega peppers
1 cup Cheddar cheese
3 eggs, beaten
2 cups milk
1 cup Bisquick
½ tsp. salt

Clean seeds from peppers. Chop peppers and cover bottom of casserole. Cut cheese in cubes and cover peppers. Beat eggs with milk and Bisquick. Add salt. Pour over cheese and peppers. Bake at 350° for 45 minutes.

Preparation:	15 min.	Easy	Serves: 8
Cooking:	45 min.	Serve immediately	

Kathleen M. Pearson

BRIE QUICHE
"Use your food processor for easy mixing"

6 oz. Brie cheese, crusts removed
8 oz. cream cheese
2 Tbsp. butter, softened
3 Tbsp. whipping cream
2 eggs
salt, white pepper, and cayenne,
  to taste
½ cup chopped chives or
  scallions or more, if desired
1 8" pie shell

Preheat oven to 375°. With a mixer, beat the cheeses, butter and cream until there are no lumps. Beat in eggs. Season and stir in chives. Pour into pastry shell and bake for 30 minutes or until quiche is puffy and top is brown.

Preparation:	20 min.	Easy	Serves: 6
Cooking:	30 min.	Can do ahead	Can freeze

Shelagh B. Richards

70

BEEF

COUNTRY FRENCH CASSOULET
"Add a cup of wine for the cook"

2 lbs. smoked sausage, cut in
   2" pieces
3 lbs. beef stew meat, cut into
   1" cubes
¼ cup flour
1 tsp. salt
½ tsp. pepper
3 medium onions, coarsely
   chopped (1½ cups)
3 garlic cloves, minced
¾ cup stuffed green olives,
   halved
½-1 tsp. thyme leaves
2 15½-oz. cans kidney beans,
   drained
2 cups whole fresh mushrooms
2-3 cups dry red wine

In 5-quart Dutch oven brown sausage. Remove from pan with slotted spoon and set aside. In large bowl combine flour, salt, and pepper; coat beef stew meat. Add beef, onions and garlic to Dutch oven; cook until beef is evenly browned and tender (15 minutes). Heat oven to 350°. In 5-quart casserole, or ovenproof Dutch oven, combine sausage, beef mixture and remaining ingredients, except wine. Add 2 cups wine. Cover and bake at 350° for 3 to 3½ hours until meat is tender, stirring occasionally and adding more wine if needed. Casserole may be uncovered during last 45 minutes to thicken cassoulet, if desired.

Preparation: 30 min.	Easy	Serves: 10-12
Cooking: 3-3½ hrs.	Can do ahead	Can freeze

Robert Popovich

MEATLOAF WELLINGTON

"Very attractive in its pastry shell"

Sour Cream Pastry:
2¼ cups flour
1 tsp. salt
12 Tbsp. unsalted butter,
  cut into small pieces
1 egg
½ cup sour cream

Glaze:
1 egg
2 Tbsp. milk

Meatloaf Filling:
4 Tbsp. butter
½ lb. fresh mushrooms,
  chopped
3 lbs. ground meat (veal, beef,
  ham, lamb or any
  combination)
½ cup chopped onions
¼ cup chopped fresh parsley
½ cup milk
1 cup grated Cheddar or Swiss
  cheese
salt and pepper, to taste
sour cream (optional)

Preheat oven to 375°.

Sour Cream Pastry:
In a large bowl, place the flour and salt and add the butter. Work the mixture until it is like the texture of coarse meal. In a small bowl, mix egg and sour cream and add to flour and butter. Work into a soft ball. Wrap in plastic wrap and refrigerate one hour. Remove from refrigerator and cut dough in half. Roll out one piece to be used for bottom crust. Keep other half refrigerated. Save scraps for decorations. Mix egg and milk for the glaze; brush over top. Add decorations, brush glaze over, then prick the pastry.

Meatloaf Filling:
In large skillet, melt butter; add mushrooms. Sauté for 5 minutes; add meat. Stir until brown. Drain meat. Cook until liquid is completely gone. Place in large bowl, then stir in onion, parsley, milk and cheese. Cool. Add salt and pepper to taste.

Grease jelly roll pan with butter and lay a sheet of pastry on pan. Shape meat into loaf from one end to the other. Cover with top sheet of pastry, tucking in under bottom edge and pressing together. Glaze, decorate and glaze again.

Bake for 45 minutes. Can be served with sour cream.

Preparation:	30 min.	Moderately difficult	Serves: 6
Cooking:	45 min.	Serve immediately	

Marianne Caspary

1-2-3 BEEF WELLINGTON
"An elegant Wellington"

1 6 lb. fillet of beef
1 box Sara Lee patty shells
1 large can deviled ham, or
   spreadable paté
1 small can sliced mushrooms

Preheat oven to 425°. Thaw patty shells. Bake fillet of beef for 25 minutes and let cool to room temperature. This can be done the morning of serving entrée. Spread deviled ham or paté on top of roast, placing sliced mushrooms on top also. Roll out thawed patty shells on lightly floured surface. Wrap shells around roast, putting seal on bottom and closing ends. Roast at 450° for approximately 25 minutes for rare. Additional pastry decorations or fluted mushrooms can be added to decorate.

Preparation: 20 min.	Easy	Serves: 8
Cooking: 50 min.	Can do ahead	

Mrs. Mark E. With

MARINATED FLANK STEAK
"Get out the grill"

1 flank steak, scored
⅓ cup vinegar
¼ cup ketchup
1 Tbsp. Worcestershire sauce
2 Tbsp. soy sauce
2 Tbsp. oil
1 clove garlic, crushed
1 tsp. dry mustard

Combine vinegar, ketchup, Worcestershire sauce, soy sauce, oil, garlic and mustard. Pour over steak and marinate at room temperature at least one hour. Grill over hot coals about 10 minutes. Brush with marinade while grilling.

Preparation: 10 min.	Easy	Serves: 4
Cooking: 10-15 min.	Can do ahead	

Mary Jo Hottenstein

MUSTARD-COATED FLANK STEAK
"A unanimous hit"

⅔ cup Dijon mustard
¼ cup soy sauce
2 Tbsp. heavy cream
2 tsp. thyme, dried and
   crumbled
2 tsp. fresh ginger, minced
½ tsp. crushed peppercorns
2 1¼-lbs. flank steaks

Mix first 6 ingredients. Put steaks on large plate. Brush mixture over both sides of steaks. Cover with plastic wrap and refrigerate for 6 hours or overnight. Heat grill. Cook steaks for 6 minutes per side for medium-rare. Cut diagonally across grain to serve.

Preparation: 15 min.	Easy	Serves: 6
Cooking: 12 min.	Must do ahead	

Mary Jo Hottenstein

AVOCADOS AND BEEF

"Can be salad or sandwich"

2 avocados, peeled and sliced
2 lbs. left-over roast beef, rare and sliced
1 sweet red onion, sliced very thin
½ cup vegetable oil
¼ cup olive oil
½ cup wine vinegar
2 tsp. Dijon mustard
2 tsp. salt
¼ tsp. pepper
chopped parsley

In a casserole dish arrange layers: avocado, beef, onion, repeat. Mix remaining ingredients; pour on top of meat mixture. Marinate several hours.

*Wine suggestion: Bourgogne Blanc

Preparation: 10 min.   Easy   Serves: 6
                          Must do ahead

Betsy Maloney

EASY BEEF STROGANOFF

"Clever people can also cook this on their ranges"

4 Tbsp. butter
2 lbs. sirloin beef, cut in 2x½" strips
½ cup tomato juice
dash of garlic salt
½ lb. sliced mushrooms
1 can cream of mushroom soup
2 tsp. salt
⅛ tsp. pepper
1 cup sour cream
rice or noodles

Using an electric skillet, melt butter at 400°. Add strips of sirloin beef and sauté in melted butter. Add tomato juice and garlic salt. Cover, vent open, and cook at 200-225° for 30-40 minutes. Add mushrooms, soup, seasoning and sour cream. Heat thoroughly. Serve over rice or noodles.

Preparation: 15 min.   Easy   Serves: 4-6
Cooking: 40-50 min.   Can do ahead

Judie Vescio

LEFTOVER ROAST BEEF-STEW

leftover beef, cubed
1 small onion, sliced
2 stalks celery, sliced
2 carrots, sliced
1 small green pepper, chopped
salt and pepper, to taste
fine herbs, to taste
thyme, to taste
dash Tabasco sauce, to taste
Worcestershire sauce, to taste
1 potato, cubed
1 cup gravy, leftover or fresh

Put all ingredients in a pan, except potato. Cover with water. Bring to a boil. Cover, turn down heat and simmer until tender, about ½ hour. (You can freeze at this point.) When ready to serve, heat thoroughly, and add potatoes. Bring to a boil, then turn down heat and simmer until potatoes are done, about 15 minutes. Adjust vegetables to amount of meat. Put in gravy.

Crust:
1 cup flour
2 tsp. baking powder
¼ tsp. salt
¼ cup Crisco shortening
a little milk to make a soft
   dough

Crust:
Blend dry ingredients with Crisco. Add milk, knead a little, and roll about ¼" thick. Cut in squares. Place on top of meat stew in casserole dish. Bake for 30 minutes at 350°.

Preparation: 20 min.	Easy	Serves: 4-6
Cooking: 45 min.	Can do ahead	Can freeze

Mary Ellen Whitinger

INFALLIBLE RARE ROAST BEEF

"This really works - try it!"

1 roast beef with or without
   bones - ANY SIZE

In the morning, preheat oven to 375°. Put roast in and cook for 1 hour. Turn off heat. Leave roast in oven. Do not open door. Thirty minutes before serving, turn oven back on to 375°. If you need the oven for something else, take it out to "rest" and cover with aluminum foil.* Every slice is uniformly pink and gorgeous.

*NOTE: The first five times you do this takes courage!

	Easy	Serves: Any number
Cooking: 1½ hrs.	Must do ahead	

Barbara A. Blaxter

BOEUF EN DAUBE

"Also known as Beef Stew"

4 lbs. beef pot roast
salt and pepper, to taste
1 clove garlic, mashed
2 large onions, sliced
1 cup celery, sliced
2 carrots, sliced
¼ cup parsley, chopped
2 tsp. salt
8 whole peppercorns, slightly
  crushed, but still in large
  pieces
½ cup red wine vinegar
1 cup dry red wine
1 10½-oz. can condensed beef
  broth
¼ cup margarine
½ cup tomato purée
1 Tbsp. cornstarch
rice

Sprinkle roast with salt and pepper and rub with garlic. Place beef in bowl. Add onions, celery, carrots, parsley, salt, peppercorns, vinegar, wine and broth. Let stand at room temperature for 2 hours. Drain meat and reserve marinade. In Dutch oven, melt margarine and brown meat on all sides. Add marinade and bring to a boil. Lower heat and simmer for 2½ hours or until meat is tender. Remove roast. Mix tomato purée and cornstarch together. Add to marinade. Stir over low heat until thickened. Cut beef into small pieces and stir into marinade mixture. Serve over rice.

Preparation: 2 hrs. 45 min. Easy Serves: 6 (large)
Cooking: 3-3½ hrs.   Must do ahead Can freeze

Denise Doyle

ZESTY CHILI CON CARNE

"Very, very good basic chili"

1 lb. ground beef
1¼ cups minced onion
3 Tbsp. butter or beef
  drippings
2½ cups cooked kidney beans
  (or #2 can)
1⅓ cups condensed tomato
  soup (1 can)
1 cup stewed tomatoes
1 medium fresh green pepper,
  chopped
1 Tbsp. flour
3 Tbsp. water
1 tsp. salt
1 tsp. sugar
1½ - 2 Tbsp. chili powder

In soup pot, cook beef and onion until browned in hot butter or drippings. Add kidney beans, tomato soup, stewed tomatoes, and green pepper and cook over medium heat for 10 minutes. Make a paste out of flour, water, salt and sugar and blend in chili powder. Add to beef mixture and cook over low heat, stirring frequently, for 45 minutes.

Preparation: 10 min. Easy Serves: 8
Cooking: 1 hr.   Can do ahead Can freeze

Warren R. Kinneer

CHILI

"Zippy with chopped green chilies"

2 Tbsp. salad oil
2½ cups chopped onion
2 cloves garlic, crushed
2 lbs. ground beef
1 28-oz. can tomatoes
1 6-oz. can tomato paste
1 4-oz. can chopped green
  chilies
3 Tbsp. chili powder
1 Tbsp. ground cumin
1 bay leaf
2½ tsp. salt
6 whole cloves
¼ tsp. cayenne pepper
1 30-oz. can red kidney beans,
  drained

Sauté onions and garlic in oil for about 5 minutes. Add beef and brown. Drain. Add the remaining ingredients, except beans. Simmer, covered, over low heat for 2 hours. Add the drained beans. Cook until heated.

Preparation:	25 min.	Easy	Serves: 8
Cooking:	2½ hrs.	Can do ahead	Can freeze

Patricia I. Berini

FAMILY DINNER BAKE

1½ lbs. ground chuck
1 medium onion, sliced
2 medium celery stalks, sliced
2 16-oz. cans tomato sauce
¼ lb. fresh mushrooms, sliced
½ cup water
½ tsp. salt
½ tsp. fennel seeds
½ tsp. sugar
¼ tsp. pepper
3 medium potatoes, peeled and
  thinly sliced
½ 8-oz. pkg. Mozzarella
  cheese, shredded

In large skillet over medium heat, cook the beef, onion, and celery until browned. Stir in the tomato sauce, mushrooms, water, salt, fennel seeds, sugar, and pepper. Over high heat bring to boiling, then reduce to low. Cover and simmer for 5 minutes, stirring occasionally. Into a 9x13" baking pan, spoon ⅓ of the ground beef mixture; arrange half of the potato slices on top. Repeat layering, ending with the beef mixture. Cover the dish with foil. Bake at 375° for one hour.

Remove from oven, discard foil and sprinkle with cheese. Return to oven until the cheese melts.

NOTE: This can be prepared in the morning and baked at dinner time. It is especially nice when you don't know how many there will be for dinner.

Preparation:	40 min.	Easy	Serves: 6-8
Cooking:	1 hr. 5 min.	Can do ahead	

Missy Zimmerman

SLOW-OVEN BAKE BARBECUE CHUCK ROAST IN FOIL

"A godsend for a busy day"

3 lbs. lean, boneless, chuck
   roast, fat removed
1 11-oz. can cream of mushroom soup
1 envelope Lipton onion soup
   mix

Barbecue Sauce:

1 cup ketchup
2 Tbsp. prepared mustard
¼ cup cider vinegar
⅓ cup dark brown sugar
2 tsp. Worcestershire sauce
½ tsp. salt
¼ tsp. Tabasco sauce

noodles

Preheat oven to 300°. Place a double thickness of heavy-duty aluminum foil in a jelly roll pan or 9x13" baking dish. Place meat on foil in pan. Mix the mushroom soup, onion soup mix, and barbecue sauce together. Pour over meat. Seal foil tightly, leaving about 1" clearance between meat and foil. Bake for 2½ - 3 hours or longer, or until meat is almost falling apart. Let sit for 10 minutes before slicing. Serve with the sauce over noodles.

Barbecue Sauce:
Combine all ingredients in a small pan and heat to combine flavors. (Great as a sauce for any barbecue!)

Preparation: 15 min.	Easy	Serves: 4-6
Cooking: 3 hrs. or more	Can do ahead	Can freeze

Mary Anne Riley

BEEF AND TORTILLA CASSEROLE

"A Mexican lasagna"

10-12 corn tortillas
1 lb. ground beef
1 onion, quartered and chopped
1 bell pepper, quartered and
   chopped
1 clove garlic, minced
1 tsp. salt
½ tsp. oregano
1 14½-oz. can tomatoes
½ cup tomato sauce
1 cup sour cream
1 cup canned pinto beans,
   drained
8 oz. Monterey Jack or Cheddar cheese, grated

Cut each tortilla into 3 strips. In a skillet, sauté beef with onions and peppers and garlic. Add salt and oregano. Combine tomatoes, tomato sauce, and sour cream in blender or processor. Butter a 9x13" casserole dish and layer ingredients: tortilla strips, sauce, beans, meat, cheese. Repeat layers, ending with cheese on top. Casserole may be made several hours ahead and refrigerated. Bake for 20-30 minutes at 350°. Cut in squares and serve.

Preparation: 40 min.	Easy	Serves: 6-8
Cooking: 20-30 min.	Can do ahead	

Mary Jo Hottenstein

SPANISH SWISS STEAK

"Delicious new flavor from an old standby"

2-3 lbs. round steak, cut 1"
  thick
flour seasoned with salt and
  pepper
oil for browning
approx. ⅓ cup red wine
1 10¾-oz. can tomato soup
1 10-oz. can enchilada sauce,
  mild or medium-hot
4-6 Tbsp. olive juice
2-3 tsp. sugar
1 large onion
12 or more stuffed green
  olives, sliced
1 medium-sized each green and
  red bell peppers, cut in ½"
  strips

Cut round steak into serving
pieces. Coat each side of meat
with seasoned flour and use a
mallet to pound it into meat.
Brown meat pieces on each side
in a small amount of oil. Remove
meat and pour off any oil that is
left in pan. Pour wine into pan
and deglaze (use a spatula to
remove bits and pieces from bottom of pan). Mix the soup and
enchilada sauce together and
add olive juice and sugar. Add
this to pan. Lay meat pieces in
this mixture. Sprinkle top with the
chopped onions, sliced olives
and peppers. Cover and bake in
a 350° oven for 2 hours or until
meat is tender. Serve over rice.

Preparation: 30 min.   Easy   Serves: 6
Cooking: 2 hrs.   Can do ahead

Mrs. Phyllis R. Grine

ITALIAN STYLE MEATLOAF

"Bravo!"

3 lbs. ground chuck
½ cup Italian bread crumbs
2 eggs
½ tsp. salt
½ tsp. pepper
1 tsp. onion powder
3 cups Mozzarella cheese
1 cup thinly sliced pepperoni
  (optional)
4 cups spaghetti sauce

Mix first six ingredients together
well. Take mixture and pat out on
board to form a flat 9x13" size.
Sprinkle 2 cups Mozzarella
cheese evenly over flattened mixture. (Then sprinkle pepperoni, if
desired). Pour 2 cups spaghetti
sauce over mixture. Then roll
lengthwise like a jelly roll, seal
ends. Place in a 9x13" baking
dish and pour remainder of

sauce on top. Bake at 350° for 50 minutes, covered. Take out of oven
and sprinkle with remaining 1 cup cheese. Put back in oven, uncovered,
for 15 minutes. You may serve sauce in pan as gravy.

Preparation: 15 min.   Easy   Serves: 6-8
Cooking: 65 min.   Can do ahead   Can freeze

Lynn Popovich

PIZZA DELIGHT
"Layered with goodness"

1 lb. ground beef
2 8-oz. cans pizza sauce
1 4-oz. can sliced mushrooms, undrained
1 tsp. crushed oregano
1 tsp. garlic salt
2 cups rotini or macaroni, cooked and drained
⅔ cup milk
2 cups shredded Mozzarella cheese
¼ lb. thin sliced salami (Genoa is best) or pepperoni

Brown beef and drain. Stir in pizza sauce, mushrooms, oregano, and garlic salt. Bring to a boil and remove from heat. Combine rotini and milk. Spray 2-quart casserole with PAM. Put layers in as follows: pasta, meat sauce, cheese. Repeat. Bake, covered, at 350° for 25-30 minutes. Uncover and garnish with meat slices. Place back in oven for 5-7 minutes.

Preparation: 30 min.   Easy   Serves: 6
Cooking: 30-40 min. Can do ahead Can freeze

Clee McBee

COMPANY MEATLOAF
"Use super lean for less fat"

1 cup cracker crumbs
1½ lbs. ground beef
1 6-oz. can tomato paste
2 eggs, beaten
1 cup finely chopped onion
⅓ cup finely chopped green pepper
¾ tsp. salt
⅛ tsp. pepper
1½ cups small curd cottage cheese
1 4-oz. can mushroom pieces
1 tsp. dried parsley

Combine ½ cup cracker crumbs with beef, tomato paste, eggs, onion, green pepper, salt and pepper. Pat half of the mixture into the bottom of an 8″ square pan. Combine remaining ½ cup cracker crumbs with cottage cheese, mushrooms and parsley. Spread over meat mixture in pan. Top with remaining meat mixture. Bake in a preheated 350° oven for 1 hour. Let stand 10 minutes.

Preparation: 20 min. Easy   Serves: 6
Cooking: 1 hr.   Can do ahead

Susan L. Nitzberg

CORNED BEEF CASSEROLE
"A satisfying Sunday supper"

1 15½-oz. can corned beef
  hash
½ of a 16-oz. jar meatless
  spaghetti sauce
1 3-oz. pkg. cream cheese, cut
  into cubes
1 cup shredded natural Cheddar cheese
4 eggs, beaten
¼ tsp. dried oregano, crushed
dash pepper

Pat corned beef hash on bottom and up the sides of a greased 1½-quart casserole dish. Pour in spaghetti sauce; top with cubed cream cheese. Sprinkle with Cheddar cheese. Bake in 350° oven for 30 minutes. Combine eggs, oregano and pepper; pour into partially baked casserole. Bake for 20 minutes. Let stand 5 minutes.

Preparation: 10 min.   Easy   Serves: 4
Cooking: 50 min.   Serve immediately

Dorothy S. Anderson

MEAL-IN-A-CASSEROLE
"One variation of Shepherd's Pie"

1 lb. ground beef
1 small onion, chopped
1 can mushroom soup
1 can corn
4 cups mashed potatoes
butter
Parmesan cheese

Brown ground beef, add chopped onion. Continue to cook until onion is translucent. Remove from heat and add soup and corn. Put this mixture in a greased 2-quart casserole. Put mashed potatoes on top of meat mixture, dot with butter and sprinkle with Parmesan cheese. Bake at 350° for 30-45 minutes.

Preparation: 30 min.   Easy   Serves: 4-6
Cooking: 30-45 min.   Can do ahead   Can freeze

Sandra L. Kuriger

81

LAMB

PHYLLIS' LAMB

1 6-lb. boned leg of lamb

Marinade:
⅓ cup lemon juice
½ cup olive oil
⅓ cup chopped parsley
1 Tbsp. oregano
2 cloves garlic, minced
1 tsp. salt
1 tsp. pepper

Crumb mixture:
¼ cup clarified butter
¼ cup bread crumbs
½ cup Parmesan cheese
2 Tbsp. parsley
2 Tbsp. marjoram
1 Tbsp. basil
1 tsp. salt
1 tsp. pepper
1 Tbsp. lemon juice

Mix marinade ingredients together and marinate lamb overnight. Remove lamb from marinade and let come to room temperature. Grill over hot coals until pink in center, about 15 minutes or longer per side. Place lamb on cookie sheet and cover with crumb mixture. Broil until lightly brown. Slice lamb against grain in ¼" slices and arrange on serving platter with slices overlapping.

| Preparation: | 15 min. | Easy | Serves: 8-10 |
| Cooking: | 30-45 min. | Must do ahead | |

Phyllis Lynch

POTATO MOUSSAKA

3 medium onions, chopped
6 Tbsp. butter or margarine
1 lb. ground lamb
2 Tbsp. chopped parsley
½ tsp. ground thyme
2 tsp. salt
¼ tsp. pepper
2 Tbsp. flour
¼ cup water or white wine
3 eggs
1 cup light cream
2 lbs. potatoes, peeled and
   thinly sliced
¼ cup fine dry bread crumbs

Sauté onions in 2 Tbsp. of butter in a large skillet. Add meat and sauté for 3-5 minutes. Stir in all seasonings and 1 Tbsp. flour. Add the water/wine and cook, stirring constantly, for 2 minutes. Remove from heat and cool. Separate two of the eggs. Beat two egg yolks with 2 Tbsp. cream and stir into meat mixture. Beat egg whites until stiff and fold into meat mixture. Heat 3 Tbsp. butter in large skillet. Add potatoes and cook, turning several times, for 10 minutes. Cover and cook on low for 10 minutes longer. Butter a 10-cup baking dish with remaining butter. Sprinkle with bread crumbs. Layer meat mixture and potatoes at least twice (end with potatoes). Bake, uncovered, at 350° for 30 minutes. Beat remaining flour, cream and egg together in small bowl. Pour over top of casserole and bake 10 minutes longer.

Preparation: 25 min.   Moderately difficult   Serves: 6
Cooking: 1 hr.

Clee McBee

LAMB MANCHU

1 leg of lamb
4 cloves of garlic
½ cup honey
½ cup boiling water
1 cup soy sauce
¼ cup white wine
cooked rice

Have butcher bone and roll lamb. Cut in two pieces of equal thickness. Dissolve honey in boiling water; add garlic and soy sauce. Put lamb into glass or enamel pan (not metal), fat side down. Pour half of sauce over lamb, then turn over and pour on rest of sauce. Cover with wax paper and let stand in refrigerator for 24 hours. Put lamb in roasting pan, fat side up. Put ½ cup marinade and ½ cup water in pan. Cook 1 to 1¼ hours. It should be rare; at least pink. Remove lamb. Add wine to roasting pan and cook 5 minutes. Slice lamb, pour sauce over it and serve with rice.

Preparation: 10 min.   Easy   Serves: 10-12
Cooking: 1¼ hrs.   Must do ahead

Alice T. Barber

SWEET AND SOUR LAMB

2 lbs. lamb
12 small onions
1 cup ketchup
1 cup soup stock
2 Tbsp. brown sugar
¼ cup lemon juice (OR 2 Tbsp. vinegar)
2 Tbsp. Worcestershire sauce
cooked rice

Cut lamb into large or small pieces and place in a casserole with the onions. Mix remaining ingredients and pour over meat. Place in slow 300° oven for 2 hours. Serve with rice.

NOTE: Can use the small onions from a jar. Can also use beef bouillon for soup stock.

| Preparation: | 15 min. | Easy | Serves: 6-8 |
| Cooking: | 2 hrs. | Can do ahead | Can freeze |

Geraldine S. Holst

ARIZONA LEG OF LAMB

1 medium leg of lamb
1 cup dry red wine
½ cup orange juice
1 Tbsp. chili powder
¼ cup diced green chiles
2 Tbsp. olive oil
1 medium onion, chopped
2 cloves garlic, minced
1 tsp. ground cumin
⅞ tsp. salt

Remove fat and skin from meat. Place in glass baking dish. Combine remaining ingredients and pour over lamb. Marinate 24 hours in refrigerator, turning occasionally. Place lamb on rack in roasting pan, reserving marinade. Place in oven preheated to 450°. Bake 15 minutes, then reduce heat to 350° and pour marinade over meat. Cook 25 minutes per pound until meat thermometer registers 140° for rare, or until desired degree of doneness.

| Preparation: | 15 min. | Easy | Serves: 6 |
| Cooking: | 2-3 hrs. | Must do ahead | |

Diana Morrow

LAMB STEW

3 lbs. lamb, cubed
1 medium onion, chopped
¼ cup flour
½ tsp. pepper
2 tsp. salt
2 cups Spice Island chicken stock
1 cup sour cream
1 Tbsp. dillweed

Brown lamb and onion with flour, salt and pepper. When browned, add stock and simmer, covered, for 2 hours. Add more stock if necessary. Remove lid to simmer off extra liquid if necessary. Just before serving, add sour cream and dill. Do not boil. Serve over rice or noodles.

| Preparation: | 20 min. | Easy | Serves: 4-6 |
| Cooking: | 2¼ hrs. | Can do ahead | |

Catherine Clarke Johnson

STUFFED ZUCCHINI

4 large zucchini
2 lbs. lean ground lamb (or beef)
½ cup chopped onion
1½ cups Minute Rice (may use brown, if desired)
1 16-oz. jar tomato (spaghetti) sauce
16 oz. grated Parmesan cheese or Mozzarella cheese

Cut zucchini in half lengthwise and then in half crosswise. Parboil until tender, about 5 minutes. Drain and set aside. Brown ground meat with onion. Add rice and tomato sauce. Remove from heat, cover, and let stand for 5 minutes. Scoop out soft centers of zucchini; chop and add to meat mixture. Arrange shells in 9x13" pan. Fill each shell with heaping amounts. Sprinkle top with cheese. Add enough water or oil to pan to keep them from sticking. Bake at 350° for 35-40 minutes.

Preparation: 30 min.   Easy   Serves: 4-6
Cooking: 35-40 min. Can do ahead

The Cookbook Committee

SWEDISH DILL LAMB

3 lbs. lamb breast or shoulder of lamb
boiling water (to proportion of 1 Tbsp. salt to each quart)
4-6 white peppercorns
1 bay leaf
5 dill sprigs (fresh only)

Dill Sauce:
2 Tbsp. butter
2 Tbsp. flour
1½ cups stock (above)
2½ Tbsp. chopped dill
1½ Tbsp. white vinegar
2 Tbsp. sugar
1 egg yolk, beaten
salt, to taste

Trim excess fat and scald lamb in boiling water (see note in ingredients). Drain and place in Dutch oven or large casserole dish. Add boiling water (salted) to cover. Bring to a boil and skim. Add rest of ingredients, cover, and simmer for 1½ hours or until meat is tender. Drain and reserve stock. Cut meat into serving pieces. Place on hot platter with more sprigs of dill. Serve with Dill Sauce and boiled potatoes.

Dill Sauce: Melt butter; add flour and stir until smooth. Add stock and cook until smooth. Simmer for 10 minutes. Add dill, vinegar, sugar and salt. Remove from burner and stir in egg yolk. Serve immediately.

Preparation: 30 min.   Moderately difficult   Serves: 6-8
Cooking: 1½ hrs.   Serve immediately

Mary Louise Johnson

ROAST PORK WITH APRICOT STUFFING

"A tart and tangy stuffing"

8 oz. dried apricots, coarsely chopped
20 oz. water
5¼ oz. sugar
4 lb. pork loin center rib roast
salt, to taste
freshly ground pepper, to taste
4 oz. butter
3 oz. celery, minced
10 oz. onions, minced
7 oz. bread, cubed
4½ oz. walnuts, finely chopped
¼ tsp. thyme
¼ tsp. marjoram
½ tsp. chives, chopped
½ tsp. parsley, chopped
12 oz. pork jus

Bring apricots and water to a boil. Cover and simmer until apricots are tender. Stir in sugar until dissolved. Cut long slits between ribs on meaty side of pork roast to form pockets. Rub salt and pepper into surface and slits of roast. Sauté celery and onions until tender. Stir in apricots and their liquid, bread cubes, walnuts, thyme, marjoram, chives and parsley. Mix thoroughly. Fill the slits made in the roast with the apricot stuffing. Roast the pork, stuffed side up, on a rack in open roasting pan at 350° for 1-1½ hours. Cut back bone from roast, slice and place on a warm platter. Serve with pork jus and garnish with watercress.

Preparation: 20 min.   **Easy**   **Serves: 8-10**
Cooking: 1-1½ hrs.   **Can do ahead**

Norbert Bomm, Exec. Chef
Orchard Cafe
Vista International Hotel

STIR FRY PORK WITH SNOW PEAS

½ lb. uncooked pork tenderloin
   or boneless lean pork or pork
   chops
1 Tbsp. peanut oil
½ lb. fresh snow peas
1 scallion, chopped
½ cup sliced bamboo shoots
1 tsp. soy sauce
1 Tbsp. dry Sherry
¼ tsp. salt

Marinade:
1 tsp. cornstarch
1 Tbsp. soy sauce
2 Tbsp. dry Sherry
½ tsp. salt
1 tsp. sesame seed oil

Slice pork ⅕" thick,* then cut into 1x2" pieces. Combine marinade and mix well. Add pork; toss to coat well. Marinate pork for 30 minutes. Heat oil in wok or skillet over high heat. Add pork, stir-fry for 2 minutes. Add remaining ingredients; stir-fry for 2 minutes longer. Serve hot.

*It slices easier if partially frozen, or have your butcher slice it for you.

NOTE: Can be prepared up to 2 hours ahead, but do not add snow peas. When serving, add peas and stir-fry for 1 minute.

Preparation: 45 min.   Easy   Serves: 2
Cooking: 4-5 min.   Can do ahead

Anna Kao's Chinese Cooking Class

PORK IN SWEET PEPPER SAUCE

2 pork tenderloins
salt and pepper
1 Tbsp. olive oil
4 Tbsp. chopped onion
1 red bell pepper, trimmed and
   cut into 1" cubes
1 green bell pepper, trimmed
   and cut into 1" cubes
1 tsp. chopped garlic
1 cup chicken broth
½ tsp. cumin
1 bay leaf
2 Tbsp. butter
2 Tbsp. lemon juice

Cut tenderloins into 2" slices. Flatten pieces lightly with mallet. Sprinkle with salt and pepper. Heat oil. Add meat in single layer and cook about 5 minutes over medium-high heat. Turn slices and cook 5 minutes. Reduce heat and cook 5 minutes, turning meat occasionally. Put meat on warm serving dish and keep warm. Cook onions and peppers in small amount of reserved oil until wilted. Add garlic and cook briefly. Add broth, cumin, and bay leaf and cover and simmer

for 5 minutes. Discard bay leaf. Put mixture in blender. Add butter and lemon juice and blend to fine texture. Pour mixture in skillet; add pork slices and bring to simmer. Serve immediately.

Preparation: 30 min.   Easy   Serves: 6
Cooking: 30 min.   Serve immediately

Mary Jo Hottenstein

ROAST PORK LOIN

1 7-lb. loin of pork
½ cup flour, divided
1½ tsp. cloves
1 tsp. salt
1 tsp. poultry seasoning
½ tsp. paprika
½ tsp. cinnamon
¼ tsp. pepper
1 cup water
1 cup milk OR apple juice
salt and pepper

Preheat oven to 450°. Wipe pork with damp cloth. Sift ¼ cup flour and seasonings together (or stir with fork to blend). Rub seasoning mixture into surface of roast. Place pork in large roaster and roast at 450° for 10 minutes. Reduce oven to 300°; add 1 cup water to pan and roast, covered, about 3½ hours. Meat thermometer should register 180°. Remove cover and roast another 5-10 minutes. Remove meat to warm platter. Skim excess fat from pan. Heat remaining ¼ cup flour in skillet until lightly browned. Add the pan drippings, blend and gradually add the milk. Cook until thickened, stirring constantly. Season with salt and pepper, if desired. May need to adjust amount of liquid for desired consistency of gravy.

NOTE: May need to roast at 325°.

Preparation: 5 min.   Easy   Serves: 12
Cooking: 3 hrs. 45 min.

Carolyn S. Hammer

ITALIAN STYLE PORK CHOPS AND POTATOES
"Your family should enjoy this"

6 large pork chops
1-2 potatoes per person
salt, to taste
pepper, to taste
parsley flakes
1 6-oz. can tomato sauce
2 Tbsp. tomato paste
water

Fry pork chops in skillet, seasoning to taste until browned on both sides. In bottom of roaster or large casserole dish place raw potatoes (each sliced into 3 pieces). Salt and pepper to taste. Sprinkle with parsley flakes. Remove pork chops from skillet, and add to skillet the tomato sauce and tomato paste. Fill tomato sauce can with water and add to above sauce and paste. Simmer in pork chop drippings until tomato paste is completely dissolved. Pour over potatoes. Add enough water to just cover top of potatoes. Place pork chops on top and bake in a 350° oven for about 1 hour.

NOTE: Can be baked slowly in a 300° oven for 2½ hours.

Preparation: 20 min.   Easy   Serves: 6
Cooking: 1-2½ hrs.   Can do ahead

Dorothy Truckey

88

PORK CHOP AND POTATO HOT POT
"A wonderful one dish dinner"

4 pork chops (2 lbs.)
1 tsp. salt
⅛ tsp. pepper
1 medium onion, sliced
4 medium potatoes, peeled and
    sliced
1 10¾-oz. can condensed
    cheddar cheese soup,
    undiluted

Preheat oven to 350°. Wipe pork chops with damp towels. Lightly pound each side of pork chops and trim excess fat. Heat fat in skillet. Brown chops well on both sides, sprinkling with salt and pepper. Drain well on paper towel. Place chops in a 2-quart shallow casserole dish. Arrange onion slices, then potato slices over top. Spoon cheese soup over all and bake, covered, for 1 hour or until meat and potatoes are tender.

Preparation: 15 min.   Easy   Serves: 4
Cooking: 1 hr.   Can do ahead

Louise Johnston

ROAST LOIN OF PORK IN SHERRY CREAM SAUCE

3-4 lbs. boneless pork loin roast
2 Tbsp. dried basil
1½ Tbsp. fennel seeds
4 dried bay leaves
garlic powder, to taste
salt and pepper, to taste
2 large onions, sliced
1 cup thickly sliced carrots
1¼ cups dry Sherry

Cream sauce:
½ cup Sherry
2 Tbsp. butter
2 Tbsp. flour
1 cup whipping cream
1 cup fresh sliced mushrooms
salt and pepper

Preheat oven to 300°. Spray roasting pan with PAM. Rinse roast and place in pan, fat side down. Sprinkle basil, fennel, bay leaves, garlic, salt and pepper evenly over meat. Cover roast with sliced onions and surround it with the carrots. Pour the dry Sherry over all and cover the pan with a tight-fitting lid. Bake roast in preheated oven for 40 minutes per pound or until the meat tests fork tender.

Cream sauce:
Remove meat to an ovenproof platter, cover with foil and let stand 15 minutes before slicing while making the sauce. After discarding vegetables and bay leaves, deglaze roasting pan with ½ cup of Sherry, scraping browned bits from the bottom of pan. Bring liquid to a simmer; cook until reduced by half and add butter that has been mixed with the flour (this flour mixture should resemble coarse meal). Cook, while stirring constantly, until flour is brown. Still stirring slowly, add cream and mushrooms. Simmer for 5 minutes while continuing to stir constantly. Season to taste with salt and pepper. Serve with roast.

Preparation: 20 min.   Moderately difficult   Serves: 6-8
Cooking: 2 + hrs.

Terri West
Wesleyan Community Services

PORK TENDERLOIN A LA ASPARAGUS

"Asparagus soup is the secret ingredient"

8 pieces (2 lbs.) pork tenderloin
1 Tbsp. butter
1 10-oz. can cream of
  asparagus soup
½ cup milk
½ cup chopped onion
1 3-oz. can mushrooms, drained
  OR ½ lb. fresh
½ tsp. curry
dash pepper

Pound pork to flatten. Remove fat. Brown in butter and set aside. In same skillet, blend soup, milk and the rest of the ingredients. Return meat to skillet. Cover and simmer for 45 minutes. Serve sauce on meat.

Preparation: 25 min.
Cooking: 45 min.

Easy
Serve immediately

Serves: 6-8

Karen Rossin

ROAST PORK

"White wine adds moistness"

5-6 lb. pork roast
salt
ground pepper
1 tsp. sugar
pinch of cayenne
rosemary
1 cup white wine

Heat oven to 450°. Rub roast liberally with salt and ground pepper. Sprinkle sugar and cayenne pepper on roast. Cook for 10 minutes. Reduce heat to 300°. Sprinkle with rosemary. Pour wine over roast and cook 30 minutes per pound. Baste several times, adding wine as needed.

Preparation: 5 min.
Cooking: 2½-3 hrs.

Easy

Serves: 4-6

Barbara Burton

FAST FREDDIE'S SPARERIBS

1 rack pork spareribs
vegetable oil
sauce*
pineapple slices for garnish

*Sauce:
1 part soy sauce
2 parts cider vinegar (or Chinese red vinegar)
3 parts sugar
4 parts water

Slice spareribs into three strips. Trim fat from ribs. Cut between ribs into 1½" long pieces (each with piece of bone attached). Brown spareribs on both sides with oil. Remove spareribs and discard excess oil. Make sauce by mixing ingredients together. Pour sauce into pan used to brown spareribs and bring to a boil. Add ribs to sauce. Over medium heat keep stirring constantly to prevent burning, and heat until sauce is thick enough to adhere to ribs. Garnish with pineapple. Serve warm or cold.

Preparation: 30 min.
Cooking: 25-30 min.

Moderately difficult
Can do ahead

Dr. Freddie Fu
Physician
Pgh. Ballet Theatre and Pitt Panthers

90

GRILLED PORK CHOPS

"Tasty marinated chops"

¼ cup fresh lemon juice
2 Tbsp. vegetable oil
3 cloves garlic, minced
1 tsp. salt
¼ tsp. ground thyme
¼ tsp. dried oregano
¼ tsp. black pepper
6 pork chops, 1" thick

In a shallow dish, blend all ingredients, except meat. Add pork chops. Cover and chill 12 hours, or overnight, turning meat occasionally. To serve, remove meat from marinade. Grill over hot coals 15-20 minutes per side or until done. Baste chops with marinade during grilling.

Preparation: 5 min.   Easy   Serves: 6
Cooking: 15-20 min.   Must do ahead

Gretchen Hansen

MARTA'S BRUNCH PIE

"So easy - sort of like a sandwich"

2 prepared pie crusts, unbaked
½ lb. sliced Swiss or Muenster cheese
1 lb. "chipped" ham (or sliced as thin as you can get it)
2 tsp. Poupon mustard

Place one pie crust in pie plate (follow package directions). Place some slices of cheese to cover bottom. Then evenly layer all ham slices. Spread mustard on ham. Top with remaining cheese. Place top crust on pie. Trim as needed. Fold and crimp edges. Cut decorative slits in top crust. Bake at 350° for about 30 minutes or until golden brown.

Preparation: 10 min.   Easy   Serves: 6
Cooking: 30 min.   Can do ahead

Clee McBee

KIELBASSI AND BEER SAUCE

"A real Pittsburgh dish"

3 lbs. Kielbassi, cut in ½" slices
1 cup chopped green onion
12 Tbsp. butter
flour to thicken
4 tsp. dry mustard
4 tsp. caraway seeds
2½ tsp. cayenne pepper
½ tsp. salt
4 cups milk
6 cups (24 oz.) American cheese, cubed
3 cups (12 oz.) Swiss cheese, shredded
2⅔ cups Iron City beer
6 lbs. cooked linguine

Cook Kielbassi until brown. Drain on paper towel. Drain fat from pot. In same pot, cook green onions in butter until tender. Stir in flour until mixture thickens, making a roux. Add mustard, caraway seeds, cayenne pepper and salt. Stir in milk and cook until thickened. Add cheese, beer and Kielbassi. Stir until all cheese is melted. Serve hot over already preportioned linguine.

Preparation: 10 min.   Moderately difficult   Serves: 12-15
Cooking: 20 min.   Can do ahead

Mario's Southside Saloon

HAM PIE

"Unusual with a puffy pancake topper"

2 sweet potatoes, peeled and
   thinly sliced (white can be
   substituted)
3 cups cooked ham, diced
3 medium apples, peeled,
   cored and sliced
½ tsp. salt
½ tsp. pepper
3 Tbsp. brown sugar
¼ tsp. curry powder
⅓ cup water or apple juice
1 cup pancake mix
1 cup milk
½ tsp. dry mustard
2 Tbsp. butter, melted

Preheat oven to 375°. Layer half of the potatoes, ham and apples in a greased 2-quart casserole. Combine salt, pepper, sugar and curry and sprinkle half over layers in dish. Repeat with same ingredients. Pour water or juice over all. Cover and bake at 375° for 40 minutes (potatoes must be tender). Remove from oven. Mix last 4 ingredients together and pour on top of casserole. Place back in oven, uncovered, for 20 minutes or until top is puffed and golden.

Preparation: 30 min.   Easy   Serves: 6
Cooking: 1 hr.   Can do ahead   Can freeze

Beatrice Cooper

BARBEQUE RIBS

3-4 lbs. pork loin back ribs
2 Tbsp. caraway seeds
1 envelope dry onion soup mix
1 onion, chopped
1 Tbsp. Worcestershire sauce
1 tsp. paprika
½ cup brown sugar
8 oz. tomato sauce
1 cup ketchup
2 Tbsp. vinegar
1 tsp. salt
1 tsp. yellow mustard
½ tsp. pepper
¼ tsp. garlic powder

Put ribs in large pot and add enough water to cover meat. Add caraway seeds and dry onion soup mix. Cover and simmer for 1½ hours. In small saucepan, simmer remaining ingredients for ½ hour. After ribs are cooked, remove from water and put onto a cookie sheet and baste with sauce. Bake at 325°, turn and baste every 15 minutes, for 45 minutes.

Preparation: 15 min.   Easy   Serves: 6
Cooking: 2½ hrs.   Can do ahead

Linda Marie Peterson

HAM BALLS

"Could also be an appetizer"

½ lb. ground ham
¾ lb. ground pork
1 cup bread crumbs
1 egg
1 cup milk

Sauce:
1 cup brown sugar
¼ cup vinegar
¾ cup water
1 tsp. dry mustard

Combine ham, pork, bread crumbs, egg and milk. Mix thoroughly and form into balls or loaves. Place in baking dish and pour sauce over meatballs. Bake in a 350° oven for 1 hour. Baste often.

Sauce:
Cook all ingredients until sugar is dissolved.

Preparation: 20 min.   Easy   Serves: 6-8
Cooking: 45 min.   Can do ahead

Karen Rossin

HAM CASSEROLE

"A super Sunday evening supper"

1 can cream of celery soup
1 small onion, chopped
½ cup milk
1 cup sharp Cheddar cheese,
   shredded
2 cups macaroni (8 oz.)
2 cups diced cooked ham
   (about 1 lb.)

Place soup, onion, milk, and ½ cup of the cheese in blender and blend until smooth. Save ½ cup cheese for top. Cook macaroni for 8 minutes. Mix macaroni, ham and sauce in a casserole dish. Sprinkle remaining cheese on top of casserole. Bake at 350° in greased 1½ quart casserole dish for 25 minutes.

Preparation: 20 min.   Easy   Serves: 6
Cooking: 25 min.   Can do ahead   Can freeze

Marie Feiertag

GREEN CHILE STEW

"Hot stew for a cold night"

24 green chiles (fresh or canned)
2 Tbsp. olive oil
2 lbs. pork loin, cubed
2 large onions, finely chopped
3 cloves garlic, minced
3 cups stewed tomatoes
1 6-oz. can tomato paste
2 cups water
½ tsp. cumin
2 tsp. salt

If chiles are fresh, parch and peel them. Remove the ribs, seeds, and tops. In a large stewing pot, heat olive oil. Add pork cubes and lightly brown. Add onions and garlic and brown. Cut chiles into 1" slices and add to pork and onions. Add remaining ingredients and cook about 1 hour until stew is thickened. Adjust seasonings.

Preparation: 20 min.   Easy   Serves: 6-8
Cooking: 1 hr.   Can do ahead   Can freeze

Mary Jo Hottenstein

VEAL

VEAL WITH GREEN PEPPERCORNS

"A company treat"

Veal scallops, allow about ¼
   lb. per person OR you can
   use raw sliced turkey breast
   in similar amounts
salt and pepper, to taste
¾ cup flour
4 Tbsp. butter
4 Tbsp. oil
2½ cups thinly sliced fresh
   mushrooms
1½ cups dry white wine
1 cup heavy cream
1½ tsp. Dijon mustard
1 rounded Tbsp. green peppercorns (drained if purchased
   packed in vinegar water)

Toss scallops with salt, pepper
and flour. Heat 2 Tbsp. each of
butter and oil until it stops foaming; sauté mushrooms until tender. Remove mushrooms. Add
remaining butter and oil and heat
until it stops foaming. Sauté scallops, a few at a time, and remove
from pan. Add wine, and deglaze
pan, reducing liquid to about ¾
cup. Add cream, mustard and
peppercorns, stirring constantly
until slightly thickened. Return
scallops and mushrooms to pan
and heat with sauce about 2
minutes.

Preparation: 15 min.	Moderately difficult	Serves: 4-6
Cooking: 15 min.	Can do ahead	

Rusty McBride

VEAL SUPREME

1¼ lb. veal, cut in 1" thick
   cubes
4 Tbsp. flour
1 tsp. salt
⅛ tsp. pepper
4 Tbsp. melted butter
1½ cups thinly sliced onions
1 4-oz. can mushrooms or 1 cup
   sliced fresh
¾ cup sour cream
ginger, to taste
paprika, to taste
celery seed, to taste
oregano, to taste

Dredge meat in flour, salt and pepper mixture. Melt butter in skillet, add onions and brown. Remove onions and brown meat. Place meat in casserole, cover with mushrooms and onions; add cream and seasonings. Bake until meat is tender—about 40-50 minutes at 350°.

Preparation: 15 min.   Easy   Serves: 6
Cooking: 40-50 min.   Serve immediately

Shirley W. Neal

BRAISED HERB-FLAVORED VEAL TIDBITS WITH MUSHROOMS
"Very tender tidbits"

3 Tbsp. butter
2 Tbsp. vegetable oil
1½ lbs. boneless veal shoulder,
   cut into 1½" cubes
1 medium onion, finely
   chopped (½ cup)
1 clove garlic, finely chopped
2 Tbsp. flour
½ cup dry white wine or
   Inglenook Blanc de Blanc
½ cup canned Italian plum
   tomatoes (with juice), cut up
1 cup water
1 tsp. rosemary, crumbled
⅛ tsp. sage leaf, crumbled
1 tsp. salt
freshly ground pepper
½ lb. mushrooms, sliced
1 Tbsp. butter
1 Tbsp. vegetable oil

Heat the butter and oil in a Dutch oven, over medium heat. When mixture foams and then subsides, add veal, a little at a time so pan is not crowded. Remove pieces as they brown, then return veal to pan. Add the onion and garlic; cook, stirring occasionally, until golden. Sprinkle flour over contents of pan, stirring for 1 minute. Add the wine and let bubble for a few seconds. Add tomatoes, water, rosemary, sage, salt and a few twists of pepper. Lower heat; cover. Simmer, stirring occasionally, for 1 hour or until the meat is fork-tender. While meat is cooking, prepare mushrooms. Heat the remaining Tbsp. of butter and oil in a large skillet. Sauté mushrooms, turning frequently, until the liquid has evaporated from skillet. Add to meat about 5 minutes before end of cooking.

Preparation: 15 min.   Moderately difficult Serves: 6
Cooking: 1 hr. 10 min.   Serve immediately

Mrs. D. Ryan Cook

VEAL MARSALA
"Great served with linguine"

1-1½ lbs. veal scallopini
½ cup seasoned bread crumbs
3 Tbsp. butter
1 medium onion, sliced
1 medium green pepper, sliced
1-2 Tbsp. parsley
1 clove garlic
1 tsp. salt
¼ tsp. pepper
1 3-oz. jar mushrooms
1 cup chicken soup stock
½ cup water
⅓ cup Marsala wine

Cut veal into 2" cubes. Coat veal with bread crumbs (keep leftover crumbs). Brown in skillet for 5-10 minutes in butter. Blend all vegetables and seasonings with soup stock, water and wine. Add to meat and cook for 10 minutes, covered, on moderate heat. Turn meat and cook on low heat for 25-30 minutes, turning once during cooking.

Preparation: 30 min.
Cooking: 45 min.
Easy
Serve immediately
Serves: 4-6

Ray A. Yonko
Parental Stress Center, Inc.

VEALBALLS STROGANOFF
"Boasts a creamy wine sauce"

½ cup fresh bread crumbs
½ cup chicken broth
1 lb. ground veal
1 egg, beaten
¼ tsp. ground cumin
⅛ tsp. nutmeg
salt
2 Tbsp. butter
½ cup chopped onion
¼ lb. mushrooms, sliced
1 Tbsp. paprika
¼ cup Sherry
¼ cup heavy cream
¾ cup sour cream
buttered noodles

Soak bread crumbs in ¼ cup chicken broth. Combine veal, egg, and soaked bread crumbs. Add cumin, nutmeg, and salt. Mix well and shape into 1½" balls. Should make about 40. Heat butter and cook meatballs over medium-high heat, turning until they are completely browned (about 5 minutes). Add onions, mushrooms, and paprika. Cook about 1 minute and cover. Simmer 5 minutes. Add Sherry and remaining ¼ cup chicken broth. Stir in heavy cream, cover, and simmer 10 minutes. Stir in sour cream and just bring to a boil. Serve hot over buttered noodles.

Preparation: 20 min.
Cooking: 20 min.
Moderately difficult
Serve immediately
Serves: 4

Mary Jo Hottenstein

VEAL CHOPS INVERNESS

4 veal* chops, 1" thick

Marinade:
2 cloves garlic, minced
⅓ cup oil
¼ tsp. pepper
3 Tbsp. soy sauce
2 Tbsp. ketchup
1 Tbsp. wine vinegar

*Boneless chicken breast can
  be substituted for veal.

Marinate veal chops overnight.
Grill over charcoal for 4-6
minutes, turning once and basting. DO NOT OVERCOOK!
Should feel slightly spongy when
touched.

Preparation:	10 min.	Easy	Serves: 4
Cooking:	10 min.	Must do ahead	

Lorraine P. Trice

VEAL ROIESE

1½ lbs. cleaned and de-veined
   veal
4 slices Prosciutto ham
4 slices Provolone cheese
flour
oil or clear butter
2 oz. cooking Sherry
4 oz. cooked, sliced
   mushrooms
4 artichoke hearts, halved
2 oz. heavy cream
4 oz. brown gravy

Cut veal into 8 pieces, 2-3" in
diameter. Pound veal to less than
¼" thickness. Top each
individual slice with one slice of
Prosciutto ham and one slice of
Provolone cheese. Top with
remaining piece of veal. Flour
lightly. Pan fry for 2 minutes in
oil or clear butter. Remove fat;
add Sherry, mushrooms,
artichoke hearts, and brown
gravy. Bring to a boil and add
heavy cream. Remove the meat
and place on platter. Continue to let the sauce boil to desired thickness.
Pour the mixture over the veal and garnish as desired.

Preparation:	20 min.	Easy	Serves: 4
Cooking:	15 min.	Can do ahead	

Domenic More
Tivoli Restaurant

SPINACH ANGEL HAIR AND RED PEPPER CREAM SAUCE

1 lb. spinach angel hair pasta
1 lb. diced veal
olive oil
1 oz. fresh dill
8 oz. sundried tomatoes
6 oz. pignola nuts
32 oz. red pepper cream sauce
  (recipe below)
Parmesan cheese, to taste

Cook pasta to al dente and set aside. In a skillet, sauté veal in olive oil. Add dill, sundried tomatoes, and pignola nuts and sauté. Add red pepper cream sauce and heat. Toss with pasta until warm. Divide evenly onto 8 warm dishes; sprinkle with Parmesan cheese. Serve.

Red Pepper Cream Sauce:
6 roasted red peppers
2 cups white wine
32 oz. heavy cream
salt and pepper, to taste

Red Pepper Cream Sauce: Char your peppers on a grill, then place in a paper bag. Peel the charred skin off under cold water. Place peppers in saucepan with white wine and cook until almost dry. Add heavy cream and reduce by one-fourth. Purée in food processor until smooth; season and set aside until ready to use.

Preparation: 45 min.
Cooking: 12-15 min.

Moderately difficult
Can do ahead

Serves: 8

Gregory Powell
Wooden Angel Restaurant

POULTRY

BONELESS FRIED CHICKEN FILLETS
"Kids love this"

4 whole chicken breasts, split and cut into strips
4 eggs
3 cups Progresso seasoned bread crumbs
1 cup matzo meal* (Streits)
2 Tbsp. dried parsley
1 Tbsp. garlic powder or garlic salt
2 cups vegetable or sunflower oil

*If you are unable to find the matzo meal, you may substitute 1 cup of bread crumbs. (Matzo meal is usually found with kosher foods.)

Prepare chicken as described. Beat eggs in a shallow bowl. Combine bread crumbs, matzo meal, parsley, and garlic salt in a baggie or plastic bag and shake to mix. In frying pan, add the oil and heat over a medium-high flame. While pan is heating, start placing chicken strips in the egg mixture and then into the bag of bread crumbs. Mix and shake to coat. Place coated chicken into hot frying pan and cook, turning once, until golden brown, approximately 2-3 minutes on each side.

NOTE: Oil in pan should not be too hot - food should cook nicely without the bread coating burning.

Preparation: 20-30 min.	**Easy**	**Serves: 4-6**
Cooking: 30 min.	**Can do ahead**	**Can freeze**

Donna M. Adipietro

99

CAROLYN'S CHICKEN KIEV

⅔ cup butter
½ cup bread crumbs
2 Tbsp. grated Parmesan
  cheese
1 tsp. basil
1 tsp. oregano
½ tsp. garlic
¼ tsp. salt
¼ tsp. pepper
1-1½ lbs. boneless chicken
  breasts
¼ cup dry white wine
¼ cup chopped onion
¼ cup chopped parsley

Preheat oven to 375°. Melt butter. In a small bowl, combine bread crumbs, cheese, basil, oregano, garlic, salt and pepper. Dip chicken in butter, then roll in crumbs. Place in a 9″ square baking dish. Bake for 25 minutes. Combine wine, onion and parsley with remaining butter. Pour over chicken. Cook 5 minutes more. Serve with sauce spooned over chicken.

NOTE: This can be a low cholesterol dish by using Promise margarine instead of butter and by eliminating the Parmesan cheese.

Preparation: 15 min.   Easy   Serves: 2-3
Cooking: 30 min.   Can do ahead
                                          Kathleen A. Harrison

LIGHT CHICKEN-BROCCOLI-PEPPER STIR FRY
"You'll love the combination of spices"

1 lb. chicken breasts,
  boned and skinned
2 lbs. broccoli, trimmed and
  broken into flowerets (do not
  use stems)
non-stick vegetable oil spray
1 Tbsp. olive oil
2 large red or green bell
  peppers, cut lengthwise
1 large onion, quartered
2 large garlic cloves, minced
1 tsp. dried basil
½ tsp. dried thyme
½ tsp. ground pepper
¼ tsp. dried rosemary
½ tsp. salt
4 Tbsp. grated Parmesan cheese

Have all ingredients prepared and ready before starting. Pound chicken breasts to ¼″ thickness, then cut into ½″ thick strips. Cover broccoli flowerets with cold water. Spray large, heavy skillet with vegetable spray. Add olive oil and heat over high heat for 1 minute. Add peppers, onions, garlic, basil, thyme, pepper and rosemary to skillet. Stir-fry for 2 minutes. Drain broccoli (do not shake off excess water) and add to skillet. Stir-fry for 2 minutes. Cover and simmer for 2 more minutes over medium heat. Add chicken and salt. Cover and steam for about 2 minutes until chicken is cooked through. Uncover and stir-fry over high heat until liquid evaporates. Sprinkle with Parmesan cheese.

NOTE: Remember that this is a light menu (reduced calorie). It will not be as rich as most stir-fry dishes.

Preparation: 30 min.   Easy   Serves: 4-6
Cooking: 15 min.   Serve immediately
                                          Mary Jo Hottenstein

MY KANSAS CHICKEN

2 whole chicken breasts, split,
  skinned, and boned
salt and pepper, to taste
3 Tbsp. sweet butter
½ cup Chablis wine
1½ Tbsp. Worcestershire sauce
1 4-oz. can sliced mushrooms
⅛ cup grated Parmesan cheese
¼ cup sour cream

Season chicken breasts with salt and pepper. Melt butter in a 10" skillet and sauté chicken breasts until golden on each side, about 12-14 minutes. Remove chicken to warm platter. Deglaze pan with wine and add Worcestershire sauce, mushrooms, cheese and sour cream. Stir constantly until heated through. Do not boil. Serve sauce over chicken breasts.

Preparation: 10 min.   Easy   Serves: 4
Cooking: 15-20 min.   Can do ahead   Can freeze

Barbara Ann Martz

CHICKEN FONTINELLA WITH LEMON-MUSHROOM SAUCE

<u>The chicken:</u>
¾ cup seasoned bread crumbs
¾ cup grated Romano cheese
4 boneless chicken breasts,
  skinned, split and flattened
  lightly
salt and pepper, to taste
flour for dredging
3 eggs, beaten
5 oz. butter
5 oz. grated Fontinella

<u>The sauce:</u>
1½ oz. butter
2 cups sliced mushrooms
1 bunch chopped green onion
  (include half the green)
1 oz. dry white wine
1½ oz. flour
2 cups chicken stock
juice of 1 lemon
salt and pepper, to taste
lemon slices and curly endive
  for garnish

<u>The chicken:</u> Preheat oven to 375°. Combine bread crumbs and Romano cheese. Season chicken breasts with salt and pepper; dredge in flour, then dip in beaten eggs and coat with bread crumb mixture. Heat butter in skillet and sauté until brown on both sides. Place in ovenproof pan and bake approximately 10 minutes. Then remove chicken, top with grated Fontinella and place back in oven until cheese melts.

<u>The sauce:</u> When chicken is first placed in oven to cook, put butter, mushrooms and green onion in a small saucepan and cook until mushrooms are tender. Add wine and let cook for 1 minute. Stir in flour, then chicken stock and lemon juice. Bring to a boil, then reduce to simmer and season with salt and pepper. Put sauce on bottom of plate, place chicken on top. Garnish with lemon slices and curly endive.

Preparation: 35 min.   Easy   Serves: 4
Cooking: 20 min.   Can do ahead

Jeffrey A. Rudek, Sous Chef
Edgeworth Club

ONE DISH CHICKEN AND GRAVY

"Easy and good family dinner"

¼ cup butter
4 whole chicken breasts, split, boned and skinned
¼ cup flour
1 1-lb. bag frozen baby onions
1 lb. carrots, peeled and sliced
⅔ cup undiluted Carnation milk
1 can cream of mushroom or cream of chicken soup
1 cup grated Cheddar cheese
¾ tsp. salt
⅛ tsp. pepper
½ cup white wine
¼ lb. sliced mushrooms
paprika

Preheat oven to 425°. Melt butter in a 9x11" baking dish in oven. Dip chicken in flour. Place chicken in melted butter. Bake, uncovered, for 30 minutes. Turn chicken and bake 15 minutes longer. Pour off excess fat. While chicken is baking, parboil onion and carrots. Drain and add to chicken. Mix rest of ingredients together; pour over chicken. Sprinkle with paprika (may be frozen at this point). Cover dish with foil. Reduce heat to 325° and bake for 15-20 minutes or until bubbly.

NOTE: 1 small can of carrot fingers and 8-10 small, cooked onions may be substituted for the carrots and onions.

Preparation: 30 min.   Easy   Serves: 8
Cooking: 1 hr.   Can do ahead   Can freeze

Maureen T. Senetra

BREAST OF CHICKEN TAKOMA PARK

½ cup all-purpose flour
2 Tbsp. Old Bay seasoning
1 egg white, beaten
2 Tbsp. stone-ground mustard (such as Pommery)
½ cup finely ground walnuts
½ cup fresh bread crumbs
2 skinless, boneless chicken breast halves (6 oz. each)
3 Tbsp. olive oil
1 Tbsp. unsalted butter
juice of ½ lemon

In a shallow bowl, combine the flour and Old Bay seasoning. In a second shallow bowl, blend egg white with mustard. In a third shallow bowl, combine walnuts and bread crumbs. One at a time, dredge each chicken breast in the flour and shake off excess. Next, dip breast into egg and mustard to coat. Finally, dip into walnut/bread crumb mixture. Press mixture onto chicken so the coating adheres to both

sides. In a medium skillet, heat olive oil over moderately high heat. Cook on one side until crisp and brown, about 3 minutes. Then turn; reduce heat until moderately low and cook until the chicken has just lost its pinkness inside, about 5 minutes. To serve, slice the breast on the diagonal and fan out decoratively on 2 warm plates. Melt butter in skillet and add lemon juice, then drizzle over chicken.

Preparation: 20 min.   Easy   Serves: 2
Cooking: 10 min.   Serve immediately

John Gregory King, Chef
Allegheny Country Club

MID EAST MEDLEY

4 quarts water
1 small onion, chopped
2 medium carrots, chopped
3 stalks celery, chopped
1 bay leaf
6 peppercorns
4 cloves
½ tsp. salt
5 whole chicken breasts
   (remove skin from 4 of 5)
⅓ cup olive oil
¼ cup lemon juice
1 Tbsp. chopped dill, fresh
   (OR 1½ tsp. dry)
1 16-oz. can small pitted
   olives, drained
1 Tbsp. grated Parmesan
   cheese
1½ lbs. asparagus
2 Tbsp. capers

In stew pot, place first 8 ingredients. Bring to a boil, reduce heat and simmer for 10 minutes. Add chicken breasts. Simmer for 20 minutes on lowest heat. Remove chicken to cool. Bone and cube when cool. Place in large bowl. Meanwhile, blend olive oil and lemon juice with dill by hand. Let sit 15 minutes. Strain out the stewed vegetables, reserving 2 Tbsp. of juice. Add olive oil dressing and reserved stew juice to chicken cubes. Add strained stewed vegetables. Add olives and cheese. One hour before serving, cook asparagus, then slice into 1″ sections. Lightly toss into salad. Add capers. Should stand at room temperature for ½ hour.

Preparation: 1 hr.   Moderately difficult   Serves: 10
                            Must do ahead

Susan D. Craig

POACHED CHICKEN BREASTS WITH TARRAGON SAUCE
"Wonderful cold summer entrée"

1 cup water
½ cup dry white wine
1 tsp. tarragon
1 bay leaf
1 lb. skinned and boned
   chicken breasts (4 halves)
½ cup yogurt
2 tsp. chopped shallots
1 tsp. Dijon mustard
½ tsp. tarragon

In a medium saucepan, bring the water, wine, tarragon, and bay leaf to a boil over high heat. Add the chicken breasts and simmer for 12 minutes, or until the breasts are cooked. Remove from the poaching liquid and chill. Combine the remaining ingredients in a small bowl. Serve the sauce with the chilled chicken breasts.

NOTE: If you prefer a warm variation, the breasts can be pounded and sautéed in butter. The sauce should be served chilled.

Preparation: 20 min.   Easy   Serves: 4
Cooking: 10-15 min. Must do ahead

Missy Zimmerman

BOULDER CHICKEN
"Well worth the time"

3 whole chicken breasts, boned
4 eggs, well beaten
seasoned Italian bread crumbs
½-1 stick butter or margarine
1-2 lbs. fresh mushrooms,
   sliced
8-12 oz. Provolone cheese
   slices
1 can chicken broth

Cut chicken breasts in bite-sized pieces. Add chicken pieces to eggs; marinate overnight in covered bowl. Roll chicken pieces in bread crumbs. Heat half of the butter, more can be added if needed. Slowly sauté chicken pieces over low-medium heat until chicken is white, turning frequently, about 15 minutes, until golden brown. Remove chicken to warm plate. Sauté the mushrooms in the remaining butter. In a 3-quart ungreased casserole, layer chicken pieces, mushrooms, cheese; repeat layers. Pour chicken broth over all. Top with additional bread crumbs. Bake, uncovered, for 25 minutes at 350°.

Preparation: 1 hr.   Easy   Serves: 6
Cooking: 25 min.   Must do ahead

Susan Stalling DePree

HOT TOMATO VINAIGRETTE CHICKEN

Tomato Vinaigrette:
1 Tbsp. olive oil
1 clove garlic, crushed
¼ tsp. crushed red pepper
   flakes
½ tsp. dried basil
1 3″ strip lemon peel
½ tsp. sugar
1 16-oz. can tomatoes, undrained
1 Tbsp. red wine vinegar
½ tsp. salt
1 Tbsp. chopped parsley

Tomato Vinaigrette:
In medium saucepan (NOT ALUMINUM), heat olive oil over medium heat. Add garlic, crushed red pepper and basil. Cook for 1 minute, stirring constantly. Add lemon peel, sugar and tomatoes with juice (broken into small chunks). Simmer 20 minutes. Remove from heat; stir in vinegar, salt and parsley. Remove lemon peel and set mixture aside.

2 whole chicken breasts, split,
   skinned and boned
1 Tbsp. olive oil
1 Tbsp. butter
1 Tbsp. chopped parsley

Place chicken breast halves between 2 sheets of wax paper and pound to ¼-½″ thickness. In large skillet, heat oil and butter over medium-high heat. Add half the chicken. Cook about 3 minutes on each side. Keep warm in a 200° oven. Cook remaining chicken, remove to platter and keep warm. Add tomato vinaigrette to skillet; heat for 2 minutes, stirring constantly. Pour over chicken and sprinkle with parsley. Serve hot.

Preparation: 20 min.   Easy   Serves: 4
Cooking: 30 min.   Serve immediately

Vernon D. Schauble

CHICKEN CACCIATORE

"Great family meal"

2 Tbsp. margarine
2 whole chicken breasts, split
  and boned
½ cup chopped onions
1 green pepper, chopped
1 clove garlic, minced
1 large can Italian tomatoes
1 large can tomato sauce
½ tsp. salt
½ tsp. oregano
½ tsp. basil
¼ tsp. cayenne pepper

Cook chicken in margarine. Add onions, peppers and garlic. Brown until tender. Add other ingredients and simmer for 1-1½ hours. Serve over rice or noodles.

Preparation: 10-15 min.   Easy   Serves: 4
Cooking: 1½ hrs.   Can do ahead

Suzanne Blackburn

CHICKEN CHARDONNAY

"So easy, yet so elegant"

4-6 boneless chicken breasts,
  pounded
flour for dredging
butter
5-6 green onions, chopped
2 cloves garlic, pressed
½ cup Chardonnay
¼ cup fresh lemon juice
salt and pepper, to taste (white
  pepper suggested)

Lightly flour chicken and brown in butter until golden, about 5 minutes on each side. Place in warm oven. Add 3 Tbsp. butter to the pan. Sauté onions and garlic in butter. Add wine, lemon juice, salt and pepper. Simmer on low for 5 minutes. Add chicken to sauce, cover, and simmer for 5-10 minutes. Serve with rice.

Preparation: 20 min.   Easy   Serves: 4-6
Cooking: 20 min.   Serve immediately

Lisa Zambri

DIJON CHICKEN

3 whole chicken breasts,
  split and boned
salt and pepper, to taste
garlic powder, to taste
¾ cup sour cream
¾ cup Dijon mustard
½-¾ cup Italian-style fine
  bread crumbs

Lightly sprinkle chicken with salt, pepper and garlic powder. Combine sour cream and mustard in shallow dish, mixing well. Dip each chicken breast into mustard mixture and dredge in bread crumbs. Arrange chicken in a single layer in a baking pan. Bake at 375° for 50 minutes or until tender.

Preparation: 10 min.   Easy   Serves: 6
Cooking: 50 min.   Can do ahead

Katharine T. Harbison

CHICKEN BREASTS WITH CHAMPAGNE

4 whole chicken breasts, split,
  skinned and boned
¼ cup flour
1 tsp. salt
½ tsp. pepper
½ cup butter
½ lb. fresh mushrooms, sliced
1 cup whipping cream
6½ oz. bottle French
  champagne
8 large mushroom caps
2 Tbsp. butter

NOTE: Use no substitutions.

Slightly pound breast halves between wax paper to flatten. Mix flour, salt and pepper. Roll chicken breasts in flour mixture and shake off excess. Heat ½ cup butter in large skillet and cook chicken over low heat until lightly browned on both sides. Add mushrooms, cover and cook for 10 minutes. Remove any excess butter with a spoon. Add cream and simmer for 10 minutes on low heat. Transfer breasts to warm serving platter.

Sauce: Add to liquid in skillet, ¼ cup champagne. Bring to a rapid boil, stirring constantly, until sauce is reduced to a creamy consistency (if sauce becomes too thick, add a little milk). Serve chicken on a platter. Spoon sauce over breasts and garnish with mushroom caps that have been sautéed in butter.

Preparation: 25 min.   **Moderately difficult**   Serves: 6-8
                         Serve immediately

Lynn Popovich

BRANDY CHICKEN WITH PECAN RICE
"Surprisingly easy and good"

3 whole chicken breasts, split,
  skinned and boned
salt and pepper, to taste
2 garlic cloves, minced
2 Tbsp. butter
2 cups water
1 6¼-oz. pkg. long grain and
  wild rice
⅔ cup heavy cream
2-3 Tbsp. Brandy
¼ tsp. salt
¼ cup sliced scallions
¼ cup coarsely chopped pecans

Pound chicken breasts to ¼" thickness; season with salt and pepper. Cook chicken and garlic in 1 Tbsp. butter in a large skillet over medium heat until lightly browned (about 2 minutes per side). Meanwhile, turn water and remaining butter into a medium saucepan. Stir in contents of rice and seasoning packets; bring to a vigorous boil. Cover tightly and simmer until all liquid is absorbed (about 5 minutes). Remove chicken from skillet and keep warm.

Add cream, brandy and salt to skillet. Cook over medium-high heat until thickened to desired consistency. Stir scallions and pecans into rice. Serve rice with chicken; spoon sauce over chicken.

Preparation: 30 min.   **Easy**   Serves: 6
                         Serve immediately

Sally G. Heimbrook

LEMON CHICKEN WITH MUSHROOMS AND ARTICHOKES

2 whole chicken breasts, split,
  boned and skinned
juice from 1 lemon
4 Tbsp. butter
¼ cup olive oil
1 clove garlic, crushed
½ cup flour
½ lb. sliced mushrooms
½ cup sliced green onions
½ cup dry white wine
1 cup heavy cream
1 cup chicken broth
1 can artichoke hearts,
  quartered
½ tsp. red pepper, crushed
½ tsp. black pepper
1 tsp. salt
1 Tbsp. basil
1 lb. linguine
Parmesan cheese

Cut chicken breasts into strips and marinate overnight in lemon juice. In large skillet, melt butter and olive oil. When hot, add garlic and sauté for 2 minutes. Do not let brown. Remove garlic and discard. Dredge chicken pieces in flour and add to hot oil mixture. Sauté until chicken is done, about 5 minutes. Remove chicken from pan and set aside. Sauté mushrooms and green onions for 3 minutes. Remove from pan and set aside. Add wine and scrape up any particles remaining in pan. Cook for 1 minute. Add cream and broth and simmer for 2 minutes. Return chicken, onions, and mushrooms to pan. Add artichoke hearts, red pepper, black pepper, salt, and basil and simmer for 3 minutes. Serve over linguine with Parmesan cheese.

Preparation: 30 min.   **Moderately difficult**   **Serves: 4-6**
Cooking: 20 min.   **Can do ahead**

Phyllis Lynch

CHICKEN PAPRIKA

1 cup flour
2½ tsp. paprika
¼ tsp. cayenne pepper
¼ tsp. ginger
¼ tsp. basil
¼ tsp. nutmeg
2½ tsp. salt
½ tsp. ground pepper
4 whole chicken breasts, boned,
   skinned and cut in 2" pieces
1 stick butter
1 clove garlic, minced
2½ cups chicken broth
2 cups sour cream, room
   temperature
2 Tbsp. Worcestershire sauce
2 Tbsp. dry Sherry
1 can water chestnuts, drained
   and sliced

Preheat oven to 350°. Combine flour, paprika, cayenne pepper, ginger, basil, nutmeg, salt and pepper in a paper bag. Shake chicken pieces in flour mixture in bag, shake off excess flour and brown in ¾ stick butter. Transfer chicken pieces to baking dish. Add remaining butter to pan and sauté garlic. Blend in chicken stock, sour cream, Worcestershire sauce, Sherry and chestnuts. Heat, stirring constantly (DO NOT BOIL). Pour over chicken. Bake, uncovered, for 1 hour.

| Preparation: 35 min. | Easy | Serves: 8 |
| Cooking: 1 hr. | Can do ahead | |

Mary Jo Hottenstein

LEMON CHICKEN

"As good as in any Chinese restaurant"

1 lb. boneless chicken breasts
   or chicken tenders, cut into
   1½ x 1½" pieces
2½ Tbsp. peanut oil
1 tsp. cornstarch
1 tsp. salt
2 tsp. finely grated lemon peel
⅓ cup chicken stock
1 6-oz. pkg. LaChoy frozen
   pea pods
½ cup fresh mushrooms, sliced
2 tsp. fresh lemon juice
½ Tbsp. cornstarch mixed with
   ½ Tbsp. water
pinch of white pepper
salt, to taste

In a small bowl, combine chicken, 1 Tbsp. of the oil and the cornstarch. Blend well. Heat remaining oil with salt in wok or skillet until very hot. Add chicken and sauté until meat is white. (Recipe can be prepared ahead to this point.) Sprinkle with lemon peel. Add stock, pea pods and mushrooms; cook an additional minute. Combine remaining ingredients and pour over chicken. Continue cooking, stirring constantly, until sauce thickens. Adjust the seasoning with salt and white pepper. Transfer to a chafing dish and serve immediately over boiled rice.

| Preparation: 20 min. | Easy | Serves: 4 |
| Cooking: 10 min. | Serve immediately | |

Marilyn Linford

108

ITALIAN CHICKEN WITH PEPPER SAUCE
"This is a low-cholesterol recipe"

1 pkg. boneless, skinless
   chicken breast fillets
2 egg whites, slightly beaten
½ cup Italian bread crumbs
½ cup plain bread crumbs
1 tsp. basil
1 tsp. minced garlic
1 tsp. lemon-pepper seasoning
1 tsp. thyme
1 tsp. oregano
virgin olive oil
1 pkg. Knorr white sauce
1 jar roasted or fried sweet
   peppers, diced

Remove excess fat from chicken; cut fillets into 1½" wide strips. Pound to ¼" thickness. Dip in egg whites, then into mixture of bread crumbs, herbs and spices. Heat ¼" olive oil in skillet. Sauté chicken until brown on both sides. Place in oblong baking dish and bake in 350° oven for 15-20 minutes. While baking, prepare white sauce according to package directions. When thickened, add diced peppers. Pour sauce over chicken and serve immediately.

Preparation: 30 min.	Easy	Serves: 4-6
Cooking: 15-20 min.	Serve immediately	Can freeze

Carol S. Metzger

SPINACH FETA CHICKEN BREASTS
"Wonderful"

1 large pkg. fresh spinach
3 whole chicken breasts,
   split, skinned and boned
2-3 Tbsp. butter
3 cloves garlic, crushed
1-1½ cups Feta cheese
2 cups Italian bread crumbs
½ cup oil

Sauce:
½ cup butter
2 cups sliced fresh mushrooms
1 cup white wine
1 cup chicken broth
1 Tbsp. lemon juice
1 Tbsp. flour

Cook spinach according to package directions; drain. Pound chicken breasts between plastic wrap until ¼" thick. Sauté spinach in 2-3 Tbsp. of butter with garlic for about 5 minutes. Divide spinach mixture and spread one-sixth on each chicken breast. Crumble Feta cheese on each, then roll and seal with toothpicks. Dip into bread crumbs and cover lightly. Brown all chicken breasts in oil, turning frequently, for about 6-7 minutes. Remove and place in baking dish. Bake for 20-30 minutes at 350°. Just before chicken is done, melt ½ cup butter in skillet and sauté mushrooms for 3-4 minutes. Add white wine, chicken broth, lemon juice and flour to mushrooms and simmer until it cooks down, about 10 minutes. Pour mushroom sauce (will not be thick) over chicken and serve immediately.

Preparation: 30 min.	Moderately difficult	Serves: 6
Cooking: 20-30 min.	Serve immediately	

Lynn Popovich

AUNT NILA'S CHICKEN BREASTS

6 whole chicken breasts,
  boned and skinned
½ cup flour or bread crumbs
1 cup butter, divided
salt and freshly ground pepper,
  to taste
1½ cups sliced mushrooms
½ cup Marsala wine
¼ cup chicken stock
½ cup shredded Mozzarella
  cheese
½ cup grated Parmesan cheese
basil, to taste
oregano, to taste

Preheat oven to 450°. Flatten and dredge chicken breasts in flour or bread crumbs. Brown in butter, lightly, for 3-4 minutes on each side. Place browned breasts in a 9x13" casserole dish. Salt and pepper to taste. Sauté mushrooms and sprinkle them over the chicken. Stir wine and chicken stock into pan drippings. Simmer for 10 minutes. Pour over chicken. Sprinkle with cheeses, basil and oregano. Bake for 10-15 minutes or until cooked through and very hot.

Preparation: 40 min.   Easy   Serves: 12
Cooking: 25-30 min.   Can do ahead

Judy Jones

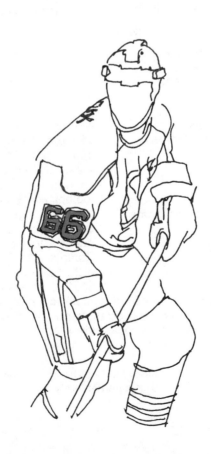

110

CHICKEN "GEORGE"

"Very good, very rich, very easy"

Sauce:
1/4 lb. butter
6 Tbsp. flour
4 cups scalded Half & Half
2 tsp. salt
1/2 tsp. white pepper

4 Tbsp. butter
2 green peppers, diced
1 cup sliced mushrooms
3 cups chicken, cooked and
  diced
1/2 cup cooked ham,
  diced (optional)
3 pimientos, diced (optional)
1/4 cup Sherry

Sauce: Melt butter. Stir in flour. Cook and stir for 1 minute on low heat. Add Half & Half. Stir in salt and pepper. When mixture reaches boiling point, turn down heat and cook for 10 minutes, stirring occasionally.

While sauce cooks, sauté peppers and mushrooms in butter until tender, but do not brown. Add to sauce. Add chicken, then pimiento and ham, if desired. Stir in Sherry right before serving.

Preparation: 1 hr.   Easy   Serves: 6
Cooking: 20 min.   Can do ahead   Can freeze

Patricia Stover

CHICKEN CRESCENTS

"Simply delicious"

1 can crescent rolls
3 oz. cream cheese, softened
2 Tbsp. margarine, melted
2 cups cooked chicken, cubed
1 Tbsp. chopped pimiento
1 Tbsp. chopped green pepper,
  sautéed
1-2 Tbsp. chopped mushrooms,
  sautéed
1/4 tsp. salt
1/8 tsp. pepper
2 Tbsp. milk
1/2 Tbsp. chopped parsley
1 Tbsp. chopped chives
seasoned croutons, crushed
4 Tbsp. margarine

Separate the rolls into 4 rectangles. Seal perforations by pressing together. Blend cream cheese and 2 Tbsp. of margarine together. Add chicken; mix, then add pimiento, green pepper, mushrooms, salt, pepper, milk, parsley and chives. Spoon 1/2 cup chicken mixture onto each crescent roll rectangle. Pull up corners and twist top. Melt 4 Tbsp. of margarine; dip crescent into it and then into crushed croutons. Bake at 350° for 20-30 minutes.

Preparation: 40 min.   Moderately difficult   Serves: 4
Cooking: 30 min.   Can do ahead

Jane Birnie

111

CHICKEN SPECTACULAR

"The name says it all"

2-3 cups cooked chicken, cut
   into bite-sized pieces
1 can cream of celery soup
1 small jar pimientos, chopped
1 small onion, chopped
1 cup Hellmann's mayonnaise
1 can sliced water chestnuts
2 cups French-style green beans
2 Tbsp. lemon juice
1 box Uncle Ben's long grain
   and wild rice
½ tsp. curry powder
1 cup grated Cheddar cheese
slivered almonds

Combine all ingredients, except cheese and almonds. Put into a 9x13" pan. Top with cheese and almonds. Bake at 350° for 45 minutes.

Preparation:	1 hr.	Easy	Serves: 6-8
Cooking:	45 min.	Can do ahead	Can freeze

Karen Rossin

SESAME CHICKEN

½ cup Parmesan cheese
2 cups seasoned bread crumbs
4 Tbsp. sesame seeds
2-3 lbs. chicken fryers,
   cut into pieces
margarine, melted

Mix Parmesan cheese, bread crumbs and sesame seeds. Dip chicken in margarine and then into the Parmesan cheese mixture. Bake for 1½ hours, uncovered, at 350°

Preparation:	10 min.	Easy	Serves: 6-8
Cooking:	1½ hrs.	Can do ahead	

Margee Denver

CORNISH HENS A LA ORANGE

6-8 cornish hens*
4 Tbsp. butter
6 oz. frozen concentrated
   orange juice
¾ cup water
2 Tbsp. steak sauce
2 Tbsp. honey
1 tsp. salt
1 tsp. rosemary

*Frying chicken pieces can be
   substituted for the hens.

Cut hens in half and rinse well. Brown hens in butter. Remove from pan. Stir remaining ingredients into skillet; heat to boiling. Return hens to skillet. Reduce heat and cover. Simmer, basting several times with sauce, for 1 hour and 20 minutes. After hens have cooked for 1 hour, remove ¾ of the sauce from the skillet. Put sauce in microwave on High for 5 minutes (or until sauce is thick enough for glazing). Glaze hens for final 20 minutes of cooking.

Preparation:	25 min.	Easy	Serves: 8
Cooking:	1 hr. 20 min.	Can do ahead	

Angie C. Haskell

HONEY CHICKEN

"A gentle curry-honey flavor"

3 lbs. chicken pieces
4 Tbsp. butter
½ cup honey
¼ cup prepared mustard
1 tsp. salt
1 tsp. curry

Wash and dry chicken pieces; can use boned breasts. Melt remaining ingredients in roasting pan. Roll chicken in sauce. Bake at 375° for 1 hour.

Preparation: 10 min.   Easy   Serves: 6
Cooking: 1 hr.   Can do ahead

Barbara Burton

LONE STAR BARBEQUE CHICKEN

"You should have most ingredients on hand"

1 chicken, quartered
salt and pepper, to taste
¼ cup butter
garlic, to taste
chopped onion, to taste
¼ cup lemon juice
¼ cup vinegar
¼ cup ketchup
¼ cup Worcestershire sauce

Wash and drain chicken. Season with salt and pepper. Place in large pan so pieces do not overlap. Melt butter in saucepan; add garlic and onions and sauté until transparent. Add remaining ingredients and bring to a boil. Broil chicken until golden brown on both sides. Add sauce to chicken and cook, uncovered, in a 325° oven for 1 hour or until tender. Baste often.

Preparation: 15 min.   Easy   Serves: 4
Cooking: 1 hr. 10 min.   Can do ahead

Kay Moiles

CHICKEN ENCHILADAS

"Double and do ahead for a crowd"

2 cups chopped cooked chicken
1 4-oz. can chopped, mild
   green chiles
1 7-oz. jar green chile salsa
½ tsp. salt
2 cups whipping cream
12 corn tortillas
salad oil for frying tortillas
1½ cups Monterey Jack
   cheese, grated

Combine chicken, green chiles, and chile salsa and mix well. In medium-sized bowl, mix salt and whipping cream. Heat ½" oil in small skillet. Dip each tortilla into the hot oil for 5 seconds; drain on a paper towel. Dip each tortilla into cream, then fill with chicken mixture. Roll and place in an ungreased baking dish, seam side down. Pour remaining cream over all of the enchiladas and sprinkle with cheese. Bake, uncovered, in a 350° oven for 15-20 minutes.

Preparation: 30 min.   Easy   Serves: 6
Cooking: 15-20 min.   Can do ahead   Can freeze

Annemarie Gordon

TURKEY CHILI

1 small onion, diced
½ green pepper, diced
2 lbs. ground turkey breast
2 10-oz. cans stewed tomatoes,
   diced (reserve liquid)
2 1-lb. cans kidney beans
2 12-oz. jars chili sauce
1 tsp. thyme
1 tsp. lemon-pepper seasoning
1 tsp. basil
1 tsp. chili powder
2 Tbsp. brown sugar
1 Tbsp. mustard
½ cup ketchup

Sauté onion and pepper together; add turkey and brown. Drain. Add stewed tomatoes, reserving liquid for later. Add kidney beans, chili sauce, and remaining ingredients. Simmer for 30 minutes, adding stewed tomato liquid if more liquid is desired.

| Preparation: 15 min. | Easy | Serves: 6 |
| Cooking: 30 min. | Can do ahead | Can freeze |

Carol S. Metzger

COLD CURRIED CHICKEN/CHUTNEY RICE

"Great on a warm summer's night"

6 whole chicken breasts, split,
   skinned and boned
2 Tbsp. butter or margarine
2 Tbsp. flour
1 pint chicken stock, hot
1 pint light cream
1 Tbsp. curry powder
salt and pepper, to taste
2 egg yolks, slightly beaten
cooked rice, enough for
   12 servings
½-1 cup chutney

Parboil chicken breasts until tender; set aside. Melt the butter and stir in flour. Stirring constantly, add hot stock, cream, curry powder, salt and pepper. Add a few spoonfuls to the egg yolks, then pour back into cream mixture. Cool and pour over chicken. Refrigerate for several hours. Serve cold over cold chutney rice.

Chutney Rice: Mix cooked rice with enough chutney for flavor. Chill.

| Preparation: 30 min. | Easy | Serves: 12 |
| | Must do ahead | |

Gretchen R. Burnham

𝕮𝖎𝖇𝖎·𝕱𝖔𝖈𝖚𝖘·𝕾𝖕𝖑𝖊𝖓𝖉𝖊𝖗

FISH & SEAFOOD

ORANGE ROUGHY WITH SPINACH PESTO
"Looks difficult, but easy"

1 10-oz. pkg. frozen chopped
  spinach
1 cup (4-oz.) shredded part-skim
  Mozzarella cheese, divided
¼ cup grated Parmesan cheese
1 small clove garlic, minced
2 Tbsp. chopped onion
1 Tbsp. pine nuts (optional)
2 tsp. dried basil
¼ tsp. dried marjoram
⅛ tsp. white pepper
3 Tbsp. Chablis or other dry
  white wine
⅓ cup plain low-fat yogurt
6 4-oz. skinned orange roughy
  fillets

Pierce the package of spinach with a fork; microwave on High for 4 minutes. Drain well by pressing between paper towel layers. Combine spinach, ½ cup Mozzarella cheese, and the next 9 ingredients in blender or food processor. Process at medium speed until smooth. Arrange fish in single layer in a 12x8x2" baking dish, with spinach mixture spread evenly on top. Cover with wax paper and microwave on High for 3 minutes. Give dish a half-turn and sprinkle with remaining ½ cup cheese. Microwave on High for 3-4 minutes or until fish turns opaque. Let stand, covered, for 3-5 minutes. Fish is done if it flakes easily.

NOTE: Fish can be baked in conventional oven at 350° for 30 minutes.

Preparation: 15 min.   Easy   Serves: 4-6
Cooking: 10-15 min.   Can do ahead

Diane Abell

LOUISIANA FILLETS

2 Tbsp. butter or margarine
2 Tbsp. lemon juice
2½ lbs. fillets - sole, trout,
   snapper or catfish
¾ tsp. lemon and pepper spice
⅛ tsp. crushed red pepper
⅛ tsp. garlic powder
½ tsp. salt

Preheat oven to 350°. Melt butter with lemon juice in a shallow pan. Coat both sides of fillets with butter mixture. Lay fillets side by side, overlapping slightly if necessary, in pan. Mix spices together. Sprinkle over fillets. Bake for 20-25 minutes, depending on size of fillets and type of fish (catfish bakes the longest).

NOTE: The pan may blacken, but that's fine. The liquid will keep the fish moist.

Preparation: 10 min.   Easy   Serves: 5-6
Cooking: 25-30 min.   Serve immediately

Susan Craig

FLOUNDER FAVORITE
"Make as much as you need"

Fillets of flounder (or trout)
sliced fresh tomatoes
Italian seasoning
salt
pepper
Parmesan cheese
herb-seasoned croutons,
   crushed
butter

Line glass baking dish with sliced tomatoes. Lay fillets over this. Sprinkle seasoning and cheese over fish. Crush croutons in blender or food processor and sprinkle heavily over top. Dot with butter. Bake at 400° for 15-17 minutes.

Preparation: 15 min.   Easy   Serves: 1 fillet per person
Cooking: 15 min.   Can do ahead

Barbara Laman Gaudio

FLOUNDER FILLET WITH DILL VEGETABLE
"Fish in foil"

2 Tbsp. margarine
1 tsp. dill weed
2 cloves garlic, minced
1 carrot, cut in thin strips
1 fresh tomato, diced
1 lb. fresh flounder fillet

Melt margarine in skillet over low heat. Add dill and garlic. Stir to prevent browning. Add carrots and sauté for 7 minutes. Add tomato and continue to sauté for 5 minutes. Place flounder fillet in the center of a square of foil.

Pour carrot-tomato mixture over the fish. Fold foil so that fish is completely enclosed. Place in baking dish and bake for 7-10 minutes in a 325° oven.

Preparation: 15 min.   Easy   Serves: 3-4
Cooking: 20-25 min.   Serve immediately

Catherine Connell
D. T. Watson Rehabilitation Hospital

WALNUT STUFFED TROUT

"Heads or tails - on or off? You call it!"

6 very fresh trout, boned,
  heads on*
1 cup walnuts
2 shallots
½ bunch parsley
¼ cup butter
½ tsp. pepper
½ tsp. salt
½ cup butter
Lemon, parsley, seedless
  grapes for garnish

*Heads can be removed if you
  wish.

Rinse and dry the trout. Make stuffing: chop walnuts in a food processor until they are fine (reserve 6 for garnish). Remove. Chop shallots with metal blade. Add parsley and chop. Add softened butter, seasonings and walnuts and mix. Spread this mixture inside of trout. Reserve 1 Tbsp. of stuffing for each trout for garnish. Sauté each trout in butter about 8-10 minutes on each side or until nicely brown. Serve on platter with reserved stuffing and a walnut on each trout — garnish with lemon, parsley and seedless green grapes.

Preparation: 15-30 min. Easy   Serves: 6
Cooking: 16-20 min. Can do ahead

Mary Lee Parrington

SALMON STEAKS WITH CUCUMBER SAUCE

"Delicious hot or cold"

4 salmon steaks
1 cup white wine
1 lemon, thinly sliced
1 onion, thinly sliced
6 whole peppercorns
several parsley sprigs

Cucumber sauce:

1 cucumber, peeled and seeded
2 Tbsp. mayonnaise
½ cup sour cream
1 Tbsp. lemon juice
salt and white pepper

Preheat oven to 350°. Place salmon in ovenproof pan and pour wine over steaks. Add remaining ingredients, except cucumber sauce. Cover with buttered wax paper, greased side down. Bake in oven for 15 minutes. Serve with cucumber sauce.

Cucumber sauce:
Grate cucumber in food processor, transfer to a mixing bowl. Add the remaining ingredients and mix thoroughly. Serve at room temperature over hot salmon. Or serve chilled over cold salmon.

Preparation: 5-10 min. Easy   Serves: 4
Cooking: 15 min.   Can do ahead

Tina Morrison

HALIBUT SUPREME

"This is an excellent family dinner"

2 Tbsp. butter
2 Tbsp. flour
1 cup milk
salt and pepper
1 cup grated Parmesan cheese
1½ - 2 lbs. halibut steak
paprika

Melt butter in a saucepan. Add flour. Stirring constantly, slowly add milk and seasonings. Continue to stir until thickened, then add grated cheese. Remove from heat. Arrange halibut in buttered baking dish, pour cheese sauce around, sprinkle with paprika and bake at 350° until halibut is tender.

Preparation: 15 min.   Easy   Serves: 6
Cooking: 20-25 min.

Betty G. VanKirk

DANA'S SHRIMP

"A shrimp lovers' delight"

2 cups cooked long grain rice,
   not instant
2-3 cups cooked shrimp
6 Tbsp. ketchup
½ tsp. Tabasco sauce
several shakes of Worcestershire sauce
1 pt. whipping cream
1 stick melted butter

Mix all ingredients together and put in baking dish. Bake at 350° for 1 hour.

Preparation: 30 min.   Easy   Serves: 6
Cooking: 1 hr.   Can do ahead

Mrs. Robinson F. Barker

SOLE AND BANANAS

"Fish & bananas? Try it, you'll like it!"

4 large sole fillets
flour
salt and pepper
¼ cup butter
½ cup dry white wine
2 Tbsp. lemon juice
2 Tbsp. brown sugar
½ tsp. ginger
2 bananas, quartered
   lengthwise
toasted slivered almonds

Dust fillets with mixture of flour, salt and pepper. In a skillet, melt the butter. Add fillets and brown 2-3 minutes on each side, until golden and flaky. Remove to heated platter. In the same skillet, add wine, lemon juice, brown sugar, ginger, and bananas and simmer for 2 minutes. Arrange bananas around fish. Pour sauce over all. Sprinkle with almonds. Serve immediately.

Preparation: 10-15 min.   Easy   Serves: 4
Cooking: 5 min.   Serve immediately

Tina Morrison

SCALLOPS WITH JULIENNE VEGETABLES

"A creamy wine sauce"

2 medium carrots
2 small zucchini
2 small leeks
1 small turnip (optional)
8-10 large white mushrooms
2 sticks butter*
2 lb. large sea scallops
1 cup dry white wine
1 lemon
1 cup heavy cream
salt, to taste
pepper, to taste
nutmeg, to taste
1 Tbsp. fresh dill

*Margarine may be used in place of butter, but taste is slightly different.

Cut vegetables in julienne strips. Melt 4 Tbsp. butter in skillet. Add vegetables and sauté until tender, but crisp. In another skillet, melt 6 Tbsp. butter. When hot, sauté scallops, deglaze with wine, stir and scrape butter from sides and bottom of pan. Simmer 2 minutes. Flake the remaining butter, adding slowly to scallops. Squeeze in juice of 1 lemon while stirring constantly. Add vegetables and heavy cream. Stir and simmer for another 3-4 minutes to reduce liquid. Season with salt, pepper and a dash of nutmeg. Serves nicely on cooking shells. Sprinkle with dill.

Preparation: 20 min.   Easy   Serves: 8
Cooking: 15 min.   Serve immediately

Lynn Popovich

SHRIMP AND SCALLOPS ROMANOFF

"Very elegant"

¼ cup butter
flour for dredging
1 lb. shrimp, peeled and
   deveined
1 lb. scallops
½ tsp. white pepper
1 clove garlic, crushed
salt, to taste (optional)
½ cup white wine
1 Tbsp. lemon juice
1 cup cream
1 egg, lightly beaten
½ cup shredded Parmesan
   cheese
½ lb linguine, cooked
¼ cup sour cream
1 Tbsp. caviar or black olives

Melt butter in a large skillet. Dredge shrimp in flour and place in skillet, adding scallops, pepper, garlic and salt. Cook until seafood is tender, but not soft. Add wine and lemon juice. Simmer for 1 minute and add cream, egg, and shredded cheese. When completely heated, pour over linguine. Serve with a dollop of sour cream and dot center with caviar or olives.

Preparation: 10 min.   Easy   Serves: 6
Cooking: 20 min.

Linda D. Orsini

SCALLOPS AU GRATIN

"A classy presentation in baking shells"

1 lb. scallops
½ cup white wine
1 cup water
3 Tbsp. butter or margarine
3 Tbsp. flour
½ tsp. salt
¼ tsp. paprika
1 beaten egg yolk
¼ cup shredded Cheddar
   cheese
1 cup fresh soft bread crumbs
2 Tbsp. melted butter or
   margarine

Boil scallops in white wine and water for 2 minutes. Drain, save liquid. Melt butter, stir in flour and seasonings. Add to liquid. Cook and stir until thick and bubbly. Add small amount of mixture to egg yolk - then return mixture. Add cheese, stir until melted. Add scallops. *Turn into 6 large baking shells or into individual casseroles. Combine bread crumbs with melted butter**. Sprinkle over scallops. Bake at 400° for 5-10 minutes until bubbly.

*May use 1½ quart casserole dish instead of individual casseroles.
**May omit melted butter, if desired.

Preparation: 10 min.   Easy   Serves: 6
Cooking: 5-10 min.   Can do ahead

Anne S. Courneen

SHRIMP CURRY

"Some like it HOT"

2 lbs. medium shrimp
½ cup butter or margarine
1 large onion, sliced
1 clove garlic, minced
3 ribs celery, sliced
1 green pepper, sliced
½ cup flour
3 cups milk
1 tsp. salt
¼ tsp. pepper
cayenne, to taste
¼ tsp. tumeric
1 Tbsp. curry powder
2 Tbsp. freshly-squeezed
   lemon juice
rice

Clean shrimp, split lengthwise. Melt butter or margarine in a large skillet and sauté shrimp until light pink. Add onion, garlic, celery and green pepper and sauté until soft. Lower heat and stir in flour. Add milk and stir until smooth. Add seasonings, cook until thickened, stirring occasionally. Stir in lemon juice. Serve with rice.

| Preparation: | 30-45 min. | Moderately difficult | Serves: 6 |
| Cooking: | 15-20 min. | Serve immediately | |

Marilyn J. Sittig

SHRIMP WITH ROSEMARY

"Has a delicate flavor"

2 Tbsp. olive oil
1 lb. (16-20) raw shrimp, peeled
   and deveined
2 Tbsp. finely minced onion
½ cup dry Vermouth
1 Tbsp. finely chopped rosemary leaves
1 cup heavy cream
1 tsp. unsalted butter
pinch of salt
½ tsp. ground black pepper

Heat olive oil in a skillet on moderately high heat. Sauté shrimp on both sides. Remove from pan, set aside, turn heat to moderately low. Add minced onion and cook until transparent. Add Vermouth and chopped rosemary and reduce by ⅔. Add heavy cream, cook down by ½. Add shrimp to sauce, stir in butter, season with salt and pepper. To serve, use slotted spoon and place equal number of shrimp on warm serving plates. Spoon remaining sauce over shrimp.

| Preparation: | 15 min. | Easy | Serves: 2-3 |
| Cooking: | 30 min. | | |

John Gregory King, Chef
Allegheny Country Club

ORIENTAL SHRIMP

"A wonderful tasty shrimp kabob"

2 lbs. large shrimp, fresh or
  frozen
½ cup safflower oil
¼ cup soy sauce
¼ cup lemon juice
1 medium onion, chopped
2 Tbsp. chopped crystallized
  ginger
2 cloves garlic, minced

Thaw shrimp, if frozen; shell and devein. Mix all ingredients, except shrimp, in a large bowl. Mix well, then add shrimp. Cover and refrigerate overnight or at least 2-3 hours. Drain marinade and reserve for basting.* Thread shrimp on skewers. Grill 3 inches above heat (medium heat).

*Basting constantly, cook shrimp 6-8 minutes per side or until they become opaque.

Preparation: 10 min.   Easy   Serves: 4-6
Cooking: 12-15 min.   Must do ahead

Christine K. Wells

SHRIMP SCAMPI

¾ cup butter or margarine
¼ cup finely chopped onion
3-4 garlic cloves
¼ - ⅓ cup fresh parsley,
  chopped
1 lb. shrimp, uncooked and
  deveined
¼ cup dry white wine or
  Vermouth
2 Tbsp. (or more) lemon juice
salt, to taste
pepper, to taste

Melt butter. Add the onion, garlic and parsley. Cook over low heat until the onion is translucent. Add the shrimp and stir for 2-3 minutes or until done. Transfer shrimp to a platter and keep warm. Add wine and lemon juice to the butter mixture. Simmer for 2-3 minutes. Pour over shrimp. Season with salt and pepper.

Preparation: 30 min.   Easy   Serves: 4-6
Cooking: 15-20 min.

Francye Kinney

SEWICKLEY SHRIMP

"Very mellow tasting"

1 lb. fresh peeled shrimp
flour
4 Tbsp. olive oil
1 clove garlic, crushed
2 Tbsp. butter
shallots or Vidalia onions
juice from 1 lemon
¼ cup dry white wine
lemon wedges for garnish

Coat the shrimp in flour. Heat pan without olive oil; when hot, add oil and shrimp. Keep turning swiftly until flour is brownish. Add garlic. Add butter (or if you wish to keep cholesterol down, add more olive oil). Add shallots or onions and fry until tender in sauce. Add lemon juice. Add wine. Serve at once with wedges of lemon and either plain French bread or garlic bread.

Preparation: 5-10 min.   Easy   Serves: 4-6
Cooking: 6-8 min.   Serve immediately

Vivian Brown

122

BAKED CRAB IMPERIAL
"Now this is GOOD"

4 Tbsp. butter or margarine
4 Tbsp. flour
2 cups milk
1 tsp. salt (optional)
⅛ tsp. pepper
½ tsp. celery salt
dash of cayenne
1 egg yolk, beaten
2 Tbsp. dry Sherry
1 cup soft bread crumbs
1 lb. crabmeat
1 tsp. minced parsley
1 tsp. minced onion

Topping:
¼ cup buttered crumbs
paprika

Melt butter or margarine. Add flour and blend. Gradually add milk and seasonings. Cook over low heat, stirring constantly until thickened. Gradually add egg yolk, stirring constantly. Cook for 2 minutes. Remove from heat and add Sherry, soft bread crumbs, crabmeat, parsley, and onion. Gently mix and pour into a well-greased 1½ quart casserole or ramekins. Top with buttered crumbs and sprinkle with paprika. Bake in hot oven of 400° for 20-25 minutes or less for ramekins.

Preparation: 30 min.   Moderately difficult   Serves: 6-8
Cooking: 20-30 min. Can do ahead

Mrs. Richard Marsh

JAMBALAYA

1 cup diced cooked ham
1 cup chopped onion
¾ cup sliced celery
1 medium green pepper, cut in strips
1 clove garlic, minced
2-4 Tbsp. oil
1 10¾-oz. can chicken broth
1 15-oz. can Hunt's tomato sauce
¾ cup water
1½ cups chopped, cooked chicken
¾ cup uncooked rice
2 Tbsp. minced parsley
1 bay leaf
¼ tsp. thyme
¼ tsp. Worcestershire sauce
⅛ - ½ tsp. cayenne (to taste)
1 lb. medium shrimp, cleaned, deveined and parboiled

Cook ham, onion, celery, green pepper, and garlic in oil in a large skillet until onion is soft. Add remaining ingredients, except shrimp. Bring to a boil. Cover and simmer for 40 minutes or until rice is cooked, stirring once or twice. Add shrimp during last 5 minutes or so of cooking.

NOTE: This dish can be made without the ham, or chicken, or shrimp; or can be made with any two of them; but the combination of all three is best.

Preparation: 30-40 min.   Easy   Serves: 4-6
Cooking: 40-45 min.   Can do ahead

Bonnie J. Weber

SEAFOOD MARINARA

"Use whatever you've caught"

2 medium onions, chopped
¼ green pepper, chopped
2 Tbsp. vegetable oil
1½ cups water
1 16-oz. can whole tomatoes,
  undrained and chopped
1 8-oz. can tomato sauce
½ cup chopped fresh parsley
3 cloves garlic, chopped
½ tsp. salt, or to taste
¼ - ½ tsp. black pepper, or to
  taste
1½ lb. cleaned, uncooked
  seafood (see NOTE)
1 lb. pasta, cooked (linguine is
  best)
grated Parmesan cheese

In a large saucepan, sauté onions and green pepper in oil until transparent. Stir in all other ingredients except seafood, cheese, and pasta. Simmer 1½ hours, stirring frequently. You may refrigerate at this stage for up to 2 days. Add seafood and simmer 20 minutes. Serve over cooked pasta and sprinkle with cheese.

NOTE: For seafood choose any combination of three — ½ lb. each to make 1½ lbs.:

shrimp	crab	clams
scallops	lobster	
white fish	squid	

Preparation: 20-25 min.	Easy	Serves: 4-6
Cooking: 2 hrs.	Can do ahead	

Joyce Scalercio

JAMBALAYA

"Rich and spicy"

6-8 slices bacon
1 medium onion, chopped
2 medium green peppers, cut
  in 1″ strips
1 cup raw rice (not instant)
2-3 tsp. minced garlic
1 large can tomatoes, chopped
  coarsely
1 tsp. thyme
1 tsp. salt
¾ tsp. black pepper
¼ tsp. red pepper
1½ cups chicken stock
½ lb. smoked ham (small strips)
1 lb. medium shrimp (raw and
  shelled)

In a Dutch oven, fry bacon to render fat, but not until it is crisp. Remove bacon and save. Add onion to bacon fat and cook until golden - about 5-6 minutes. Add green pepper and cook 3 minutes more. Add 1 cup rice. Stir to blend well. Add garlic, tomatoes, bacon, thyme, salt, black and red peppers and stir thoroughly. Pour in chicken stock and bring to boil. Add ham. Cover and place in a 350° oven for 20 minutes. Add shrimp and push them under mixture. Cover and bake 15 minutes more. Do not overcook as rice will get soggy.

Preparation: 30 min.	Moderately difficult	Serves: 6
Cooking: 35 min.	Serve immediately	

Jennifer C. Jose

BAKED SEAFOOD SALAD

"Serve as main dish for luncheon or light dinner"

½ cup chopped green pepper
¼ cup minced onion
1 cup chopped celery
1 cup flaked crabmeat
1 cup cooked or canned shrimp
1 cup mayonnaise
½ tsp. salt
1 tsp. Worcestershire sauce
2 cups corn flakes, crushed
2 Tbsp. butter or margarine
paprika, to taste
lemon slices

Combine green pepper, onion, celery, crabmeat, shrimp, mayonnaise, salt and Worcestershire sauce; mix lightly. Place mixture in individual shells or a shallow 9x13" baking dish. Sprinkle with crushed corn flakes and paprika. Dot with butter. Bake at 350° for about 30 minutes. Serve with lemon slices.

Preparation: 25 min. Easy Serves: 6-8
Cooking: 30 min. Can do ahead

Mabel E. Heinecke

CREAMY SALMON BOATS

"Great for lunch or dinner"

3 medium baking potatoes
1 8-oz. pkg. cream cheese, softened
½ cup mayonnaise
¼ cup finely chopped onion
⅓ cup sliced pitted ripe olives
½ tsp. dill weed
½ tsp. salt
1 6½-oz. can pink salmon

Preheat oven to 350°. Bake potatoes and cut in half lengthwise. Scoop out insides, leaving shell. Place scooped out potatoes in bowl and add all other ingredients, except the salmon. Mix well. Fold in salmon. Spoon mixture into the potato shells. Bake for 15-20 minutes.

Preparation: 15 min. Easy Serves: 6
Cooking: 20 min.

Teresa A. Surgeon

SEAFOOD SANDWICH SPREAD

"A can of this, a can of that equals a delicious spread"

1 3-oz. pkg. cream cheese, softened
1 Tbsp. sour cream
1 Tbsp. mayonnaise
1 tsp. green onion, shredded
½ - 1 cup relish
1 tsp. chives
1 small can shrimp, drained
1 small can salmon, drained
1 small can tuna, drained
1 small can crabmeat, drained
dash garlic powder, optional

In a food processor, beat cream cheese until fluffy. Add sour cream, mayonnaise, green onions, relish and chives. Add seafood and blend. Chill. Serve on croissants or tiny cocktail buns.

Preparation: 15 min. Easy Yield: 2½ cups
Can do ahead

Judy Young

SANDWICHES

HAM AND ASPARAGUS GRILLED SANDWICHES

¼ cup cream cheese, softened
2 Tbsp. mayonnaise
¼ tsp. Fines herbs
1 tsp. parsley
2 slices firm bread (rye, sourdough, whole wheat, pumpernickel)
soft margarine, vegetable oil or butter-flavored PAM
4 very thin slices baked ham
3 fresh asparagus spears, blanched

Mix the cream cheese, mayonnaise, Fines herbs and parsley together. Spread 1 side of each bread slice with a thin layer of margarine, oil or spray with PAM. Turn bottom slice over and place ham on uncoated side of bread so it hangs over by half. Cover entire ham slice with cream cheese. Place asparagus spears on the half over the bread slice. Fold the ham slices over like a blanket. Top with remaining slice of bread and grill on griddle, in pan or in a sandwich toaster.

Preparation: 20 min.   Easy   Serves: 1
Cooking: 5-10 min.   Serve immediately

Clee McBee

MUSHROOM TOPPED MUFFINS
"Great flavor"

10 slices Canadian bacon or ham
4 Tbsp. butter
½ cup chopped onion
6 cups fresh sliced mushrooms
1½ cups sour cream
⅓ cup milk
1 tsp. paprika
1 tsp. lemon juice
⅛ tsp. pepper
¼ tsp. salt
5 English muffins, split, buttered and toasted

Brown bacon. Remove from pan and set aside. Sauté onion and mushrooms in skillet in butter over low heat for about 5 minutes. Stir in sour cream, milk, paprika, lemon juice, pepper and salt. Heat through. Place one slice of bacon on muffin half. Spoon sauce over.

Preparation: 30 min.   Easy   Serves: 5
Cooking: 20 min.   Serve immediately

Betty T. Galey

WATERCRESS SANDWICHES

¼ lb. unsalted butter, room
  temperature
1 tsp. fresh lemon juice
1 tsp. fresh watercress, finely
  chopped
whole wheat/white bread
radish slices, garnish

Whip butter until fluffy. Add juice and then gently fold in water-cress. Chill several hours to allow flavors to blend. Cut rounds from bread and spread generously with watercress mixture. Top with a slice of fresh radish or leaf of watercress.

Preparation: 20 min.   Easy   Yield: 1 doz. sandwiches
                  Must do ahead

Penny Lawrence

BROCCOLI REUBEN SANDWICH

1 large bunch broccoli, cut into
  flowerets
½ tsp. chopped scallion,
  optional
2 cups fresh mushrooms, sliced
butter or margarine, softened
8 slices rye bread (i.e., New
  York deli-style)
4 slices Swiss cheese
1 cup sauerkraut, well-drained
bottled Thousand Island
  dressing

Microwave or steam broccoli until crisp-tender. Meanwhile sauté scallions and mushrooms in but-ter. Drain. Spread butter on one side of each slice of rye bread. Grill 4 slices of rye bread on heated griddle while layering each slice with Swiss cheese, mushrooms, broccoli and sauer-kraut. Spread Thousand Island dressing on unbuttered sides of the 4 remaining slices of bread, butter side up. Flip sandwich and cover to grill and melt cheese.

Preparation: 15-20 min.   Easy   Serves: 4
Cooking: 10-15 min.   Serve immediately

Vince Abromitis

TUNA OR CHICKEN CRESCENT ROLL-UPS

½ onion, chopped
2 Tbsp. margarine
1 8-oz. can water chestnuts,
  diced
½ cup sour cream
¼ cup bread crumbs
1 egg, beaten
½ cup Swiss cheese (or
  Mozzarella), grated
¼ tsp. black pepper
2 cups diced chicken or tuna
2 pkgs. crescent rolls

Sauté onion and margarine; add diced water chestnuts. Remove from heat and add sour cream, bread crumbs, beaten egg, cheese, pepper and tuna or chicken. Roll up in crescent rolls. Bake at 350° for 15 minutes.

Preparation: 15 min.   Easy   Yield: 16
Cooking: 15 min.   Serve immediately

Sylvia Bowen

CHICKEN & SWISS EXTRAORDINAIRE

"Have your knife and fork ready"

3 whole chicken breasts,
  skinned and boned
1 tsp. Accent seasoning
½ cup flour
¼ cup vegetable oil
6 thick slices French bread
6 slices Swiss cheese
1 Tbsp. butter or margarine
½ lb. mushrooms, sliced
1 tsp. salt
⅔ cup white wine
¼ tsp. pepper

Cut chicken breasts in half. Sprinkle chicken with Accent. Roll in flour. Brown chicken in vegetable oil over medium-high heat in large skillet. Cover and cook for 25-30 minutes over medium heat. Place bread slices, topped with one slice of Swiss cheese each, on baking sheet. Heat in oven at 275° until cheese is melted. Meanwhile, remove cooked chicken and keep warm. To juices in skillet, add butter or margarine, mushrooms, and salt. Cook 3 minutes until mushrooms are tender. Pushing mushrooms aside, add wine and pepper. Return chicken to pan. Simmer until sauce is slightly thickened. Place chicken on bread and cheese slices. Spoon mushrooms and sauce over chicken.

| Preparation: 15 min. | Easy | Serves: 6 |
| Cooking: 40 min. | Can do ahead | Can freeze |

Deborah Elstner-Benz

FABULOUS CHICKEN SANDWICH

"No mayonnaise means low-calorie"

2 whole cooked chicken breasts,
  skinned and boned
2 Tbsp. white wine
1 Tbsp. red pepper, chopped
  and roasted (pimientos can
  be used)
1 Tbsp. oil
2 tsp. parsley, minced
1 tsp. wine vinegar
½ tsp. fresh dill
½ tsp. capers
salt and pepper, to taste
4 split French bread baguettes,
  6-8" long each
lettuce and tomato slices,
  optional

Shred chicken breasts and place in a large bowl. In food processor, blend all other ingredients, except baguettes. Pour over chicken and stir to combine. Best if chicken marinates at least 1 hour. Spoon onto split bread. Serve with lettuce and tomato slices if desired.

| Preparation: 20-30 min. | Easy | Serves: 4 |
| | Can do ahead | |

Lynn Popovich

PEPPERONI LOAF

"Freshly grated imported Romano is best"

1 loaf frozen bread dough
6 oz. Mozzarella cheese, sliced
6 oz. imported Provolone cheese, sliced
8 oz. pepperoni, sliced
1 egg, beaten with fork
Romano or Parmesan cheese, grated

Thaw bread dough and let rise in large, oiled bowl or pan, covered, until at least double in size (4-5 hours or overnight). Roll into a rectangle ⅛" thick on a floured board. Place Mozzarella, Provolone, and pepperoni on rectangle. Sprinkle with ½ of the beaten egg. Sprinkle generously with the grated Romano. Roll like a jellyroll, pinch seam closed, and place seam down on an oiled jellyroll pan. (Roll may be placed straight, in a circle, or in a horseshoe shape.) Pinch ends closed. Brush half of beaten egg on sides and top. Place oiled waxed paper and towel on loaf and let rise for 30-40 minutes. Bake at 400° for 20 minutes, then at 350° for 10 minutes, until golden brown. Cool 5 minutes and slice.

Preparation: 30 min.   Moderately difficult   Serves: 6-8
Cooking: 30-40 min.   Must do ahead   Can freeze

Rose C. Witteman

OPEN FRENCH ROLL SANDWICH

"Count on more than one per person"

1 14-oz. pkg. French rolls (12 per pkg.)
2 eggs, beaten
⅔ cup water
½ cup parsley
¼ cup Dijon mustard
½ tsp. oregano
½ tsp. ground pepper
1 lb. lean ground beef
1 lb. ground sausage
1 med. onion, chopped
1 stick butter
1 garlic clove, minced

Preheat oven to 400°. Cut rolls in half lengthwise, remove and save centers. Should have shells about ¼" thick. Mix next 6 ingredients in bowl with the breadcrumbs from center of rolls. Brown and drain beef, sausage and onion and combine with bread mixture. Fill hollowed-out rolls with this mixture and put onto ungreased baking pan. Melt butter and add garlic. Brush or drizzle over filling and edges of bread. Bake 10-15 minutes until browned.

Preparation: 30 min.   Easy   Serves: 12
Cooking: 10-15 min.   Can do ahead   Can freeze

Anne F. Dithrich

LO-CHOLESTEROL MEXICAN PIZZA

½ cup + 1 Tbsp. cornmeal
1½ cups all-purpose flour
1 Tbsp. baking powder
½ tsp. salt
¾ cup skimmed milk
¼ cup light olive oil
1 12-oz. jar taco sauce
1 15½-oz. can Mexican chili
  beans, undrained
1 pepper, cut into thin rings
1 cup shredded imitation cheese
  or Monterey Jack

Heat oven to 450°. Spray a 14" round pizza pan with PAM. Sprinkle 1 Tbsp. cornmeal evenly onto prepared pan. Mix ½ cup cornmeal, flour, baking powder and salt. Combine milk and oil. Add this to flour mixture, stir with fork until mixture forms a ball. Press dough into prepared pan, shaping edge to form rim. Bake for 15 minutes. Spread taco sauce evenly over partially baked crust. Top with beans, pepper rings and cheese. Continue baking for 10 minutes until cheese melts.

NOTE: Dough will be sticky and you may want to flour your hands.

Preparation: 20 min.   Easy   Serves: 4
Cooking: 25 min.   Can do ahead   Can freeze

Shirley B. Connolly

MORNING PIZZA

"A very hearty pizza"

1 lb. bulk pork sausage
1 8-oz. pkg. refrigerator crescent
  rolls
1 cup loose-pack frozen hash
  browns, thawed
1 cup shredded sharp Cheddar
  cheese
5 eggs, beaten
¼ cup milk
½ tsp. salt
⅛ tsp. pepper
¼ tsp. oregano
2 Tbsp. freshly grated Parmesan

Cook sausage and drain. Separate rolls and form a "shell" in a lightly greased pizza pan. Form sides and seal perforations. Spoon crumbled sausage over dough. Sprinkle potatoes over sausage. Sprinkle half of the Cheddar cheese over potatoes. Combine the eggs, milk, salt, pepper, and oregano and pour over all. Sprinkle rest of Cheddar cheese on top. Bake at 375° for 25 minutes. Sprinkle Parmesan cheese on top and bake until done (about 5-10 minutes).

Preparation: 15-20 min.   Easy   Serves: 6-8
Cooking: 30-40 min.   Can do ahead   Can freeze

Clee McBee

SPOONBURGERS

"Terrific for tailgate parties or picnics"

2 lbs. extra-lean ground beef
1 large onion, chopped
1 cup thinly sliced celery
1 1-lb. can stewed tomatoes
1 1-lb. can whole kernel corn
1 4½-oz. can chopped ripe
  olives
1 bottle chili sauce
2 tsp. salt, or to taste
2 tsp. garlic salt, or to taste
¼ tsp. pepper
1 bay leaf
16 split hamburger buns,
  buttered

Brown beef in a large pot. Add onion and celery and cook 5-10 minutes longer. Stir in tomatoes, corn (with liquid), olives, chili sauce, and spices. Simmer for 20 minutes to blend flavors. Spoon onto buns.

| Preparation: 30 min. | Easy | Serves: 8-16 |
| Cooking: 40 min. | Can do ahead | Can freeze |

Clee McBee

HOT TURKEY SURPRISE

2 cups chopped turkey
1 apple, unpeeled and chopped
1 small onion, finely chopped
6 oz. Swiss cheese, grated
½ cup chopped walnuts
mayonnaise
salt and pepper, to taste
delicatessen rolls or French
  bread, buttered

Blend first 5 ingredients with mayonnaise. Season to taste. Spread on rolls. Wrap tightly in foil. Bake at 350° for 20 minutes.

| Preparation: 15 min. | Easy | Serves: 4-6 |
| Cooking: 20 min. | Serve immediately | |

Gretchen S. Hansen

AUTHENTIC PORK BARBECUE

1 pork loin roast (4-5 lbs.)
1 medium onion, chopped
1 cup cider vinegar
¾ cup ketchup
½ cup Worcestershire sauce
1 Tbsp. dry mustard
¼ cup honey (preferred) OR
  brown sugar
1 tsp. salt
1 tsp. Tabasco sauce

Place the pork loin, fat side up, in a roasting pan - no rack. In a medium bowl, combine remaining ingredients and pour over roast. Cover and marinate 3 hours minimum or overnight in refrigerator. Preheat oven to 325°. Place roast in oven, uncovered, and cook for 2½ hours or until meat thermometer registers 170°. Remove from oven and let stand

20 minutes or longer. Chop meat coarsely and mix with remaining sauce from pan. Serve on soft rolls.

| Preparation: 30 min. | Easy | Serves: 8-10 |
| Cooking: 3½ hrs. | Must do ahead | |

Susan T. Henry

BEEF BARBECUE SANDWICHES

"Great for a crowd"

6 lbs. beef chuck roast
1 stick celery, chopped
3 large onions, chopped
1 14-oz. bottle ketchup
3 Tbsp. barbecue sauce
1½ cups water
3 Tbsp. vinegar
2 Tbsp. chili powder
2 Tbsp. salt, or to taste
1 tsp. Tabasco sauce
1 tsp. pepper

Cut beef in 5-6 chunks and place in a roaster or Dutch oven just big enough for size of meat. Combine the remaining ingredients and pour over meat. Heat to boiling on top of range. Cover and bake in 300° oven for 6 hours or until meat is tender enough to shred with a fork. Remove fat and pull meat into shreds. Makes great sandwiches or topping for noodles.

| Preparation: 15 min. | Easy | Serves: 50 |
| Cooking: 6 hrs. | Can do ahead | Can freeze |

Linda M. Prepelka

STROMBOLI

"A great alternative to pizza"

1 loaf frozen bread dough
1 cup sliced mushrooms
½ cup diced onion
½ cup diced green pepper
1 Tbsp. butter
¼ lb. sliced ham
¼ lb. sliced Genoa salami
¼ lb. Provolone cheese, grated
1½ oz. sliced pepperoni

Thaw dough. Sauté mushrooms, onions, and green pepper in butter. When dough is thawed, pat to form a 14" rectangle. Cover center third of rectangle with ham, salami, cheese and pepperoni. Sprinkle with mushrooms, onions and green pepper mixture. Cut each side into 8 equal strips, just to the edge of filling.

Fold strips to center, alternating sides. Overlap ends of strips just enough to pinch together. Let rise in warm place until double in size. Bake at 350° for 45 minutes.

| Preparation: 1 hr. | Moderately difficult | Serves: 6-8 |
| Cooking: 45 min. | Must do ahead | |

Dorothy Truckey

OPEN-FACE HOT TUNA ROLLS

½ lb. aged Cheddar cheese, cubed
2 7-oz. cans tuna, rinsed and drained
6 hard-boiled eggs, chopped
4 Tbsp. chopped green pepper
2 Tbsp. chopped green olives
2 Tbsp. chopped onion
1 cup mayonnaise
12 buns, split

Combine ingredients. Spread on split buns and broil until slightly brown and bubbly.

| Preparation: 10 min. | Easy | Serves: 12-15 |
| Cooking: 5 min. | Can do ahead | |

Holly Worth

SAUCES & ACCOMPANIMENTS

WALNUT ZUCCHINI PESTO SAUCE

2 medium zucchini, trimmed
  and diced
1 small onion, peeled and
  diced
2 cloves garlic
½ cup parsley, stems removed
½ cup fresh basil, stems
  removed
2 cups walnut pieces
½ cup freshly grated Romano
  cheese
1 cup virgin olive oil
¼ tsp. salt and pepper
cooked pasta of your choice

Combine zucchini, onion, garlic, parsley, basil and walnuts in food processor. Process to a coarse texture. Add Romano cheese and process while drizzling in oil. Season with salt and pepper. To serve: warm slightly and toss with your favorite pasta.

Preparation: 20 min.　　Easy　　　　　　Serves: 6
　　　　　　　　　　　　Can do ahead

Martin Thomas
Season's Cafe

SCALLOPED PINEAPPLE

1 2-lb. can crushed pineapple
⅓ can of water
2 eggs, beaten
3 Tbsp. cornstarch
⅓ cup sugar
butter
cinnamon

Combine all ingredients in saucepan. Cook on top of stove until thick. Pour into buttered casserole, dot with butter and sprinkle with cinnamon. Bake ½ hour at 350°.

Preparation: 15 min.　　Easy　　　　　　Serves: 6-8
Cooking:　　 30 min.　　Can do ahead

Mary Culbertson-Stark

APPLE-ONION DRESSING

"Great as stuffing for pork, veal, duck or goose"

4-6 Tbsp. butter, bacon fat, or
   fat rendered from uncooked
   holiday goose
1 cup onions, coarsely
   chopped
½ cup celery slivers
¼ cup water
4 cups soft bread crumbs,
   made from raisin bread*
2 cups apples, peeled and cubed
1 tsp. salt
1 tsp. poultry seasoning
black pepper

*May use plain bread for the
   crumbs and add ¼ cup raisins

Heat fat in heavy skillet or pan. Sauté onions and celery slivers for 3-4 minutes. Remove from heat and add water. In large mixing bowl, mix the bread crumbs and apple cubes. Add the contents of the skillet and seasonings and toss all together lightly.

NOTE: Good as stuffing for pork, veal, duck or 10-lb goose.

| Preparation: 20 min. | Easy | Yield: 6 cups |
| | Can do ahead | |

Diane D. Abell

AUNT RUTH'S CRANBERRY RELISH

"Very festive in color and taste"

2 cups sugar
1½ cups water
1-2 sticks cinnamon
1 navel orange, cut in
   bite-sized chunks
   with skins on
1 lemon, cut in bite-sized
   chunks with skins on
1 apple, cored and cut in bite-
   sized chunks with skins on
1 lb. whole cranberries
1 box dried mixed fruit, cut up
1 handful raisins
1 handful nuts
3-4 Tbsp. Brandy, Cognac or
   orange liqueur (optional)

Place sugar and water in large saucepan over medium heat and stir until sugar is completely dissolved. Add cinnamon, orange, lemon and apple. Boil 2-3 minutes. Add all cranberries. Boil until cranberries begin to pop. Take off stove and add remaining ingredients. Let stand until it begins to cool. Serve either refrigerated or at room temperature.

| Preparation: 15 min. | Easy | Serves: 10-12 |
| Cooking: 10-15 min. | Can do ahead | Can freeze |

Judy B. Scioscia

24 HOUR PICKLES

"More than just pickles"

1 cup water
1 cup cider or rice wine vinegar
1 cup sugar
2 Tbsp. dry Sherry
1 tsp. salt
3 Tbsp. ginger, freshly peeled and minced
1 medium Granny Smith apple or Asian pear, peeled, cored and cut into ¼" wedges
2 medium celery stalks, cut diagonally in ¼" slices
2 zucchini, unpeeled and cut in ¼" rounds
1 carrot, peeled and cut in ¼" rounds
½ red bell pepper, seeded and cut in ¼" strips
½ cucumber, peeled, seeded and cut into ½x2" sticks
12 small cauliflower flowerets
3 large mushrooms, cut in ¼" slices

Stir first five ingredients together in large bowl, or 2 quart jar, until salt and sugar dissolve. Mix the remainder of the ingredients with the sauce. Cover and refrigerate overnight.

NOTE: Can be prepared up to 6 days ahead. Keep refrigerated.

Preparation: 30 min.   Easy   Serves: 12-14
                          Must do ahead

Clee McBee

MIRIAM'S CREOLE SAUCE

"Great served with omelets or scrambled eggs"

2 Tbsp. butter
1 Tbsp. oil
2 medium onions, chopped
2 medium green peppers, chopped
2 cloves garlic, minced
½ tsp. salt
1 cup sliced mushrooms
2 8-oz. cans tomato sauce
1 large bay leaf
¼ tsp. ground thyme
Tabasco sauce, to taste
1 Tbsp. basil
1 Tbsp. sugar

Heat butter and oil in skillet. Add the onions, peppers, garlic, and salt; simmer until onion is tender. Add remaining ingredients and simmer, covered, for 20 minutes. Serve hot.

Preparation: 20 min.   Easy   Yield: 3½ cups
Cooking: 25 min.   Can do ahead   Can freeze

Paula A. Doebler

135

POTATO STUFFING

"Enough stuffing for a 15 lb. turkey"

½ cup butter or margarine
1 cup onion, finely chopped
2 cups celery, finely chopped
¾ cup parsley, finely chopped
1 Tbsp. poultry seasoning
½ tsp. paprika
½ tsp. ground sage
½ tsp. pepper
2 eggs, lightly beaten
12 cups bread cubes OR
   packaged stuffing croutons
3 cups mashed potatoes

Melt butter and sauté onions and celery for 5 minutes. Toss with remaining ingredients, except potatoes, until blended together. Add potatoes and toss lightly with fork until evenly distributed.

NOTE: Potatoes do not need butter or seasoning, just milk to moisten and make smooth mashed potatoes.

Preparation: 25 min.   Easy   Yield: 15 cups
Cooking: 20 min.   Can do ahead

Carolyn S. Hammer

CRANBERRY-APPLE CASSEROLE

"Great hot, warm or cold"

3 cups apples, peeled and
   chopped
2 cups fresh cranberries
1 cup sugar
1½ cups quick oats
½ cup brown sugar
⅓ cup flour
⅓ cup chopped pecans
½ cup melted butter
½ tsp. cinnamon

In a 2-quart casserole, combine first 3 ingredients. Mix together the remaining ingredients and spread over apple mixture. Bake at 325° for 1 hour or until light brown and bubbly.

Preparation: 15 min.   Easy   Serves: 6-8
Cooking: 45-60 min.   Can do ahead

Sally Spencer Nimick

SCALLOPED APPLES

"Can be a side dish or a dessert"

6 cups apples, peeled and
   sliced
1 Tbsp. flour
¾ cup sugar
½ tsp. cinnamon
¼ tsp. nutmeg

Grease a serving dish large enough to hold apples. Put apples in dish. Mix remaining ingredients. Sprinkle on top of apples. Bake at 350° for 30-45 minutes or until apples are soft.

Preparation: 15 min.   Easy   Serves: 4-5
Cooking: 30-45 min.   Can do ahead

Catherine Clarke Johnson

LYNN'S PICKLES

"A snap to prepare with processor"

7 cups cucumbers, sliced
1 cup green pepper
1 medium onion
2 Tbsp. salt
1 Tbsp. celery seed
2 cups sugar
1 cup vinegar

Slice and chop fine in food processor, cucumbers, green pepper, and onion. Mix all ingredients together; stir well. Marinate in refrigerator overnight.

NOTE: Will keep in refrigerator for 1 month or more.

Preparation: 20 min.

Easy
Must do ahead

Yield: 2½ cups

Maureen T. Senetra

GERMAN CUCUMBERS

"Get out your sharpest knife"

10 cucumbers
¼ cup salt
1 onion, chopped
3 Tbsp. sugar
⅔ cup cider vinegar
⅓ cup salad oil
ground pepper, to taste
chives, to taste

Remove cucumber skins and slice very thin. Put in covered dish. Add salt and mix. Refrigerate for at least 2 hours. In a covered jar, put onion, sugar, vinegar, oil, pepper and chives. Shake. Place cucumbers in colander, run cold water over them for 1 minute. Press out excess water. Put in serving dish; add dressing.

Preparation: 30 min.

Easy
Must do ahead

Serves: 8

Sandi Hennig

COOKED CRANBERRY RELISH

"Keeps indefinitely in refrigerator"

1 lb. fresh cranberries
2½ cups sugar
juice of 1 large lemon
1 cup orange marmalade
1 cup chopped nuts
  (walnuts are best)

Wash and pick over the cranberries. Place in 9x13" baking dish or pan. Stir in all of the sugar and the lemon juice. Cover pan tightly with foil. Bake at 350° for 1 hour. Remove from oven and, while hot, stir the orange marmalade in thoroughly and add chopped nuts. Chill.

Preparation: 15 min.
Cooking: 1 hr.

Easy
Can do ahead

Serves: 8

Anne S. Minster

CHICKEN MARINADE

¼ cup cooking oil
½ cup dry white wine
1 clove garlic, minced
1 medium onion, finely
  chopped
½ tsp. celery salt
½ tsp. coarse ground pepper
¼ tsp. dried thyme
¼ tsp. dried tarragon
¼ tsp. dried rosemary

Blend all ingredients in food processor or shake vigorously in covered jar. Pour over chicken pieces. Chill at least 3 hours, turning at least once. Grill or broil chicken, basting with remaining marinade.

Preparation: 10 min.   Easy   Yield: ¾ cup
                           Must do ahead

Catherine Clarke Johnson

MRS. T's BARBECUE SAUCE

"Excellent flavor enhancer for grilled meats"

1 cup ketchup
2 tsp. salt
½ tsp. Tabasco sauce
¼ tsp. chili powder
1 tsp. dry mustard
2 Tbsp. brown sugar
1 cup water
4 tsp. Worcestershire sauce
1 small onion, chopped
2 tsp. lemon

Heat all ingredients until the onion is soft. Use on chicken, ribs or any meats you barbecue.

Preparation: 10 min.   Easy   Yield: 2½ cups
Cooking: 10 min.   Can do ahead

Elaine Perry

CUCUMBER DILL SAUCE

"Delicious with salmon or on a baked potato"

1 gourmet cucumber,
  long English-LaReine
salt, to taste
1 bunch green onions
1 pint sour cream
1 small whiskey glass of sugar
1 small whiskey glass of white
  vinegar
dill weed, fresh if possible,
  to taste
black pepper, to taste

Finely chop cucumber; salt moderately and put in a sieve for "water" to drip away. Finely chop green onions. Squeeze as much water out of the cucumbers as possible. Put in a bowl. Add onions. Add sour cream, sugar, vinegar and dill weed. Mix well. Sprinkle lightly with black pepper.

Preparation: 20 min.   Easy   Serves: 8
                           Can do ahead

Virginia Carney

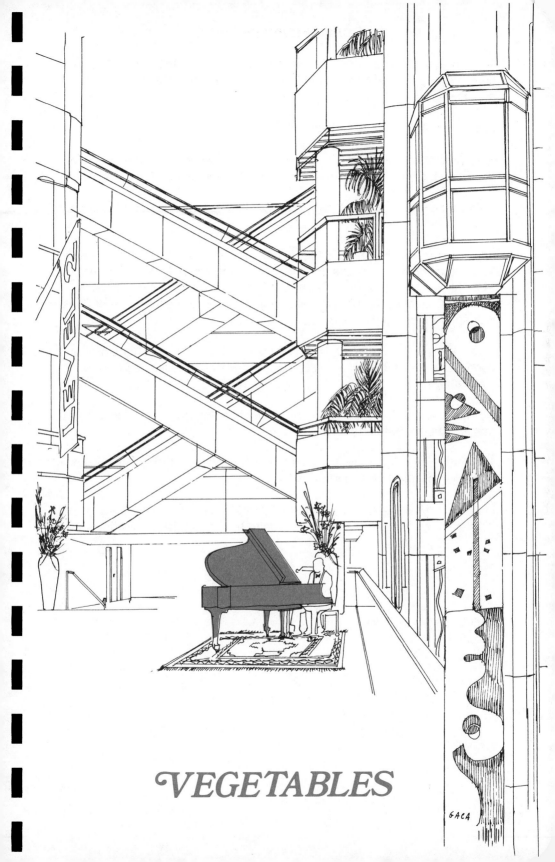

VEGETABLES

GACA

ONE OXFORD CENTRE

A prestigious 46-story office tower with an atrium of high fashion stores contains elegant restaurants and the Rivers Club, an exclusive dining and athletic facility.

Additional illustrations in this section:

This three story clock and a sunlit atrium greet visitors to the Galleria in Mt. Lebanon. It contains premier shopping, dining and entertainment facilities.

A flower shop on Carson Street in the South Side has retained its fine Victorian design.

This rose granite obelisk stands tall in the half-acre open plaza of PPG Place. The entire complex was designed by Philip Johnson and John Burgee, for PPG Industries' world headquarters. In the background is the CNG Tower, home of Consolidated Natural Gas. Its graceful design mirrors the bridges that span Pittsburgh's rivers.

Motor Square Garden is a beautiful Beaux Arts building designed by Peabody & Stearns of Boston. In 1988, it was renovated to house numerous specialty shops.

Designs from the Armenian national classroom at the University of Pittsburgh that was dedicated in 1988.

The Cathedral of Learning is home to the University of Pittsburgh's Transplant Center, the largest in the world.

Grant Street renovation is an important part of Renaissance II. Spring tulips flourish in the median planter with granite trim along the brick boulevard.

VEGETABLES

MUSHROOM PIE

"Serve this instead of potatoes or rice"

2 lbs. mushrooms
6 Tbsp. butter
salt and pepper
juice from ½ lemon
6 Tbsp. flour
1 cup chicken stock or bouillon
½ cup Madeira or Sherry wine
½ cup heavy cream
1 pie crust (mix may be used)
1 egg

Wash and dry mushrooms. In large skillet, heat 4 Tbsp. butter. Add whole mushrooms and sprinkle with salt, pepper and lemon juice. Cover skillet and cook 10 minutes, shaking pan often. Arrange mushrooms in a buttered baking dish (Use a 9" quiche dish). Use slotted spoon to remove mushrooms. To juices remaining in skillet, add 2 Tbsp. butter and the flour. Slowly stir in the chicken stock and cook, stirring constantly, until thick and smooth. Stir in Madeira or Sherry wine and the cream and season with salt and ground pepper. Pour sauce over mushrooms and cover with pie dough. Brush dough with beaten egg. Make several slits in top. (Can be refrigerated at this point, but cover with plastic wrap.) When ready to bake, remove plastic wrap and bake at 450° for 15 minutes. Reduce heat to 350° and bake 10-15 minutes longer. Serve hot.

Preparation: 30-45 min.   Easy   Serves: 6-8
Cooking: 25-30 min.   Can do ahead

Lois Anne Huston

KRAUT WITH APPLES

"Be sure to use very tart apples"

1 small head red cabbage
2 tart apples
2 Tbsp. butter
1 medium onion, sliced
2 tsp. chicken soup base
  (powder)
1 quart water
½ cup red wine vinegar
½ tsp. salt
½ cup sugar
¼ tsp. pepper
2 cloves
1 bay leaf
1 Tbsp. lemon juice
1 Tbsp. orange juice
2 Tbsp. flour

Wash and drain cabbage. Slice cabbage as for coleslaw. Wash and core apples. Peel and cut into bite-sized pieces. Heat butter. Sauté onions and apples for 4 minutes; then add soup base. Mix. Add water, vinegar, salt, sugar, pepper, cloves, bay leaf and juices. Stir. Bring to a boil. Add cabbage. Cover and simmer for 45 minutes. Just before serving, use a sifter to sprinkle flour into liquid; stir slightly to prevent lumping.

Preparation:	25 min.	Easy	Serves: 6
Cooking:	45 min.	Serve immediately	

Susan Craig

CARROT CASSEROLE

"Sweet tasty surprise"

¾ cup sugar
¼ lb. butter
3 Tbsp. flour
3 eggs
2 cups mashed cooked carrots

Mix all ingredients together and bake at 350° for 35 minutes.

Preparation:	30 min.	Easy	Serves: 4-6
Cooking:	35 min.	Can do ahead	

Laurie M. Lijoi

BELGIAN CARROTS

"Especially for garlic lovers"

2 cloves garlic
1 oz. butter
1 lb. carrots
1 tsp. (heaping) sugar
3 Tbsp. water
1 tsp. (heaping) cornstarch
1 Tbsp. water

Crush garlic and add to melted butter in large saucepan. Dice carrots and add to butter and garlic. Place sugar in center of pan, then add 3 Tbsp. water. Cook for about 1 hour on very slow burner (taking care that the water does not evaporate completely - add more if necessary). Just before serving, add cornstarch mixed to a liquid consistency with 1 Tbsp. water. This will thicken juices and serve as a sauce.

Preparation:	10 min.	Easy	Serves: 4
Cooking:	1 hr.	Can do ahead	Can freeze

Rosemary A. Beynon

ELEGANT CARROTS
"Very attractive"

1 10-oz. pkg. frozen whole
    baby carrots
¼ cup butter
¼ cup orange-flavored liqueur
    OR orange juice
2 cups seedless green grapes,
    halved lengthwise
1 Tbsp. lemon juice

Cook carrots according to package directions; drain well. Melt butter in medium-sized saucepan over medium heat. Stir in liqueur, carrots and grapes. Bring just to a boil, then reduce heat and simmer until carrots and grapes are well coated and heated through (about 10 minutes). Stir in lemon juice.

NOTE: Can partially cook ahead of time. Cook carrots, prepare grapes and be set up with butter in saucepan.

Preparation: 15 min.   Easy   Serves: 6
Cooking: 10 min.

Grace Clarke Benjamin

HONEY CARROTS
"Easy colorful side dish"

3 green onions (just white part),
    chopped
½ stick butter
1 lb. carrots, peeled and
    shredded in processor
    or grater
3 Tbsp. honey
½ tsp. thyme
¼ tsp. salt
dash pepper

Sauté onions in butter over low heat until soft. Add remaining ingredients and stir. Cover and cook over medium heat for about 5 minutes.

Preparation: 15 min.   Easy   Serves: 4
Cooking: 5 min.   Can do ahead

Anne F. Dithrich

TOMATO PIE
"A truly different way to serve tomatoes"

1 9″ deep-dish pie crust
3 large ripe tomatoes, thickly
    sliced
6 scallions, chopped
basil, salt, pepper, to taste
1 cup mayonnaise
1 cup grated sharp cheese

Bake pie crust for about 10 minutes at 350° or until brown. Layer tomatoes into pie crust. Sprinkle with scallions, basil, salt and pepper. Layer again and again until crust is full. Mix together mayonnaise and cheese and spread over top. Bake at 350° for 30 minutes or until brown and bubbly.

Preparation: 30 min.   Easy   Serves: 5
Cooking: 40 min.   Serve immediately

Kathryn R. Williamson

MUSHROOM CAKES
"Great side dish or appetizer"

1 pint fresh mushrooms,
  chopped
¼ cup whole onions, finely diced
¼ cup celery, finely diced
¼ cup carrots, finely diced
¼ cup green pepper, finely diced
1 Tbsp. + 1½ tsp. margarine
1 cup + 1 Tbsp. bread crumbs
2 oz. Provolone cheese,
  shredded
½ cup sour cream
1 egg, beaten
¼ cup Parmesan cheese
oil

Sauté vegetables in margarine until tender. Drain off excess liquid and chill. Blend the next 5 ingredients into the chilled vegetables. Portion mixture with a ¾ cup measurer and shape into patties. Coat with bread crumbs. Heat a small amount of oil in a skillet and brown mushroom cakes well on each side (approximately 3-4 minutes on each side). Serve with desired sauce and garnish.

NOTE: Suggested sauces — Dijon Cream or Cheese Sauce

| Preparation: | 30-45 min. | Easy | Serves: 4 |
| Cooking: | 10 min. | Can do ahead | *Michael Babines, C.E.C.* |

The Medical Center, Beaver

MARINATED MUSHROOMS
"Great hot or cold"

2 lbs. fresh mushrooms
½ cup lemon juice
1 cup salad oil
3 medium onions, thinly sliced
3 tsp. salt
¼ tsp. pepper
2 tsp. sugar
1 tsp. dry mustard
1 tsp. thyme
½ tsp. oregano
1 tsp. basil

Combine all ingredients and cook for 5-10 minutes over medium heat. Cool. Cover and refrigerate overnight.

| Preparation: | 10 min. | Easy | Serves: 8-10 |
| Cooking: | 5-10 min. | Must do ahead | *Laurie M. Lijoi* |

MUSHROOM FLORENTINE
"Great for a holiday buffet"

1 lb. mushrooms
¼ cup butter, melted
2 10-oz. pkgs. frozen spinach,
  cooked and well-drained
3 tsp. butter, melted
1 cup shredded Cheddar
  cheese
garlic salt, to taste

Sauté mushrooms in ¼ cup butter. In a 10" casserole, place spinach on bottom; dribble 3 tsp. of melted butter on spinach. Sprinkle one half of cheese on spinach; then place mushrooms on top and sprinkle rest of cheese on mushrooms. Sprinkle with garlic salt. Bake at 350° for 25 minutes.

| Preparation: | 20 min. | Easy | Serves: 6 |
| Cooking: | 25 min. | Can do ahead | *Judy M. Bowman* |

ASPARAGUS VINAIGRETTE

"An all occasion side dish"

1 cup salad or olive oil
⅓ cup red wine vinegar
1½ Tbsp. sugar (or to taste)
few drops garlic juice or salt
1½ tsp. pepper
¼ cup chopped onion
3 Tbsp. minced parsley
3-4 cans asparagus (green
   or white)

Combine all ingredients, except asparagus, in a blender. Marinate drained asparagus in this mixture overnight. Drain before serving.

Preparation: 15 min.	Easy	Serves: 8-10
	Must do ahead	*Joe Anne Rossin*

ASPARAGUS FORESTER

1½ lbs. fresh asparagus
2 Tbsp. butter or margarine
2 Tbsp. shallots, finely
   chopped
2 cups mushrooms, sliced
½ cup sour cream
2 tsp. prepared brown mustard
⅛ tsp. salt
⅛ tsp. pepper

Steam asparagus until crisp-tender. In medium skillet, melt butter over medium-high heat. Add shallots. Cook until soft (3-5 minutes). Add mushrooms and cook, stirring often, until soft. Stir in sour cream, brown mustard, salt and pepper. Cook until just heated through - DO NOT BOIL. Serve sauce over the asparagus.

Preparation:	20 min.	Easy	Serves: 6
Cooking:	20 min.	Can do ahead	*Christina R. Bradley*

ASPARAGUS ROLL UPS

"Elegant presentation"

2 large bunches fresh asparagus
   (or frozen, thawed)
2 Tbsp. brown sugar
12 slices bacon

Sauce:
2 tsp. butter
2 cups grated Cheddar cheese
1 egg yolk, large
¼ cup white wine
1 tsp. Dijon mustard
2 tsp. Worcestershire sauce
¼ tsp. salt
2-3 drops Tabasco sauce

Preheat oven to 425°. Cook fresh asparagus until tender, yet a little crisp; drain. Divide cooked asparagus into 6 servings (4-5 stalks each). Sprinkle each serving with brown sugar. Beginning at tips, wrap bacon around each bunch, overlapping, using 2 pieces of bacon per serving. Place each bunch on greased cookie sheet. Bake for 10-12 minutes until bacon looks done — slightly crisp. Top with cheese sauce and serve.

Sauce: Melt butter and cheese in a double boiler until creamy. Stir egg into wine and mix well. Add this to cheese mixture slowly. Whisk until blended well. Add mustard, Worcestershire, salt and Tabasco sauce. Cook until thick.

Preparation:	20 min.	Easy	Serves: 6
Cooking:	20 min.	Can do ahead	*The Cookbook Committee*

145

CAULIFLOWER-ZUCCHINI PARMESANO

"Garlic adds zip"

1 head cauliflower, separated
  into flowerets
3 medium zucchini, sliced
  ½" thick
1 cup water
1½ tsp. salt
¼ tsp. pepper
1 stick butter
1 tsp. lemon juice
1 rounded tsp. basil
1 rounded tsp. oregano
2 cloves garlic, pressed
¾ cup Parmesan cheese

In skillet, poach cauliflower in water with ½ tsp. salt for about 5 minutes. Remove flowerets, pour out water. Melt butter in skillet, then add all other ingredients except cheese (do not forget the other 1 tsp. salt). Mix well over low heat. Add zucchini first, then cauliflower. Cover. Cook on low heat for 20 minutes, stirring occasionally. Toss with Parmesan cheese before serving.

Preparation: 20 min.   Easy   Serves: 10-12
Cooking: 30 min.   Can do ahead

The Cookbook Committee

ZUCCHINI CASSEROLE

7-8 medium zucchini, cut into
  ¼" slices
1 cup water
8 slices bacon, diced
1 large onion, chopped (1 cup)
1 large clove garlic, minced
4 slices white bread, diced
2 cups shredded Cheddar
  cheese
1 tsp. salt
1 tsp. Italian seasoning
dash pepper
1 15-oz. can tomato sauce
¼ cup grated Parmesan cheese

In a large saucepan, cook zucchini in 1 cup water. Bring to a boil, cook 5 minutes and drain. In medium skillet, cook bacon until crisp. Remove from pan. Add onion and garlic to skillet and sauté until tender; drain. Preheat oven to 350°. Stir onion, garlic and bacon into drained zucchini. Add remaining ingredients except Parmesan cheese and toss until well coated. Spoon into a 9x13" pan. Sprinkle with Parmesan cheese. Bake for 20 minutes.

Preparation: 40 min.   Easy   Serves: 6-8
Cooking: 20 min.   Can do ahead

Christine M. Paavola

SUSAN REIN'S TOMATO AND ARTICHOKE CASSEROLE

"For artichoke lovers"

½ stick butter
½ cup chopped onions
2 Tbsp. chives
1 1-lb. can tomatoes, drained
1 14-oz. can artichoke hearts,
  drained and quartered
1 tsp. basil
2 Tbsp. sugar

Sauté onions and chives in butter. Add all the other ingredients and place in casserole. Bake at 325° for 10-15 minutes.

NOTE: Casserole can be made ahead and then baked before serving.

Preparation: 15 min.   Easy   Serves: 4-6
Cooking: 10-15 min. Can do ahead

Caroline M. Roberts

146

BRUSSELS SPROUTS DELUXE

1½ lbs. brussels sprouts,
 trimmed and rinsed
¼ cup butter, unsalted
1 tsp. coarse grained mustard
salt and freshly ground pepper,
 to taste
2 Tbsp. hazelnuts, toasted and
 coarsely chopped

Sprinkle cleaned sprouts lightly with water, cover with plastic wrap and microwave for 4 minutes on High (or cook in rapidly boiling water for 7-8 minutes); drain. Melt butter in a large skillet. Stir in mustard, salt and pepper. Do not have heat too high as it will splatter. Add sprouts and heat through. Mix in nuts and serve.

Preparation: 10 min.   Easy   Serves: 6
Cooking: 10 min.   Serve immediately

Clee McBee

EASY ESCALLOPED EGGPLANT

1 large (or 2 small) eggplants
1 cup cheese and garlic croutons (Pepperidge Farm)
1 cup grated sharp Cheddar
 cheese, divided in half
½ cup milk
1 Tbsp. flour
½ tsp. salt
½ tsp. pepper
½ tsp. dried basil
1 Tbsp. butter

Peel eggplant and cut into ¼" cubes. Cook in boiling salted water until tender and drain. Mix eggplant, croutons and ½ cup of cheese. Put in a lightly buttered casserole dish. Combine milk, flour and seasonings and pour over eggplant mixture. Top with remaining cheese and dot with butter. Cover and bake at 350° for 20 minutes. Remove cover and continue baking for an additional 10 minutes.

Preparation: 20 min.   Easy   Serves: 4
Cooking: 30 min.   Can do ahead

Mary Anne Riley

FRENCH BEANS — FRENCH STYLE
"Good, fast, simple"

1 lb. fresh or frozen French cut
  green beans
½ cup chopped scallions
1½ Tbsp. olive oil
freshly ground black pepper,
  to taste

Boil the beans in slightly salted water until not quite soft and are slightly crisp. Drain. In a saucepan, sauté the beans with the scallions. Stir occasionally for the next minute until beans are coated and some have begun to "catch". Serve at once with pepper.

NOTE: Can also be served cold.

Preparation:	10 min.	Easy	Serves: 6
Cooking:	15 min.	Can do ahead	Can freeze

Vivian P.T. Brown

BAKED LIMA BEANS
"Alternative to regular baked beans"

1½ cups dried lima beans
¼ lb. bacon, cut into 1" pieces
2 medium onions, sliced
salt and pepper, to taste
1 cup milk

In a pot, soak the beans in water overnight. The next day, boil beans until soft; drain. Fry bacon until cooked, but not crisp. Remove onto paper towels. Over low heat, sauté onions in bacon drippings until soft. Grease a 1½-quart casserole dish. Preheat oven to 350°. Layer beans, then onions, bacon and seasonings. Repeat until all ingredients are used. Pour milk over top and bake, uncovered, for 30 minutes or until golden on top.

Preparation:	20 min.	Easy	Serves: 4
Cooking:	50 min.	Can do ahead	

Reba Page

SERBIAN STYLE GREEN BEANS
"A very spicy green bean dish"

1 large onion, chopped
3 cloves garlic, chopped
2 medium hot banana peppers,
  diced and seeds removed
¼ cup oil
1 15-oz. can whole tomatoes
2 8-oz. cans tomato sauce
1 lb. fresh green beans OR
  1 12-16-oz. pkg. frozen
¼ tsp. paprika
salt, to taste

Sauté onions, garlic and pepper in oil until tender. Add tomatoes and sauce. Cook for 15-20 minutes. Add beans, paprika and salt. Cook until tender.

Preparation:	20 min.	Easy	Serves: 6-8
Cooking:	40 min.	Can do ahead	

Lynn Popovich

VEGETABLE/CHEESE BAKE

2 Tbsp. margarine
6 Idaho potatoes, peeled and
   diced
1½ cups zucchini squash,
   sliced thin
⅔ cup green peppers, sliced
   medium
⅔ cup whole onions, quartered
¾ cup fresh mushrooms, sliced
   thick
½ tsp. minced garlic in oil
1 cup mild barbecue sauce
⅓ cup Burgundy wine
⅓ cup water
1 bay leaf
⅜ tsp. leaf thyme
⅛ tsp. crushed peppercorns
2 cups shredded Mozzarella
   cheese

Heat margarine in heavy skillet and sauté vegetables and garlic for 3-5 minutes. Reserve. In separate saucepan, combine next 6 ingredients and simmer 10 minutes. Add sautéed vegetables and simmer an additional 10 minutes. Place ¾ cup of vegetables/sauce mixture into individual casserole dishes and sprinkle with cheese. Bake at 350° for 15 minutes, or until cheese is bubbly.

Preparation:	15 min.	Easy	Serves: 4
Cooking:	40 min.	Can do ahead	

Michael Babines, C.E.C.
The Medical Center, Beaver

BEAN SUPREME
"Unique combination of veggies"

2 10-oz. pkgs. frozen fork lima
   beans
2 10-oz. pkgs. frozen chopped
   broccoli
1 pkg. Lipton dry onion soup
   mix
1 8-oz. pkg. sour cream
1 10¾-oz. can mushroom soup
1 8-oz. can sliced water
   chestnuts

Cook vegetables together according to package directions; drain. Add other ingredients, except topping. Place in a 9x13″ pan. Sauté Rice Krispies in butter and put on top of vegetables. Bake for 30 minutes at 350°, or until heated through.

Topping:
1 Tbsp. butter or margarine
½ cup Rice Krispies*

*Chopped walnuts can be used
  instead of Rice Krispies.

Preparation:	30 min.	Easy	Serves: 12
Cooking:	30 min.	Can do ahead	

Carolyn Reed Webb

SWEET AND SOUR BAKED BEANS

"Nice bean selection"

3 large onions, cut in rings
1 cup brown sugar
1 tsp. dry mustard
1 tsp. salt
½ cup cider vinegar
2 15-oz. cans dried lima beans, drained
1 15-oz. can green lima beans
1 1 lb.15-oz. can New England style baked beans
1 15-oz. can kidney beans
8 slices bacon, fried and crumbled

Place onion rings, brown sugar, mustard, salt and vinegar in skillet. Cook for 20 minutes, covered. Add to beans. Add bacon. Pour into a 3-quart casserole. Bake for 1 hour at 350°.

Preparation: 15 min.   Easy   Serves: 12-15
Cooking: 1 hr. 20 min.   Can do ahead

Jackie Hamilton

CREAMED CORN CASSEROLE

"Children will love it"

1 15½-oz. can cream style corn
milk
1 egg
½ stick butter
1-1½ cups Ritz crackers crumbs

Place corn in casserole dish. In bottom of empty corn can, add the egg and enough milk to just cover the bottom of can. Mix well, then add to corn in casserole dish. Add ½ cup of cracker crumbs and stir. In saucepan, melt butter and the 1 cup of cracker crumbs. Stir. Sprinkle crumbs over corn and bake at 350° for 30 minutes.

Preparation: 10 min.   Easy   Serves: 4
Cooking: 30 min.   Can do ahead

Dorothy Truckey

BAKED CORN ON THE COB

"So simple — so good"

6 ears fresh corn
1 4-oz. pkg. whipped cream cheese with chives
4 Tbsp. butter, softened
¼ tsp. salt
dash pepper

Remove husks and silk from ears. Stir cream cheese into butter, add salt and pepper and blend. Place ears of corn on individual large squares of foil. Spread each ear with mixture. Fold up foil and seal. Bake in a 350°-400° oven for 30-45 minutes until corn is tender. Carefully open each ear and spoon hot chive butter over ears to serve.

NOTE: May be done on an outdoor grill. Cooking time is approximately the same.

Preparation: 5 min.   Easy   Serves: 6
Cooking: 30-45 min.   Can do ahead

Michael Orsini

POTATOES

MAURICE'S SOUTHERN SWEET POTATOES

"Sports a topping of brown sugar and nuts"

3 cups canned sweet potatoes
2 eggs, beaten
½ stick margarine, melted
1 tsp. vanilla
1 cup sugar
½ tsp. salt
½ cup milk

Preheat oven to 350°. Mix all ingredients and pour into 1½-quart casserole. Mix topping and pour evenly over potato mixture. Bake for 35 minutes at 350°.

Topping:
⅓ cup margarine, melted
1 cup brown sugar
⅓ cup self-rising flour
1 cup chopped pecans

Preparation: 15 min.	Easy	Serves: 6-8
Cooking: 35 min.	Can do ahead	

Genny Mozolak

SWEET POTATO SURPRISE

"Surprise everyone with apricots"

1 1 lb. 1-oz. can whole sweet
  potatoes, halved lengthwise
¾ cup brown sugar
1½ Tbsp. cornstarch
¼ tsp. salt
⅛ tsp. cinnamon
1 tsp. shredded orange peel
1 1-lb. can (2 cups) apricot
  halves
2 Tbsp. butter or margarine
½ cup pecan halves

Place sweet potatoes in greased 10 x 6" baking dish. In saucepan, combine brown sugar, cornstarch, salt, cinnamon, and orange peel. Drain apricots, reserving syrup. Stir 1 cup of apricot syrup into cornstarch mixture. Cook and stir over medium heat until boiling; boil 2 minutes. Add apricots, butter, and pecan halves. Pour over sweet potatoes. Bake, uncovered, at 375° for 25 minutes.

Preparation: 15 min.	Easy	Serves: 6
Cooking: 25 min.	Can do ahead	

Jebby Potter

SWEET POTATO CHIPS

"Something both colorful and different"

¼ cup margarine
½ tsp. salt
¼ tsp. pepper
¼ tsp. paprika
1 lb. (about 4) sweet potatoes
4 Tbsp. grated Parmesan cheese

Heat oven to 425°. Lightly butter a 15 x 10" cookie sheet. In small pan, melt margarine. Stir in salt, pepper, and paprika. Peel sweet potatoes and slice into thin slices. Arrange potatoes on cookie sheet evenly. Brush margarine mixture over potatoes. Bake at 425° for 25-30 minutes or until crisp and golden (turn twice so slices brown evenly). Sprinkle with cheese. Serve immediately.

Preparation: 20 min.	Easy	Serves: 4-6
Cooking: 25-35 min.	Serve immediately	

Lynn Popovich

POTATO SOUFFLÉ

"Mashed potatoes' elegant cousin"

2 lbs. potatoes
2 Tbsp. flour
2 eggs, beaten
1 clove garlic, crushed
2 Tbsp. chopped parsley
4 Tbsp. butter or margarine
nutmeg, salt, and pepper, to
  taste

Peel and boil potatoes in salted water. When very soft, drain and mash. Blend in flour, eggs, garlic, parsley and butter. Season. Put in buttered baking dish at 325° for about 30 minutes or until very hot.

Preparation: 15 min.	Easy	Serves: 4-6
Cooking: 1 hr.	Can do ahead	

Hannah Wedeen

CONFETTI MASHED POTATOES

"Put some excitement in your mashed potatoes"

7 medium potatoes
½ cup milk
¼ stick butter, room
  temperature
1 8-oz. pkg. cream cheese, at
  room temperature and cut
  into 1" cubes
½ cup chopped green onions
1 2-oz. jar chopped pimientos,
  well-drained
1 egg, well-beaten
salt and pepper, to taste

Preheat oven to 350°. Cook potatoes, then mash with milk and butter. Mix in cream cheese, onion and pimientos. Stir in egg. Salt and pepper to taste. Place in an ungreased 9 x 13" glass baking dish. (Can be done at this point up to one day ahead). Bake for approximately 25 minutes until puffed and light brown.

Preparation:	45 min.	Easy	Serves: 6-8
Cooking:	25 min.	Can do ahead	

Paula R. Hamilton

PEROGY CASSEROLE

"Great for leftover mashed potatoes"

1 12-oz. pkg. wide egg noodles
1 large yellow onion, chopped
1¼ cups melted butter
6 cups mashed potatoes
1 cup shredded cheese,
  American or Cheddar
paprika, salt, and pepper, to
  taste

Prepare noodles according to package directions. Set aside. Sauté chopped onion in butter. Combine mashed potatoes with cheese. In a 9 x 13" glass pan, spread a portion of the butter/onion mixture over the bottom. Spread 3 cups of the potatoes over the butter. Spread half of the noodles on top of potatoes. Pour ½ cup of butter/onion mixture over the noodles. Layer remaining potato mixture, then noodles, then remaining butter mixture. Sprinkle top with paprika, salt and pepper. Bake at 400° for 45 minutes.

Preparation:	20 min.	Easy	Serves: 6
Cooking:	45 min.	Serve immediately	

Chris Sunderman

AUNT HETTY'S POTATOES

"This is a sure-fire people pleaser"

4-6 baking potatoes
1 stick butter or margarine
1 pkg. dried onion soup

Slice unpeeled potatoes in ¼" slices. Spread out evenly in a 10 x 13" pan. Melt butter in saucepan and mix in onion soup. Pour over potatoes. Cover with foil. Bake at 350° for 1 hour and 15 minutes.

Preparation:	10 min.	Easy	Serves: 6-8
Cooking:	1 hr. 15 min.	Can do ahead	

Sandy L. Seymour

HASH BROWN CASSEROLE
"One of the best"

1 24-oz. box Ore-Ida frozen
  hash brown patties
½ stick butter, melted
2 cups shredded Cheddar
  cheese
1 10¾-oz. can cream of
  chicken soup
⅓ cup chopped onion
1 pint sour cream
salt and pepper, to taste

Thaw hash browns. Mix all ingredients and put into a 9 x 13" pan. Bake for 45 minutes at 350°.

Preparation: 15 min.   Easy   Serves: 10-12
Cooking: 45 min.   Can do ahead

Karen Rossin

OVEN FRIES
"Easy to decrease or increase"

vegetable cooking spray
6 Tbsp. butter
4 large Idaho potatoes
1 medium onion, minced
1 tsp. seasoned pepper
salt, to taste

Preheat oven to 425°. Spray a large open roasting pan with vegetable cooking spray; add butter. Place pan in the oven to melt the butter. Remove pan from oven. Cut unpeeled potatoes lengthwise into eight wedges. Add potatoes to melted butter in roasting pan; sprinkle with minced onion, pepper, and salt; toss gently to coat. Bake 30-40 minutes or until potatoes are tender and evenly browned, turning occasionally. Add salt to taste.

Preparation: 10 min.   Easy   Serves: 4-6
Cooking: 30-40 min.   Serve immediately

Missy Zimmerman

TWICE-BAKED POTATOES
"Good with or without the Cheddar"

3 baking potatoes, baked
½ cup sour cream
⅓ cup milk
1 Tbsp. onion, grated
1 tsp. salt
½ cup Cheddar cheese, grated

Cut potatoes in half and scoop out pulp while still hot. Add all ingredients to the scooped-out pulp, except cheese, and whip until fluffy. Fold in cheese. Stuff mixture into potato shells and bake at 350° for 30 minutes.

Preparation: 1 hr.   Easy   Serves: 6
Cooking: 30 min.   Can do ahead   Can freeze

Mary Jo Hottenstein

RICE

KOREAN MUSHROOM RICE
"Ah, so delicious"

1 cup sliced onions
3 Tbsp. oil
1 cup sliced mushrooms
2 Tbsp. soy sauce
ground pepper
2 Tbsp. sesame seeds
3 cups beef bouillon (3 cubes
   plus 3 cups water)
1½ cups long-grained rice

Sauté the onions in oil until soft. Add the mushrooms, soy sauce, pepper and sesame seeds. Cook 2-3 minutes on medium heat. Add the bouillon and mix. Bring to a boil. Stir in the rice and lower heat. Cook slowly, tightly covered, until the grains are tender and the liquid is absorbed (about 30 minutes). DO NOT STIR WHILE COOKING!

Preparation: 15 min.   Easy   Serves: 4-6
Cooking: 30 min.   Serve immediately

Christine M. Paavola

RICE CASSEROLE
"A super-easy good side dish"

1¼ cups white rice, uncooked
¼ lb. butter or margarine,
   melted
1 10-oz. can onion soup,
   undiluted
1 10-oz. can beef consommé,
   undiluted
1 cup grated Cheddar cheese

Rinse rice. Place in 2-quart casserole. Add melted butter. Add the two cans of soup and stir. Bake at 350° for 1 hour, uncovered. Sprinkle with grated Cheddar cheese. Bake until cheese melts (about 5 minutes).

Preparation: 5 min.   Easy   Serves: 6-8
Cooking: 1 hr.   Serve immediately

Anne I. Morton

JANET'S PILAF

1 cup uncooked Arborio (short
   grain rice)
2¼ cup water
¼ tsp. saffron threads
½ stick (4 Tbsp.) butter
½ tsp. salt or to taste
2 cloves garlic, minced
2 stalks celery, sliced thin
½ cup chopped onion
¼ cup shelled pumpkin seeds
   or pepitas or pignolias

Bring water to a boil. Add rice, saffron threads and salt. Cook 15 minutes until water is absorbed. Meanwhile, melt butter in pan and sauté onion, minced garlic and celery until transparent, about 6-7 minutes. Add pumpkin seeds or pepitas and stir for about a minute. Add to cooked rice and fluff with a fork.

	Easy	Serves: 6
Cooking: 15 min.	Can Do Ahead	

Janet M. Daugherty

HAM FRIED RICE
"A great and easy way to use leftovers"

2-3 Tbsp. butter
1-2 cups ham, cut in chunks
chopped green onion, to taste
parsley, to taste
1 cup raw rice
2¼ cups water
1 Tbsp. soy sauce

Melt butter in frying pan. Add ham, onion, parsley, rice and water. Bring to a boil, then reduce heat and simmer for 20 minutes until water is absorbed. Add soy sauce, stir and serve.

NOTE: You can use any leftover meat, or even shrimp, and leftover vegetables could make it more interesting.

Preparation: 15 min.	Easy	Serves: 4
Cooking: 20 min.	Serve immediately	

Missy Zimmerman

GREEN CHILI RICE CASSEROLE
"Two cheeses add flavor"

1 cup uncooked instant rice
2 cups sour cream
½ lb. Monterey Jack cheese,
   grated
1 4-oz. can diced green chilies
¾ lb. sharp Cheddar cheese,
   grated

Cook rice according to package directions. Using a 9 x 13" baking dish, layer ingredients as follows: 1st layer - rice, 2nd layer - 1 cup sour cream mixed with Monterey Jack cheese and chilies, 3rd layer - 1 cup sour cream, 4th layer - sharp Cheddar cheese. Bake at 350° for 30 minutes.

Preparation: 10 min.	Easy	Serves: 8
Cooking: 30 min.	Serve immediately	

Cynthia J. Russell

SPINACH RICE

"A great way to get your kids to eat spinach"

1 Tbsp. unsalted butter
1 small green pepper, finely chopped
1 small onion, finely chopped
2 eggs, beaten
2 cups milk
3 cups cooked rice
2 cups fresh spinach, washed and roughly chopped (about 1 lb.)
1 tsp. salt
½ tsp. freshly ground pepper

Preheat oven to 350°. In a small skillet, melt the butter, add the green pepper and onion and sauté until softened, but not brown. In a bowl, whisk the eggs and milk together until blended. Combine the rice with all ingredients. Stir gently to mix. Turn into a lightly buttered casserole. Bake for 45 minutes, until lightly brown and the custard is set.

Preparation: 25 min.   Easy   Serves: 4
Cooking: 45 min.   Can do ahead

Missy Zimmerman

ROSE'S WILD RICE

"Exotic with wild rice and pine nuts"

1 6-oz. box Uncle Ben's Long Grain and Wild Rice, Original Recipe
2 Tbsp. butter
½ cup scallions
½ cup raisins
½ cup (2½ oz.) pignoli nuts

Prepare rice with seasoning packet, according to package directions. Set aside. Melt butter in skillet. Add, and quickly sauté, the last 3 ingredients. Add rice. Toss and serve.

Preparation: 5 min.   Easy   Serves: 6
Cooking: 1 hr.   Serve immediately

Mary Lee Parrington

PASTA

LASAGNE - SOUTHWESTERN STYLE

"A whiz in your food processor"

12 oz. Monterey Jack cheese, chilled
4 oz. Mozzarella cheese, chilled
3 cups cooked chicken
2 4-oz. cans green chiles
1 med. yellow onion
8 sprigs cilantro or parsley
3 tomatoes, cored and chopped
1 Tbsp. butter
2 Tbsp. oil
½ tsp. salt
1 cup sour cream
½ cup Ricotta cheese
10 corn tortillas

In a food processor, using the shredding disc, process cheeses together. Remove. Then, using the slicing disc, coarsely chop chicken. Remove. Drain chiles. Then, using the metal blade, coarsely chop together, chiles, onion, and half of the cilantro or parsley sprigs. Remove. Do not wash work bowl. Chop tomatoes. In skillet, sauté chile mixture in butter and oil until onion is translucent. Stir in tomatoes. Add salt to taste. Set aside. Combine sour cream and Ricotta cheese.

Heat tortillas in microwave (15 seconds each) or in hot oil on stove. Using a 10″ pie plate or round quiche pan with solid bottom, make 6 layers—tortilla, sour cream mixture, chicken, chile mixture, shredded cheese, and extra chile mixture on top, topped with remaining cheeses. Bake in 350° oven for 20 minutes. Let cool for 5 minutes, then cut into pie wedges and serve.

Preparation: 30 min.   **Moderately difficult**   Serves: 4-6
Cooking: 20 min.   **Can do ahead**

Mary Jo Hottenstein

LINGUINE WITH SHRIMP SAUCE

"Absolutely delicious"

1½ lbs. medium shrimp,
  uncooked
2 16-oz. cans peeled tomatoes
⅓ cup chopped yellow onion
1 cup olive oil
2 Tbsp. minced garlic
⅛ tsp. chopped dried hot red
  pepper
1 Tbsp. dried parsley
1½ tsp. salt
1 lb. linguine (or fettucine)

Shell and devein shrimp. Rinse and drain. Drain tomatoes, reserving juice. Chop tomatoes. Sauté onion in olive oil in large pan until transparent. Add garlic and hot pepper and cook just until garlic starts to turn golden. Add parsley, tomatoes and salt. Stir. Simmer for 20 minutes, stirring occasionally, and adding some of the reserved tomato juice if it gets too thick. Boil pasta according to package directions. When pasta is almost done, turn up the heat and add the shrimp. Cover and cook for 2-3 minutes. Drain the pasta. Pour onto serving platter. Pour shrimp sauce over pasta. Serve.

Preparation: 30-35 min.   Easy   Serves: 4-6
Cooking: 25 min.   Can do ahead

Kathy Russ

SEAFOOD LASAGNE

"A special company meal"

12 lasagne noodles
2 Tbsp. butter
1 cup chopped onion
2 8-oz. pkgs. cream cheese
2 cups cottage cheese
2 eggs, beaten
2-3 tsp. dried basil
½ tsp. salt and pepper
2 10-oz. cans Campbell's cream
  of mushroom soup
⅓ cup milk
⅓ cup dry wine
1-2 lbs. shrimp, cooked, peeled
  and halved
1 lb. scallops, cooked
1 lb. fresh crabmeat, rinsed
  and picked
½ cup grated Parmesan cheese
½ cup grated Provolone cheese

Preheat oven to 350°. Grease a 9x13" casserole dish. Cook noodles according to package directions. Drain. Cover bottom of prepared casserole dish with 4 noodles. Cook onion in butter until tender, not brown. Blend in cream cheese. Stir in cottage cheese, eggs, basil, salt and pepper. Mix completely. Spread one third of this mixture over noodles in casserole dish. Combine soup, milk and wine. Fold in the seafood. Spread one third of this over cheese mixture and noodles in casserole dish. Repeat layers. Sprinkle top with the Parmesan and Provolone cheeses. Bake, uncovered, at 350° for 45-60 minutes. Let stand 15 minutes before serving.

Preparation: 1 hr.   Moderately difficult   Serves: 8
Cooking: 45-60 min.   Can do ahead   Can freeze

Jane VanKirk

159

NOODLE KUGEL

"Includes apricot, nectar and preserves"

10 oz. medium noodles
¾ stick butter
½ cup sugar
4 oz. cream cheese, room
  temperature
3 eggs
1 cup Half & Half
1 cup apricot nectar
1 cup apricot preserves

Topping:
2 cups crushed cornflake
  crumbs
¼ cup sugar
¾ cup melted butter
1 tsp. cinnamon

Cook noodles al dente in salted water. Toss noodles in butter until well coated. Cream sugar and cream cheese until smooth. Add eggs, one at a time, to the cheese mixture, mixing well after each addition. Alternately add Half & Half and apricot nectar to the mixture. Pour over buttered noodles and coat completely. Pour into greased 9x13" baking dish. Spread apricot preserves over noodles. Combine topping ingredients. Sprinkle over preserves. Bake at 350° for 1 hour.

Preparation: 20 min.　　Easy　　　　　　Serves: 12
Cooking:　　1 hr.　　　　Can do ahead　　Can freeze

Esther Neft

MICROWAVE LASAGNE

"You don't cook the lasagne noodles before"

¾ - 1 lb. ground beef
onion and garlic, to taste
1 30 oz. large jar Ragu regular
  style sauce
1 lb. Ricotta cheese
2 eggs
½ tsp. basil
¼ tsp. oregano
¼ cup Parmesan cheese
lasagne noodles
½ cup red wine
8 oz. Mozzarella cheese,
  shredded

Cook ground beef, onion and garlic in microwave on Medium-high (1 lb. - 7 ½ minutes), or brown on stove. Drain. Mix Ragu sauce with ground beef. Add a little water to jar, shake and add to Ragu sauce. Mix next 5 ingredients together. Using uncooked lasagne noodles, begin layering ingredients in a 9x13" pan. Begin with Ragu sauce mixture, noodles, cheese filling, etc. Continue to layer, ending with sauce. Sprinkle with wine. Microwave for 20 minutes on High. Sprinkle Mozzarella cheese on top. Cover with plastic wrap. Let stand for 20 minutes.

Preparation: 20 min.　　Easy　　　　　Serves: 8-10
Cooking:　　20 min.　　　　　　　　　　Can freeze

Gae C. Bradley

PASTA NOSTRA

"Delicious dinner in a dish"

3 cups medium shell pasta
2 Tbsp. olive oil
1 lb. ground chuck
2 cloves garlic, minced
1 16-oz. bottle spaghetti sauce
1 cup Ricotta cheese
½ cup sour cream
8 oz. cream cheese with chives
½ cup scallions, minced
½ green pepper, chopped
2 Tbsp. melted butter

Cook shells until al dente. Sauté meat and garlic in olive oil. Add spaghetti sauce. Combine Ricotta cheese, sour cream, cream cheese, scallions and green pepper. In a three quart casserole dish, spread half of pasta then cover with cheese mixture. Top with remaining pasta and pour on melted butter. Then cover with meat-tomato sauce. Cook for 30 minutes in a preheated 350° oven.

Preparation: 45 min.   Easy   Serves: 6
Cooking: 30 min.   Can do ahead

Marjorie B. Mann

SPAGHETTI WITH HOT SAUSAGE

"Do ahead and join the group"

2 lbs. hot sausage links
2 lbs. ground chuck
1 large onion, chopped
3 cloves garlic, crushed
  and minced
½ lb. mushrooms, sliced
  (optional)
1 pint tomato sauce,
  preferably homemade
1 12-oz. can tomato paste
6 oz. red wine
6 oz. water
1 tsp. sugar
1 28-oz. can plum tomatoes
  and liquid
4 bay leaves, crumbled
1 Tbsp. dried basil, crumbled
1 Tbsp. marjoram leaves,
  crumbled
2 tsp. oregano leaves,
  crumbled
1 tsp. thyme leaves, crumbled
2 tsp. parsley leaves, crumbled
¼ tsp. red pepper and cayenne
heavy dash paprika
freshly ground pepper, to taste
Parmesan cheese, grated
2-3 lbs. linguine, cooked
  according to pkg. directions

Cook sausage links in microwave oven or medium-hot oven until nearly cooked through. While sausage cooks, brown ground chuck in large skillet or Dutch oven. Drain off most of the fat and set aside. Sauté onions, garlic, and mushrooms in remaining fat. Add tomato sauce, paste, wine, water, sugar and tomatoes to pan and return ground meat to pan. Stir to mix well. Slice sausage links into bite-sized pieces and add to meat mixture. Cook, covered, over low heat for 45 minutes, stirring occasionally and breaking tomatoes into small pieces. Add crumbled herbs, peppers and paprika and cook for 15 minutes longer. Taste and adjust seasonings. Serve over pasta with grated Parmesan cheese.

Preparation: 30 min.   Easy   Serves: 12 +
Cooking: 1 hr. 15 min. Can do ahead   Can freeze

Carolyn S. Hammer

161

ONE-STEP VEGETARIAN LASAGNE

"A three cheese dish"

28-30 oz. jar spaghetti sauce
16 oz. cottage cheese
8 oz. plain yogurt
1 egg
½ lb. lasagne noodles, uncooked
12 oz. Mozzarella cheese
½ cup Parmesan cheese
¾ cup water

Spread 1 cup sauce in a 9x13" pan. Mix together the cottage cheese, yogurt and egg. Layer in pan as follows (using about one third of each): noodles, cottage cheese mixture, Mozzarella cheese, sauce, and Parmesan cheese. Repeat twice. Pour ¾ cup water around edges. Cover tightly with foil. Bake at 350° for 1 hour. Remove foil and continue baking for 15 minutes longer. Let stand for 20 minutes before serving.

Preparation: 30 min.   Easy   Serves: 10
Cooking: 15 min.   Can do ahead   Can freeze

Miriam R. Tuttle

DOUBLE CHEESE GOURMET CASSEROLE

"Use up your leftover ham or turkey"

1 6-oz. pkg. thin spaghetti
¼ cup butter
6 green onions and tops,
   chopped
1 4-oz. can sliced mushrooms
1½ cups diced ham
1 cup cooked, diced chicken
1 can water chestnuts
½ tsp. salt
⅛ tsp. pepper
½ tsp. celery salt
1 cup sour cream
1 cup cottage cheese
1 cup shredded Cheddar cheese

Cook spaghetti according to package directions. Melt butter in pan. Add onion and tops. Sauté. Add mushrooms. Stir in ham, chicken or turkey, water chestnuts, and seasonings. Combine sour cream, cottage cheese and Cheddar cheese with spaghetti. Add sautéed mixture and toss lightly. Bake 30 minutes at 325°. More Cheddar cheese may be added on top or crushed cereal flakes can be used.

Preparation: 20-25 min.   Easy   Serves: 6-8
Cooking: 30 min.   Can do ahead

Karen Rossin

MARTINI LINGUINE

"A meal in itself"

½ lb. butter
½ tsp. red pepper flakes
¾ cup Vodka
1 cup tomato purée
1 cup heavy whipping cream
grated Parmesan cheese, to
   thicken
3 lbs. fresh linguine, cooked

Melt butter in skillet. Add red pepper flakes and vodka. Simmer 2 minutes. Add purée and cream. Simmer for 5 minutes. Add grated Parmesan cheese to thicken sauce. Add cooked noodles to sauce and toss to coat. Each serving may be garnished with 2 olives on toothpick.

Preparation: 15 min.   Easy   Serves: 6-8
                          Serve immediately

Mario's Southside Saloon

PASTA WITH PESTO SAUCE

"It's so easy to grow your own basil"

3 packed cups fresh basil
  leaves
2 large cloves garlic
½ cup walnuts
¾ cup fresh parsley
1 cup Parmesan cheese
½ cup olive oil
¼ cup melted butter
salt, to taste
1 lb. pasta, cooked
Parmesan cheese for topping

Combine all ingredients, except pasta, in a food processor or blender. Arrange ingredients in order given to make blending easy. Work all ingredients into a smooth paste. A few tablespoons of water can be added to get a smooth consistency. Toss with hot, drained pasta. Sprinkle with Parmesan cheese.

Preparation: 10-15 min. Easy Serves: 4
Cooking: 12 min. Can do ahead Can freeze

Francine A. DeFazio

SPINACH-CHICKEN FILLING FOR PASTA

"You will need a sauce for this"

2 eggs, beaten
1 cup minced cooked chicken
1 cup chopped cooked spinach,
  drained
½ cup fresh bread crumbs
¼ cup heavy cream
⅓ cup grated Parmesan cheese
2 tsp. finely chopped parsley
1 clove garlic, finely chopped
½ tsp. nutmeg
salt and pepper, to taste

Combine ingredients and mix well. Use as a filling for ravioli, cannelloni, lasagne, shells or crepes. (Good topped with tomato sauce spiced with bay leaves and basil to taste.)

Preparation: 20 min. Easy Yield: 12 lg. shells
  Can do ahead Can freeze

Catherine Clarke Johnson

CREAMY FETTUCINE WITH SALMON

"Very rich and elegant"

8 oz. fettucine noodles
6 Tbsp. butter
½ lb. sliced fresh mushrooms
2 Tbsp. minced onion
2 Tbsp. flour
2 cups milk
2 Tbsp. cooking or dry Sherry
½ tsp. salt
¼ tsp. pepper
7¾ oz. can salmon, drained
  and separated into chunks

Prepare noodles as label directs; drain and keep warm. Melt butter in saucepan, add mushrooms and onion. Cook until tender; do not brown. Stir in flour until blended; cook 1 minute. Gradually stir in milk, Sherry, salt and pepper. Cook until thick and smooth, stirring constantly. Gently stir in salmon. Arrange noodles on a serving platter; top with salmon mixture.

Preparation: 25 min. Easy Serves: 4
Cooking: 15 min. Serve immediately Can freeze

Linda D. Orsini

FETTUCINE

"Different with anchovies and spinach"

3 lbs. fettucine
¼ cup butter, melted
2 beaten eggs
pepper, to taste
½ cup olive oil
3 cloves garlic, minced
2 10-oz. pkgs. frozen chopped
  spinach, thawed
1 cup chicken broth
8 anchovies, mashed
1 Tbsp. dried basil or 2-3 Tbsp.
  fresh
½ cup chopped parsley
1 cup grated Parmesan cheese
  (or Pecorino)
1½ cups Ricotta cheese
salt, to taste
fresh pepper, to taste

Cook pasta; drain and toss with melted butter, eggs, and pepper. Heat half of oil; add garlic and cook briefly. Add spinach and half of broth. Cook, stirring, for 5 minutes. Combine anchovies, basil, parsley, Parmesan cheese, Ricotta cheese and remaining oil and broth. Beat until smooth. Fold into spinach and heat. Season with salt and pepper. Pour over noodles onto a deep platter or bowl.

Preparation: 25-30 min.   Easy   Serves: 12
                             Can do ahead

Bonnie Casper

BROCCOLI AND SHRIMP FETTUCINE

4 Tbsp. extra virgin olive oil
1 cup mushrooms, fresh and
  sliced
1½ cups medium shrimp,
  peeled and deveined
1 cup broccoli flowerets,
  blanched and drained
1½ pints cream
4 egg yolks
3 cups imported Parmesan
  cheese, grated
½ cup butter
1¾ lbs. fettucine, cooked al
  dente and drained
4 tsp. parsley, finely minced

In large pan, sauté mushrooms, shrimp and broccoli in olive oil until shrimp are fully cooked. Beat egg yolks with cream until blended. Add cream mixture and butter to pan with shrimp. Stir constantly until smooth, gradually adding the cheese. Do not boil. Cook noodles al dente, drain and add to sauce. Toss well. Serve immediately garnished with parsley.

Preparation: 20 min.   Moderately difficult   Serves: 4
Cooking: 5 min.   Serve immediately

Glenn Ashton Taylor

SALADS

FREDERICK SAUER HOUSES

This house, one of the many structures designed by Frederick Sauer in the Pittsburgh area, is located on Center Avenue in Aspinwall. This complex of fantasy houses is made of coursed stone and yellow brick with carved eagles, lions and heads of mythical gods. He designed during the twenties and thirties.

Additional illustrations in this section:

Virgil Cantini's Fountain stands behind the East Liberty Presbyterian Church. The church was built in 1931 by the Mellon family.

A Model A Ford pickup truck and a Red Crown gas pump join other vintage autos and automotive memorabilia at the Station Square Transportation Museum.

Two playhouses built in Sewickley Heights in the nineteen thirties. The house (upper left) was designed for Miss Maude Byers-Lyon and the other for the daughters of Mr. and Mrs. John Burgwin.

"Aida" is performed by the Pittsburgh Opera. Tito Capobianco, its director, has tranformed the company into a high-profile organization with a national reputation.

The North Shore Marina occupies a stretch of newly developed shoreline along the Allegheny River.

SALADS

WRIGHT'S RASPBERRY GORGONZOLA SALAD
"This has a distinctive flavor"

Dressing:
1 cup raspberry vinegar
1 tsp. salt
1 Tbsp. poppy seeds
2 tsp. dried peppermint
1 tsp. dry mustard
½ cup honey
1¼ cups olive oil
¾ cup Wesson oil

Salad:
3 cups shredded purple cabbage
8 oz. Domestic Gorgonzola
  cheese
4 heads Bibb lettuce
1 head Escarole
1 sweet red pepper, cut into
  julienne strips
apple slices

Dressing: Combine all ingredients in a jar. Mix well to combine.

Salad: Shred cabbage and marinate in 1 cup of Dressing for 1 hour in refrigerator. Crumble Gorgonzola cheese and reserve. Wash Bibb lettuce and Escarole or other greens. When ready to serve, toss lettuce with enough dressing to coat and arrange on individual plates. Garnish with purple cabbage, red pepper strips, and apple slices. Top with crumbled Gorgonzola cheese.

Preparation: 20-25 min.   Easy   Serves: 8
                             Must do ahead

Jan Davis
Wright's Seafood Inn

PEAR SALAD
"Tart and creamy"

Dressing:
⅓ cup mayonnaise
⅓ cup sour cream
few drops orange or lemon
  extract
1 tsp. sugar (or to taste)
orange or lemon juice
1 Tbsp. raspberry vinegar,
  optional

Salad:
Bibb lettuce leaves
2 Bartlett pears, preferably red
lemon juice
½ cup seedless grapes, halved
½ cup walnut pieces

Make dressing by combining mayonnaise with sour cream. Add extract and sugar. Thin to desired consistency with juice. Add vinegar, if desired. Chill. Place lettuce leaves on individual plates. Slice pears, sprinkle with lemon juice and arrange over lettuce. Distribute grapes and walnuts. Drizzle dressing over salad and serve immediately.

NOTE: Pears can be sliced ahead and kept in chilled lemon water to cover.

Preparation: 20 min.   Easy   Serves: 6

Carolyn S. Hammer

ROCKEFELLER SALAD

Dressing:
¼ small onion, chopped
3 Tbsp. cider vinegar
2 tsp. spicy brown mustard
½ tsp. sugar
½ tsp. salt
¼ tsp. freshly ground pepper
1 cup vegetable oil

Salad:
½ lb. bacon, well cooked and
  crumbled
2 bunches Romaine lettuce,
  washed and torn into bite-
  size pieces
1 7½-oz. can hearts of palm,
  drained and quartered
1 8½-oz. can waterpack
  artichoke hearts, drained and
  quartered
4 oz. Bleu cheese, crumbled

Dressing: Purée the onion and cider vinegar together in blender or food processor. Add mustard, sugar, salt, and pepper and blend. Gradually pour in oil and mix until thick.

Salad: Mix all ingredients in serving bowl and toss with dressing to taste. Serve immediately.

Preparation: 15-20 min.   Easy   Serves: 8
Cooking: 6-7 min./bacon Serve immediately

Clee McBee

BELGIAN ENDIVE SALAD

8 small beets
8-10 heads Belgian endive
2 bunches watercress
½ cup toasted walnut pieces

Dressing:
6 Tbsp. balsamic vinegar
3 Tbsp. wine vinegar
⅔ cup safflower oil
4 Tbsp. walnut oil
6 oz. crumbled Blue cheese,
   divided
¼ tsp. cracked black pepper

Cook the beets, drain and pat dry; then slice. Clean the endive and separate leaves (do not cut until ready to serve). Wash watercress and drain. Chop or break into pieces. Toast the walnut pieces at 300° for 10-15 minutes. Line plates with leaves, cut/slice the center leaves of endive and place in the middle, top with watercress, beets, nuts and cheese. Drizzle 2 Tbsp. of dressing over each plate.

Dressing:
Blend all ingredients together in a jar by shaking well — using only half of the cheese. Use remaining cheese on top of salad or pass, letting each person serve their preferred portion of cheese.

Preparation: 40 min.   **Easy**   **Serves: 8**

Lorraine P. Trice

BROILED LETTUCE SALAD
"Super different main dish salad"

1 head of Iceberg lettuce

Topping:
½ cup tomato sauce
¼ cup vegetable or olive oil
1 Tbsp. red wine vinegar
½ tsp. garlic salt
¼ tsp. basil leaves
¼ tsp. oregano leaves
1 8-oz. can kidney beans,
   drained
3 oz. chopped salami or
   pepperoni
¾ cup shredded Mozzarella
   cheese
⅓ cup grated Parmesan cheese

Wash lettuce and cut 2 thick slices out of center of lettuce head. Place on broiler pan.

Topping: Shake tomato sauce, oil, vinegar, garlic salt, basil and oregano in covered container. Pour over each lettuce slice. Top with beans, meat and cheeses. Broil until cheese melts. Serve immediately.

Preparation: 15 min.   **Easy**   **Serves: 2**
Cooking: 5-10 min.   **Can do ahead**

Karen Z. Petley

APPLE SPINACH SALAD
"Cashews add crunch"

1 bunch Romaine lettuce
1 lb. fresh spinach
½ cup cashew nuts
2 tart Granny Smith apples,
  diced and unskinned
Dressing:
⅓ cup sugar
⅓ cup vinegar
1 tsp. celery salt
1 cup salad oil
1 tsp. salt
1 tsp. garlic salt

Toss together the Romaine lettuce, spinach, cashew nuts and apples. Mix dressing ingredients. Add enough dressing to salad to coat. Serve immediately.

Preparation: 30 min.   Easy   Serves: 6-8
                          Serve immediately   *Mary P. Newton*

TEXAS SALAD
"Olé for Doritos"

1 head lettuce
2-3 tomatoes, cut in wedges
1 lg. onion or green onions,
  chopped
¼ cup chopped green bell
  pepper
2 cups shredded Cheddar
  cheese
1 15-oz. can ranch-style beans
  or pinto beans, drained
1 8-oz. bottle French Catalina
  dressing
½ small bag Doritos

Mix first 6 ingredients and toss with dressing. Crush Doritos, add to salad and toss again.

Preparation: 20 min.   Easy   Serves: 6-8
                          Serve immediately   *Sandy Seymour*

COLD PAELLA SALAD
"No dressing to make"

1 6-oz. box long grain and wild
  rice, cooked
1 10-oz. box frozen peas,
  thawed
2 6-oz. jars marinated artichoke
  hearts, reserve oil
1 lb. cooked shrimp
1 6-oz. can small black olives,
  pitted
cherry tomatoes or tomato
  wedges

Prepare rice according to package directions. Toss all ingredients with the oil from the marinated artichoke jar and serve chilled.

Preparation: 30 min.   Easy   Serves: 4-6
Cooking: 25 min.   Must do ahead   *Peggy Standish*

CITRUS AVOCADO SALAD

4-6 cups assorted salad greens
2 oranges, peeled and sectioned
1 pink grapefruit, peeled,
    sectioned and cut in half
1 avocado, peeled and sliced
    (sprinkled with lemon juice)

Poppy Seed Dressing:

¾ cup sugar
1 tsp. dry mustard
¾ tsp. salt
½ tsp. onion powder
⅓ cup cider vinegar
1 cup vegetable oil
1 Tbsp. poppy seeds

Chill salad greens. Combine with fruit and avocado. Toss gently with enough dressing to coat well.

Poppy Seed Dressing: Blend all ingredients, except poppy seeds, in blender until smooth. Add poppy seeds, cover, and chill.

Preparation: 25 min.   Easy   Serves: 4-6

Lorraine P. Trice

FIRE AND ICE
"No oil in this dressing"

6 med. tomatoes, cut into bite-
    size pieces
1 med. Bermuda onion, sliced
1 med. green pepper, cut in
    strips
1 lg. cucumber, peeled and
    sliced (cut in half, then slice)
¾ cup vinegar
¼ cup water
1 Tbsp. + 2 tsp. sugar
1½ tsp. celery salt
1½ tsp. mustard seeds
½ tsp. red pepper (powder or
    seeded)
½ tsp. garlic salt or powder
⅛ tsp. pepper

Combine vegetables in a large bowl and set aside. Combine remaining ingredients in a small pan. Bring to a boil and let boil for one minute. Place mixture in freezer for about 3 minutes to cool a little. Pour mixture over vegetables. Cover and chill 8 hours. Serve with fresh garlic bread.

Preparation: 20 min.   Easy   Serves: 6
Cooking: 3 min.   Must do ahead

Lisa J. Miscevich

TUNA GREEN PEA SALAD

"A nice variation of tuna salad"

2 10-oz. pkgs. tiny (petite) frozen peas, thawed and drained
1 7-oz. can albacore tuna, drained and flaked
1 cup thinly sliced celery
½ cup thinly sliced green onions (scallions)
½ cup sliced water chestnuts
1 cup dairy sour cream
¼ cup fresh lemon juice
2 Tbsp. mayonnaise
salt and freshly ground pepper, to taste
6-8 lettuce leaves
½ lb. bacon, sliced into ½" pieces, fried crisp and drained
1 cup sliced almonds

Combine peas, tuna, celery, onions, water chestnuts, sour cream, lemon juice, mayonnaise, salt and pepper. Cover and refrigerate several hours before serving. Spoon mixture onto lettuce leaves and top with bacon and nuts. Serve.

Preparation: 20 min.   Easy   Serves: 6-8
                          Must do ahead

Lori O. Haley

PEPPERONI PASTA SALAD

12 oz. macaroni shells, cooked al dente and drained
1 lb. pepperoni, chopped
1 cup chopped ripe olives
1 cup pitted chopped green olives
1 green pepper, chopped
3 celery ribs, chopped
1 small onion, chopped
3 tomatoes, seeded and chopped
1½ cups grated Provolone cheese

Mix pasta, pepperoni, ripe olives, green olives, green pepper, celery, onion and tomatoes. Cover and refrigerate for 24 hours. To serve, mix salad with dressing and cheese.

Dressing: Mix all ingredients. Cover and refrigerate for 48 hours.

Dressing:
¾ cup salad oil
½ cup wine vinegar
1 tsp. salt
1 tsp. pepper
1 tsp. sugar
½ tsp. oregano

Preparation: 45 min.   Easy   Serves: 10
Cooking: 8 min.   Must do ahead

Rose C. Witteman

SEAFOOD SALAD

1 lg. loaf sandwich bread
  sliced*
butter or margarine
1 lg. onion, chopped
4 hard-boiled eggs, chopped
2 cups cooked shrimp**
1 cup cooked crab
1 cup celery, finely chopped
2½ cups Hellmann's
  mayonnaise

*Frozen bread is easier to
butter and cut.
**Shrimp may be cut into small
pieces if too large.

The night before:
Butter each slice of bread evenly
and cut crust from bread; then
cut each slice into small cubes
(about 20 per slice). Add onion
and eggs. Mix in a large bowl.
Cover and refrigerate overnight.

Next morning:
Add shrimp, crab, celery and
mayonnaise; mix well. Cover and
refrigerate several hours before
serving.

Preparation: 1 hr.   Moderately difficult   Serves: 12
                      Must do ahead

Christina Bagwell

KUMQUAT SALAD

"Exotic fruit is fun to use"

1 10-oz. jar preserved kumquats
1 3-oz. pkg. lemon-flavored
  Jello gelatin
1 avocado

Thinly slice kumquats. Be sure
seeds are removed. Prepare
lemon-flavored Jello as directed
on package. Substitute ¼ cup of
the liquid for Jello with ¼ kum-
quat syrup from jar. Peel, slice and dice avocado. Add kumquats and
avocado to Jello. Refrigerate until set (use ring mold). Place on lettuce
leaf. Garnish with parsley.

Preparation: 30 min.   Easy   Serves: 5-6
                        Must do ahead

Mary Louise Johnson

REUBEN SALAD

1 lb. drained sauerkraut
½ lb. corn beef
¼ cup sliced dill pickles
2 med. tomato wedges
¼ lb. shredded Swiss cheese
1 head lettuce
¼-⅓ cup Thousand Island
  dressing

Toss first 5 ingredients and put
in bowl. Top with head lettuce.
Heat Thousand Island dressing.
Pour over salad and toss. Serve
immediately.

Preparation: 15 min.   Easy   Serves: 8-10
                        Serve immediately

Michelle A. Wiseman

173

CHINESE-CHICKEN SALAD

"Crispy noodles make this different"

1 lb. bacon
2-3 whole chicken breasts,
  cooked, skinned and boned
1 lg. head lettuce, shredded
¾ cup chopped green onions
1 3-oz. can chow mein noodles
1 8-oz. can water chestnuts,
  drained and sliced

Oriental Dressing:

2 Tbsp. honey
⅓ cup vegetable oil
⅓ cup soy sauce
2 Tbsp. ketchup
1 tsp. dry mustard

Fry bacon until crisp and crumble; set aside. Cut chicken into small strips. In a large bowl, mix bacon pieces and chicken strips with lettuce, onions, noodles, and water chestnuts. Refrigerate until chilled or for several hours. Toss salad with dressing and serve.

Dressing: Mix all dressing ingredients. Blend well.

Preparation: 1 hr.   Easy   Serves: 8
             Must do ahead

Jane Birnie

CURRIED CHICKEN SALAD WITH HONEY & SOUR CREAM DRESSING

2 whole chicken breasts, cooked
2-3 crisp apples, peeled and
  cored
2 cups red seedless grapes,
  halved
⅓ cup minced Bermuda onion
salt and pepper, to taste

Dressing:

½ cup sour cream
½ cup mayonnaise
¼ cup honey
1 tsp. curry powder, or to taste
salt and pepper, to taste
½-1 cup cashews, optional

Discard skins of chicken and remove all chicken meat from bones. Cut into medium-size chunks. Cut apple into bite-size pieces. Mix all salad ingredients in large bowl. Mix all dressing ingredients together; add to salad in bowl and mix well. Add cashews right before serving.

NOTE: This may be made ahead and allowed to marinate in dressing.

Preparation: 30-45 min.   Easy   Serves: 6
                Can do ahead

Margaret N. Devaney

EASY COBB SALAD

"Cooking for two? — this is for you"

2 cups cubed cooked chicken
½ avocado, cubed
½ tomato, cubed
¼ cup crumbled Bleu cheese
⅛ cup chopped green onion
¼ cup Old Dutch brand sweet-
  sour dressing
crumbled bacon bits

Mix first 5 ingredients with the dressing. Top with bacon bits.

NOTE: If made ahead, add avocado just before serving.

Preparation: 15-20 min.   Easy   Serves: 2-3

Mary Anne Riley

CASHEW CHICKEN SALAD

3 cups cooked chicken
1½ cups sliced celery
3 cups cooked rice, cooled
½ cup sliced green onions
¾ cup coarsely chopped
  cashews
1 tsp. curry powder
1 tsp. salt
½ tsp. seasoned pepper
1 cup mayonnaise
2 tsp. lemon juice
¼ cup pineapple juice
pineapple slices
lettuce
tomato wedges

Mix together the chicken, celery, rice, green onions and cashews; set aside. Blend together the curry powder, salt, seasoned pepper, mayonnaise, lemon juice and pineapple juice and pour over the chicken mixture. Toss and chill well.

TO SERVE: Arrange pineapple slices on lettuce, top with salad and garnish with tomato wedges.

Preparation: 1 hr.   Easy   Serves: 6-8
                            Can do ahead

Florence C. Alling

MAIDA'S LUNCHEON SALAD

"A colorful, cheesy salad"

Dressing:
1 cup salad oil
½ cup vinegar
1 tsp. salt
1 tsp. paprika
¼ tsp. black pepper
2 tsp. oregano
parsley flakes, to taste
¼ lb. Roquefort cheese, grated

Mix all dressing ingredients together. Refrigerate overnight.

TO SERVE: Combine salad ingredients and pour dressing over. Add pitted olives when ready to serve.

Salad:
3-4 yellow parts of endive
1 head lettuce
1 cup cooked diced ham
1 cup cooked diced chicken
  breasts
¼ cup red cabbage
¼ cup green pepper
¼ lb. yellow cheese, diced
1 6-oz. can pitted black olives

Preparation: 20 min.   Easy   Serves: 6-8
                             Must do ahead

Ti DiGiorno

175

GREEN BEAN POTATO SALAD

"Perfect for a picnic"

6 small red skin potatoes
1 lb. fresh green beans,
  picked and cleaned
1 Tbsp. chopped fresh tarragon
1 Tbsp. chopped fresh parsley
6 thin slices hard salami
3 Tbsp. apple cider vinegar
½ cup olive oil
1 tsp. salt
1 tsp. ground white pepper

Boil whole potatoes in water with skin on. Cook until tender. Remove from pot and let cool. Cook green beans in salted boiling water until tender; drain beans under cold water to cool. Let beans drain; set aside.

Strip tarragon leaves from stem, chop very fine. Remove stems from parsley, wash leaves, squeeze to remove water, chop very fine. Cut slices of salami into very fine strips. Cut potatoes into quarters. In large mixing bowl, add potatoes, green beans, salami and toss gently. In a smaller bowl, mix vinegar, oil, parsley, and the tarragon. Add to green beans and toss gently. Season with salt and pepper, toss again. Cover and chill before serving.

Preparation: 25 min.   Easy   Serves: 6
Cooking: 15 min.   Can do ahead

John Gregory King, Chef
Allegheny Country Club

TOMATO SALAD CURRY

"Superb on your fresh garden tomatoes"

6 large ripe tomatoes, peeled,
  seeded and chopped
1 small white onion, grated
1 tsp. salt
¼ tsp. coarsely ground pepper
½ cup mayonnaise
2 Tbsp. minced fresh parsley
1 tsp. curry powder

Combine tomatoes, onion, salt and pepper; cover and chill for 3 hours. Combine mayonnaise, parsley and curry; cover and chill for 3 hours. To serve, spoon tomato mixture into small bowls and top each with a spoonful of mayonnaise mixture.

Preparation: 20 min.   Easy   Serves: 6-8
                              Must do ahead

Sherri Cobb

CHEF SALAD SOUTHWESTERN STYLE
"A hearty satisfying salad"

½ lb. ground beef
1 Tbsp. chopped green chile
1 6-oz. can ripe olives, pitted and sliced
1 head Iceberg lettuce, shredded
1 16-oz. can kidney beans, drained
2 tomatoes, chopped
1 avocado, diced
½ cup sour cream
2 Tbsp. Italian salad dressing
1 tsp. minced onion
¾ tsp. chili powder
½ tsp. salt
½ cup grated Cheddar cheese
½ cup coarsely crushed corn chips

Brown ground beef and green chile; drain. Combine olives, lettuce, beans, tomatoes and beef/chile mixture. Chill. Blend avocado, sour cream, Italian dressing and seasonings. Chill. Toss lettuce mixture with dressing and top with cheese and chips.

Preparation: 25 min.   Easy   Serves: 6
                        Must do ahead

Mary Jo Hottenstein

SANTA BARBARA SALAD

1 11-oz. can mandarin oranges
5 cups shredded cabbage, fresh as possible
1 cup sliced celery
½ cup raisins or chopped dates
2 Tbsp. lemon juice
1 large banana
1 tart apple, unpeeled
½ cup chopped nuts
1 8-oz. carton orange yogurt
½ tsp. salt
¾ tsp. poppy seeds

Drain oranges, saving the syrup. Combine oranges, cabbage, celery and raisins. Combine mandarin orange syrup and lemon juice. Slice the banana and apple into bite-size pieces, dip in juice mixture to prevent discoloration, then add to slaw with nuts.

Dressing: Stir 2 Tbsp. of juice mixture, yogurt, and salt until smooth. Pour over salad and toss gently. Sprinkle with poppy seeds.

Preparation: 20 min.   Easy   Serves: 8-12
                        Can do ahead

Donna L. Fisher

BROCCOLI SALAD
"A unanimous rave review"

1 head broccoli, cut into
  flowerets
1 red onion, minced
½ cup raisins
½-1 lb. bacon, cooked and
  crumbled

Dressing:
1 cup mayonnaise
½ cup sugar
2 Tbsp. white vinegar

Mix salad ingredients together.
Mix dressing ingredients together
and pour over salad.

VARIATIONS: May add 1 cup
grated Cheddar cheese or omit
raisins and add ½-1 lb. sliced
mushrooms and 8 oz. shredded
Mozzarella cheese.

Preparation: 25 min.   Easy   Serves: 6
                        Can do ahead

Patty Procopio

RICE SALAD
"Best served at room temperature"

8 cups hot cooked rice
2 cups vinaigrette (recipe
  follows)
1 sweet red pepper, thinly sliced
1 green pepper, thinly sliced
1 med. purple onion, sliced
6 scallions, finely sliced
1 cup currants
2 shallots, diced
1 10-oz. pkg. frozen peas,
  thawed
½ cup black olives, chopped
  (optional)
¼ cup parsley, chopped
½ cup fresh dill, chopped
pepper, freshly ground
salt (optional)

Vinaigrette: (yields 2 cups)
2 Tbsp. Dijon mustard
½ cup red wine vinegar
2 tsp. sugar
1 tsp. salt, or less to taste
1 tsp. pepper, freshly ground
small bunch parsley
1 cup olive oil

Mix hot rice with 1-1½ cups
vinaigrette. Cool to room temperature. Add remaining ingredients
and toss thoroughly. Adjust the
seasoning and add more
vinaigrette to taste. Serve immediately or cover and refrigerate. Bring to room temperature to
serve.

Vinaigrette: Whirl all ingredients,
except oil, in blender. With
blender running at low speed,
slowly dribble in oil until all oil is
used and mixture thickens.

Preparation: 45 min.   Easy   Serves: 12
                        Can do ahead

Carolyn S. Hammer

178

CARNAHAN JELLO SALAD

"A nice salad or dessert for children — they love it"

1 3-oz. pkg. orange Jello gelatin
1 cup boiling water
1 cup pineapple juice
1 cup mandarin oranges, drained
1 cup crushed pineapple, drained
2 cups Cool Whip topping

Put Jello in mixing bowl and add boiling water. Stir well until dissolved. Add pineapple juice. Refrigerate until Jello mixture becomes syrupy (NOT FIRMLY SET). Whip Jello mixture until light in color. Add mandarin oranges and pineapple. Blend. Fold in the Cool Whip. Pour into mold or salad dish. Refrigerate 4-5 hours until firmly set. Serve on lettuce if desired.

NOTE: You can substitute other flavors of Jello (e.g., mixed fruit or strawberry makes an attractive holiday salad).

Preparation: 15 min.   Easy   Serves: 8
                              Must do ahead

Agnes E. Shaw

SPANISH RICE SALAD

1 10-oz. pkg. yellow rice mix
½ cup chopped green pepper
½ cup chopped red pepper
8 black olives, sliced
8 green olives with pimientos, sliced
1 4-oz. can sliced mushrooms
⅓ cup diced purple onion
⅓ cup sliced green onions
1 cup cooked peas
1 12-oz. can artichoke hearts, quartered
2 Tbsp. fresh dill, minced
2 Tbsp. fresh parsley, minced
1 ripe tomato, seeded and chopped

Cook the rice according to package directions without butter. Cool. Add remaining ingredients, except the tomato, with dressing. Toss gently and refrigerate for 6 hours. Add the tomatoes just before serving. Present on lettuce leaves.

Dressing: Whisk all ingredients together and mix with salad before refrigerating.

Dressing:
4 Tbsp. olive oil
4 Tbsp. red wine vinegar
1 Tbsp. Dijon mustard
1 pkg. Sweet & Low sweetener
½ tsp. salt
freshly ground pepper
2 cloves garlic, minced
¾ tsp. dried basil

Preparation: 30 min.   Easy   Serves: 12
                              Must do ahead

Sara A. Bagley

EGGNOG CRANBERRY SALAD

"This 3 layer holiday salad looks festive and tastes delicious"

2 3-oz. pkgs. regular vanilla
   pudding mix
2 3-oz. pkgs. lemon gelatin
6 cups water
2 Tbsp. lemon juice
2 3-oz. pkgs. raspberry gelatin
2 16-oz. cans whole cranberry
   sauce, chilled
½ cup chopped pecans, optional
½ cup finely chopped celery
1 16-oz. container Cool Whip
   topping
1 tsp. ground nutmeg

In saucepan, combine vanilla pudding, lemon gelatin and 4 cups of water. Cook and stir until mixture boils. Stir in lemon juice. Chill until partially set. In separate saucepan, dissolve raspberry gelatin in 2 cups boiling water. Beat in cranberry sauce. Fold in nuts and celery. Chill until partially set. To the pudding/gelatin mixture, add Cool Whip and nutmeg. Blend well. Pour half of the pudding mixture into a 14 x 10 x 2" baking dish.

Carefully pour the cranberry layer over. Top with remaining pudding mixture. Chill 6 hours or overnight.

Preparation: 45 min.   Easy   Serves: 15
Cooking: 5 min.   Must do ahead

Linda K. Chufe

OLD FASHIONED POTATO SALAD

"One of the very best ever - pure nostalgia"

5 med. potatoes, cooked, skins
   removed, and slightly cooled
   (about 6 cups)
1¼ tsp. salt
¼ tsp. pepper

Dressing:
¾ cup salad dressing
¾ cup mayonnaise
1 tsp. sugar
2 Tbsp. dill pickle juice
1 Tbsp. vinegar
1 Tbsp. sweet pickle juice or
   sweet relish
¼ tsp. celery salt
dash onion salt
5 green onions, thinly sliced
2 Tbsp. diced sweet pickle
6 hard-boiled eggs, peeled and
   diced
1 green pepper, diced
paprika, optional
green pepper rings, optional

Dice potatoes and combine with salt and pepper in large bowl. Combine dressing ingredients and pour over still warm potatoes, mixing thoroughly. Let stand in refrigerator for at least 2 hours (overnight is preferred). Add green onions, sweet pickle, green pepper and eggs. Mix thoroughly. Garnish with additional eggs, pepper rings and paprika if desired. Serve chilled.

Preparation: 45 min.   Easy   Serves: 8
                  Must do ahead

Phyllis Ann Driver

APRICOT SPICE MOLD
"Pretty and refreshing"

2 17-oz. cans apricot halves
2 20-oz. cans crushed pineapple
1 16-oz. can apricot nectar
3 Tbsp. vinegar
1½ tsp. whole cloves
2 4" cinnamon sticks
1 6-oz. pkg. apricot Jello gelatin
1 3-oz. pkg. lemon Jello gelatin

Drain apricot halves and crushed pineapple. Reserve syrup. To reserved syrup, add enough apricot nectar to make 6 cups. To combined syrups, add vinegar, cloves and cinnamon. Bring to a boil, then simmer for 10 minutes. Strain. Pour over apricot and lemon Jellos. Stir and chill until thick (not set). Mix in halved apricots and crushed pineapple. Pour into 2 (6 cup) molds and chill until firm.

Preparation: 20 min.   Easy   Serves: 12-16
Cooking: 10 min.   Must do ahead

Gloria R. Gaydos

FRUIT-CHEESE SALAD
"Here's a surprise topper of American cheese"

mini marshmallows
1 16-oz. can sliced peaches
1 16-oz. can sliced apricots
  (use peeled apricots)
2 6-oz. pkgs. orange Jello gelatin
4 cups boiling water
2 cups cold water
1 8-oz. can crushed pineapple
1 egg, beaten
1 cup pineapple juice
2 Tbsp. cornstarch
½ cup sugar
2 Tbsp. butter
1 cup whipped cream or
  whipped topping
grated processed American
  cheese

Place layer of mini marshmallows in a 9 x 13" pan. Layer slices of peaches and apricots. Prepare the 2 packages of orange Jello with the boiling water and cold water. Cool. Add pineapple. Pour on top of fruit and refrigerate until firm. Cook together (can do in microwave) the pineapple juice, egg, cornstarch, sugar and butter. Thicken and allow to cool. Stir in the whipped cream or topping. Pour over Jello and chill. Top with grated processed American cheese.

Preparation: 30 min.   Easy   Serves: 12
                         Must do ahead

Jebby Potter

181

RASPBERRY SALAD
"Sweet and delicious"

2 10-oz. pkgs. frozen
  raspberries, thawed
1 6-oz. box raspberry Jello
  gelatin
2 cups sour cream
1½ cups water

Combine all ingredients with whisk to blend sour cream while cooking over medium heat. Bring to a boil, but don't let it boil. Pour into a 9 x 13" pan or deep bowl. Refrigerate for 24 hours.

NOTE: For a dinner party, serve on Bibb lettuce with a fresh raspberry on top.

Preparation: 5 min.   Easy   Serves: 12-16
Cooking: 10 min.   Must do ahead

Mary Ellen Whitinger

PIMIENTO SALAD
"Really different, also pretty to serve"

1 3-oz. box lemon Jello gelatin
1½ cups boiling water
1 5-oz. container pimiento
  cheese
1 8-oz. can crushed pineapple,
  undrained
½ pint whipping cream, whipped

Dissolve Jello in boiling water and add cheese. Stir until cheese is dissolved. Add pineapple (including juice) and, when contents are cooled but not congealed, fold in whipped cream. Pour into a 10 x 6" or 8" square dish and refrigerate. Cut into squares and serve on lettuce.

Preparation: 10-15 min.   Easy   Serves: 8-12
                             Must do ahead

Marjorie Fox

MANDARIN SALAD
"A new and different aspic"

1 3-oz. pkg. orange or lemon
  Jello gelatin
1 cup boiling water
1 11-oz. can mandarin oranges,
  drained - reserve liquid
¼ cup mayonnaise
¼ cup thinly sliced red
  onion rings
½ cup chopped celery

Dissolve Jello in boiling water. Drain oranges. Place reserved liquid in measuring cup and add enough water to make ¾ cup of liquid. Add to Jello. Blend in mayonnaise. Chill until very thick. Fold in onions, celery and oranges. Spoon into mold and chill until firm.

Preparation: 20 min.   Easy   Serves: 6
                          Can do ahead

Doris L. Kunkel

SALAD DRESSINGS

HOT BACON DRESSING
"Perfect over a spinach salad"

5 slices bacon
¼ cup bacon drippings
¼ cup vinegar
2 Tbsp. crumbled Blue cheese
2 Tbsp. sugar
½ tsp. salt
½ tsp. Worcestershire sauce

Cook bacon until crisp. Drain. Crumble. Combine remaining ingredients, heat and pour over salad. Toss and serve immediately.

Preparation: 20 min.   Easy   Serves: 6
                         Serve immediately

Suzette M. Truckey

PEPPERCORN DRESSING
"Black peppercorns add zest"

¾ cup + 2 Tbsp. sour cream
¼ cup mayonnaise
2 Tbsp. lemon juice
3½ tsp. coarsely cracked pepper
1 tsp. Worcestershire sauce
1 beef bouillon cube, dissolved
   in 4 tsp. warm water
pinch of salt

Combine all ingredients and whisk to blend. Transfer to a container with a tight-fitting lid and refrigerate at least 3 hours (keeps for 10 days).

Preparation: 10 min.   Easy   Serves: 8-10
                         Must do ahead

Linda D. Orsini

183

POPPY SEED DRESSING

"Try this dressing on a chicken or steak salad"

1 cup sugar
1 tsp. dry mustard
½ tsp. salt
1½ tsp. paprika
½ cup apple cider vinegar
1½ cups oil
1 tsp. grated onion
2 Tbsp. poppy seeds

Mix sugar, mustard, salt, paprika and vinegar. Slowly add oil, beating constantly, and continue to beat until thick. Add onion and poppy seeds and beat for a few minutes. Store in the refrigerator, but not near the freezing coil.

Preparation: 10 min.   Easy   Yield: 2½ cups

"A Restaurant By George"
Nags Head, NC

MUSTARD DRESSING

"Even better as a dip"

½ cup Dijon mustard
2 Tbsp. red wine vinegar
½ tsp. salt
¾ tsp. pepper
1 cup corn oil

Mix the mustard, vinegar, salt and pepper in food processor or whisk by hand. Gradually add the corn oil.

NOTE: Use on a mixed green salad, cold blanched asparagus spears or as a dip for crudites.

Preparation: 10 min.   Easy   Yield: 1½ cups
                        Can do ahead

Bonnie Casper

HONEY-LIME FRUIT SALAD DRESSING

"Limes add a unique taste"

¾ cup oil
¼ cup lime juice
1 tsp. grated lemon rind
½ tsp. paprika
⅓ cup honey
2 Tbsp. lemon juice
¼ tsp. dry mustard
2 Tbsp. sesame seeds

Combine ingredients. Beat with whisk. Chill. Serve on a fresh fruit salad.

Preparation: 15 min.   Easy   Yield: 1½ cups
                        Can do ahead

Lori O. Haley

LOW-CAL SALAD DRESSING

1 cup low-fat cottage cheese
¼ cup skim milk
1 Tbsp. lemon juice
1 Tbsp. minced onion
1 Tbsp. mustard (prepared)
2 Tbsp. fresh dill

Blend first 3 ingredients together until smooth. Stir in minced onion, mustard and fresh dill. Refrigerate 2 hours and stir before serving.

Preparation: 15 min.   Easy   Yield: 1¼ cups
                        Must do ahead

Martha D. Smith

WAIT TILIT STOPS

SWEETS

KENNYWOOD PARK'S MERRY-GO-ROUND

The Merry-Go-Round was hand carved in 1926 by a German craftsman from the William Dentzel Company of Philadelphia. The music is provided by the original Wurlitzer Band Organ. Kennywood Park, West Mifflin, is one of America's finest traditional amusement parks.

Additional illustrations in this section:

The Old Post Office, Sewickley, PA. This limestone neoclassical structure is now home to the Sweetwater Art Center and the Sewickley Valley Historical Society.

This tree has been a tradition at The Joseph Horne Company for over thirty years. Horne's has been a leading fashion department store since 1892.

A view of Mt. Washington and the Monongahela Incline.

This Bulldog greets diners at its deli-style restaurants throughout downtown Pittsburgh.

A maze of columns and tubes support Sand Castle's water rides.

The Vista International Hotel is located on Liberty Avenue downtown. A pedestrian overpass links the hotel to the David L. Lawrence Convention Center.

Fright Night transforms Phipps Conservatory into Halloween fun for everyone.

Chuckles, the Pittsburgh Zoo's Amazon River dolphin.

Alphie, the Japanese Macaque monkey, has returned to his home, the Pittsburgh Zoo, after escaping and touring Pennsylvania, West Virginia and Ohio on his own for seven months.

Recently restored by the Garden Club of Allegheny County are the Phipps Outdoor Gardens. A garden fountain is dedicated to the memory of Laura Childs Brooks.

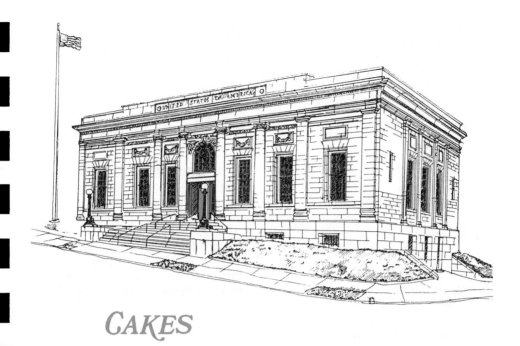

CAKES

CHOCOLATE MOUSSE CAKE

"Layers of cookies and mousse, oh my"

1 box Famous chocolate wafers
  OR chocolate circle cookies
18 oz. chocolate chips,
  semi-sweet
6 Tbsp. water
4 Tbsp. sugar
6 egg yolks
2 tsp. vanilla
6 egg whites
2 8-oz. cartons whipping
  cream*
German chocolate bar for curls
  or sprinkles

* 6 oz. liquid = 1 cup whipped—
  remainder of 2 8-oz. cartons
  can be used for topping.

Grease a 9½-10″ springform pan. Stand cookies around side and cover bottom with the cookies. Melt chocolate chips in water in microwave, stirring occasionally. Add sugar. Cool. Beat in egg yolks, one at a time. Add vanilla and beat. Beat egg whites until stiff. Fold into the chocolate mixture. Whip whipping cream and fold 2 cups into chocolate mixture. Layer pan at least 2 more layers of cookies and mousse, ending with the mousse. Cover top with remaining whipped cream. Add chocolate sprinkles or curls. Refrigerate. (May be frozen in advance—thaw before serving.)

Preparation: 1½-2 hrs.   Moderately difficult   Serves: 12 +
                          Must do ahead   Can freeze

Phyllis Strauss

187

FUDGE-NUT CAKE

"How about a garnish of whipped cream and strawberries"

1 cup all-purpose flour
½ cup sugar
¾ cup plain yogurt
¼ cup butter or margarine
¼ cup cocoa
1½ tsp. instant coffee, powder
  or granules
½ tsp. baking soda
½ tsp. baking powder
¼ tsp. salt
1 egg
1 tsp. vanilla
fudge-nut topping

Fudge-nut Topping:
¾ cup skim evaporated milk
½ cup sugar
4 Tbsp. butter or margarine
4 Tbsp. cocoa
1 Tbsp. corn syrup
1 tsp. vanilla extract
¾ cup chopped walnuts,
  pecans, macadamia nuts, or
  any favorite nuts

Preheat oven to 350°. Grease a 9" round cake pan; line bottom of pan with waxed paper. In large bowl with mixer at low speed, beat all ingredients except topping until blended, occasionally scraping bowl with spatula. Pour batter into prepared pan. Bake for 25-30 minutes until toothpick inserted in center comes out clean. Cool cake in pan on wire rack for 10 minutes. Remove cake from pan, discard waxed paper. Cool cake completely on wire rack. When cake is cool, prepare Fudge-nut Topping. Place cake on plate; quickly pour topping evenly over top of cake, allowing some of the topping to run down sides. Refrigerate cake until topping is firm (about 1 hour).

Topping:
In 2-quart saucepan over medium-high heat, heat all ingredients except vanilla and nuts. Heat to boiling, stirring constantly. Reduce heat to medium; cook 5 minutes, stirring constantly. Remove from heat and stir in vanilla. Cool about 10 minutes and stir in nuts. Pour over cake as directed above.

Preparation: 15 min.   Easy   Serves: 12
Cooking: 25-30 min.   Must do ahead

Janet L. Mackey

CHEESE CAKE

"For those who have no springform pan"

1½ cups graham cracker crumbs
¼ cup melted butter
½ cup sugar
3 8-oz. pkgs. cream cheese
1 cup sugar
5 eggs
1½ tsp. vanilla
1 pint sour cream
½ cup sugar

Mix crumbs, butter and sugar. Press into a 9x13" greased pan. Set aside. Cream cheese with electric beater, gradually adding 1 cup sugar. Add 1 egg at a time. Add vanilla. Pour mixture into crust. Bake at 350° for 30 minutes. Mix sour cream and ½ cup sugar. Spread on cake and return to oven for 5 more minutes.

Preparation: 30-35 min.   Easy   Serves: 12
Cooking: 30 min.   Can do ahead

Mickey Belas

STRAWBERRY GLAZED CHEESECAKE

"A long recipe - takes two or three days"

Position rack in center of oven and preheat to 350°. Lightly butter 1 9" or 10" springform pan.

Crust:
¾ cup coarsely ground walnuts (3 oz.)
¾ cup finely crushed graham crackers
3 Tbsp. unsalted butter, melted

Crust:
Combine walnuts, graham cracker crumbs, and butter. Press compactly onto bottom of pan.

Filling:
4 8-oz. pkgs. cream cheese, softened
4 eggs
1¼ cups sugar
1 Tbsp. fresh lemon juice
2 tsp. vanilla

Filling:
Beat cream cheese in large bowl with electric mixer until smooth. Add eggs, sugar, lemon juice and vanilla and beat thoroughly. Spoon over crust.
Set pan on baking sheet. Bake at 350° for 40-45 minutes for a 10" pan or 50-55 minutes for a 9" pan. Cake will rise and crack after you remove it from oven. Remove from oven and let it stand at room temperature for 20 minutes.

Topping:
2 cups sour cream
¼ cup sugar
1 tsp. vanilla

Topping:
Combine sour cream, sugar, vanilla and blend well. Cover and refrigerate. After cake cools, spoon on top, filling in cracks. Bake at 350° for 5 minutes. Let cool. REFRIGERATE FOR 2-3 DAYS!

Strawberry glaze:
1 qt. medium strawberries
1 12-oz. jar red raspberry jelly
1 Tbsp. cornstarch
¼ cup Cointreau
¼ cup water

Glaze:
The morning before serving, cut and hull strawberries. Dry completely on paper towels. Combine a little jelly and cornstarch and mix well. Add remaining jelly, Cointreau and water and cook over medium heat for 5 minutes. Cool. Remove cake from springform pan. Glaze berries and place decoratively on top. Drizzle glaze down sides of cake.

Preparation: 1 hr.   **Moderately difficult   Serves: 10-12**
Cooking: 1 hr.   **Must do ahead**

Patricia I. Berini

CHOCOLATE CHEESECAKE

2 cups Famous chocolate
    cookie wafers, crushed
4 Tbsp. butter, melted
¾ cup sugar
3 eggs
1½ lbs. cream cheese,
    softened
8 oz. semi-sweet chocolate,
    melted
2 Tbsp. cocoa
1 tsp. vanilla
3 cups sour cream
¼ cup melted butter
whipped cream

Crush wafers with rolling pin. Mix with butter. Press crumbs firmly against the bottom and sides of a well-buttered 9″ springform pan. Chill. Beat sugar with eggs until mixture is light and fluffy. Gradually add cream cheese. Mix well. Stir in chocolate, cocoa, and vanilla. Thoroughly beat in sour cream. Fold in butter and pour into chilled shell. Bake at 350° for 45 minutes. It will seem quite liquidy when removed from oven. Chill several hours. Remove springform pan and decorate with whipped cream.

Preparation: 30 min.   **Moderately difficult**   Serves: 10-12
Cooking: 45 min.   **Must do ahead**

Mandy Rockwell

ANGEL FOOD CAKE WITH RUM-CREAM FILLING
"Yum yum, rum and almonds"

1 angel food cake

Filling:
1 stick margarine
3 cups powdered sugar
1 tsp. vanilla
⅓ cup dark Rum
1 cup thinly slivered almonds,
    toasted

Topping:
½ pt. whipping cream
3 Tbsp. sugar
½ tsp. vanilla

Make filling by creaming the margarine and sugar together. Add vanilla and Rum. Fold in the toasted almonds. Split cake into 3 layers. Put filling between layers.

Topping:
Add sugar and vanilla to cream and whip until done.

NOTE: This tastes even better after one day.

Preparation: 30 min.   **Easy**   Serves: 10-12
                     Can do ahead

Barbara South

HO-HO CAKE

"Sounds like a cake for Santa"

1st layer: Chocolate Cake
3 cups flour
2 cups sugar
2 tsp. baking soda
½ cup cocoa
2 tsp. vinegar
1 cup oil
1 tsp. salt
2 tsp. vanilla
2 cups cold water

2nd layer: Cream Filling
5 tsp. flour
1¼ cups milk
½ cup margarine
1 cup Crisco shortening
  (not butter flavored)
¼ tsp. salt
1 cup sugar
1 tsp. vanilla

3rd layer: Icing
1 stick margarine, melted and
  cooled
1 beaten egg
1 tsp. vanilla
2 oz. Nestle's pre-melted
  baking chocolate
2 Tbsp. hot water
3 cups powdered sugar

1st layer:
Mix all ingredients together well for 2 minutes. Pour into two greased 9x13" pans. Bake at 350° for 20 minutes. Cool completely.

2nd layer:
Mix flour and milk together in saucepan. Cook and stir until thick, then cool. In a separate bowl, cream together the next 5 ingredients. Beat well with flour and milk mixture. Spread on top of cooled cake, then refrigerate.

3rd layer:
Whip ingredients together. Spread on top of filling. Refrigerate cake. Let cake stand at room temperature for 20 minutes before serving.

Preparation: 40 min.	Easy	Yield: 2 cakes
Cooking: 20 min.	Must do ahead	Can freeze

Debra Pushic Gibbs

MOSCOW CREAM CHEESE POUND CAKE

"Rich and delicious"

½ lb. butter
8 oz. cream cheese, at room
  temperature
1½ cups sugar
1½ tsp. vanilla
4 eggs
2 cups flour
1½ tsp. baking powder
mini-chocolate chips, optional

Cream together butter, cream cheese, sugar and vanilla. Add eggs, one at a time. Add flour and baking powder. Grease and flour a bundt pan. Pour in batter and bake at 325° for 70 minutes. Cool 5 minutes before removing.

VARIATION: You may add ½ bag mini-chocolate chips to batter.

Preparation: 20 min.	Easy	Serves: 12
Cooking: 70 min.	Can do ahead	Can freeze

Eve A. Rogers

SPICE CAKE
"Resembles brownies"

2 cups light brown sugar
½ cup Crisco oil
2 Tbsp. baking cocoa
2 eggs
2 cups boiling or very hot
  water
⅓ cup instant coffee
1½ Tbsp. cinnamon
1¼ tsp. ground cloves
¾ tsp. nutmeg
3 cups flour
1 Tbsp. baking soda, dissolved
  in ½ cup hot water
1 lb. dark raisins
powdered sugar (optional)

Grease and flour a 15½x10½" baking pan. (You need a 2" deep pan, but not too large). Combine first 4 ingredients in large bowl. Dissolve coffee in hot water and add, a little at a time, to the above mixture. Add the spices and mix. Add the flour, mixing together as you add. Stir the soda water into the mixture. Gently add the raisins, breaking them up first. Pour into prepared pan and bake for 40 minutes at 350° or until toothpick inserted in center comes out clean. After cake has cooled, it can be covered with a doily and sprinkled with powdered sugar.

Preparation: 20-30 min.   Easy   Serves: 10
Cooking: 40 min.   Can freeze

Catherine Crain

APRICOT CAKE
"Dots of apricot preserves could decorate frosting"

Cake:
1½ cups Crisco oil
2 cups sugar
4 eggs
2 cups flour
2 tsp. baking soda
1½ tsp. cinnamon
½ tsp. salt
2 jars junior-size apricots (baby
  food)
½-1 cup chopped walnuts

Frosting:
½ cup margarine, softened
1 3-oz. pkg. cream cheese,
  softened
1½ cups powdered sugar
1 tsp. vanilla

Cake:
Beat together the oil, sugar and eggs. Sift flour, baking soda, cinnamon and salt into mixture. Add apricots and nuts. Bake in a greased and floured bundt pan at 350° for 45-55 minutes.

Frosting:
Beat together margarine and cream cheese. Add sugar and vanilla.

Preparation: 20 min.   Easy   Serves: 12
Cooking: 50 min.   Can do ahead   Can freeze

Katharine T. Harbison

MARBLE CHEESE CAKE

"Make this for company - it looks so fancy"

6 oz. chocolate chips
½ cup sugar

Combine chocolate chips and sugar in top of double boiler. Heat over hot water until melted. Set aside to cool.

Crust:
1¼ cups graham cracker crumbs
1 Tbsp. sugar
¼ cup melted butter

Crust:
Mix all ingredients together and press into bottom and sides of a 9" springform pan.

Filling:
2 8-oz. pkgs. cream cheese, softened
¾ cup sugar
½ cup sour cream
1 tsp. vanilla
4 eggs

Filling:
Beat cream cheese. Gradually add sugar. Mix in sour cream and vanilla. Add eggs, one at a time, beating well after each one. Divide filling in half. Add chocolate mixture to one half. Pour into crust. Pour plain filling on top. Marbleize with a knife. Bake at 325° for 50-55 minutes. Cool, then refrigerate.

Preparation: 30 min.	Easy	Serves: 12
Cooking: 50-55 min.	Must do ahead	

Ruth K. Duessel

BLACK JAVA CAKE

Cake:
2 tsp. salt
2 cups flour
2 cups sugar
¾ cup cocoa
2 tsp. baking soda
1 tsp. baking powder
2 eggs
½ cup vegetable oil
1 cup black coffee
1 cup milk

Cake:
Mix all ingredients until smooth. Mixture will be very thin. Grease and flour a 9x13" cake pan (or two 9" round cake pans). Pour batter into prepared pans. Bake at 350° for 30 minutes or until toothpick inserted in cake comes out clean.

Frosting:
1 lb. powdered sugar
½-¾ cup of cocoa
¼ cup milk (or more for thinning)
½ cup margarine
1 tsp. vanilla

Frosting:
Cream all ingredients together. Frost cooled cake.

Preparation: 20 min.	Easy	Serves: 12
Cooking: 30-35 min.	Can do ahead	Can freeze

Michelle A. Wiseman

CHOCOLATE CHIP CAKE

"Try grating chocolate in your food processor"

1 box Duncan Hines butter cake mix
1 3½-oz. box instant vanilla pudding
½ cup oil
1 cup water
4 eggs
½ block (2 oz.) German sweet chocolate, grated
½ bag (6 oz.) miniature semi-sweet chocolate bits

Mix all ingredients, except grated chocolate and chocolate bits. Beat 10 minutes. Fold in chocolates. Mix well. Pour into greased and floured tube pan. Bake at 325° for 50-60 minutes.

Preparation: 25 min.   Easy   Serves: 16-18
Cooking: 50-60 min. Can do ahead   Can freeze

Anne G. Phipps

CHOCOLATE CAKE

1 Duncan Hines Devil's Food cake mix
1 pint sour cream
4 eggs
1 3½-oz. pkg. chocolate instant pudding mix
¾ cup oil
¾ cup Kahlua
1 12-oz. pkg. chocolate chips
ice cream

Mix all ingredients, except chocolate chips, for 4 minutes. Stir in chocolate chips. Bake in a greased tube pan for 1 hour at 350°. Cool and serve with ice cream.

Preparation: 10 min.   Easy   Serves: 16 +
Cooking: 60-75 min. Can do ahead   Can freeze

Eleanor H. Thomson

CHOCOLATE ICING FOR ANGEL FOOD CAKE

"Spreads beautifully"

1 cup butter (½ lb.)
2 cups powdered sugar
2 eggs, unbeaten
2 1-oz. squares unsweetened chocolate, melted
½ tsp. cinnamon
pinch of salt
4 Tbsp. coffee
angel food cake

Cream butter and sugar. Add eggs, melted chocolate, cinnamon, salt and coffee. Beat until smooth. Cut angel food cake in thirds, or half, and ice. Put layers back together and ice outside of cake.

Preparation: 15 min.   Easy   Serves: 10
                         Can do ahead

Debra Pushic Gibbs

FESTIVE CAKE
"A rich moist cake that keeps well"

Cake:
3 cups all-purpose flour
2 cups sugar
1 tsp. baking soda
1 tsp. salt
1 tsp. cinnamon
1 cup chopped almonds
3 eggs
1½ cups vegetable oil
1 tsp. almond extract
2 cups chopped firm ripe
    bananas
1 8-oz. can crushed pineapple,
    drained

Frosting:
1 8-oz. pkg. cream cheese
2 Tbsp. butter or margarine,
    softened
1½ tsp. vanilla
3 cups powdered sugar
2 Tbsp. Amaretto or Cognac
2-3 Tbsp. milk

banana slices, optional
pineapple slices, optional
whole roasted almonds, optional

Cake:
Mix first 5 ingredients well; then add chopped almonds. In another bowl, beat eggs slightly; combine with oil, almond extract, bananas and pineapple. Add to dry ingredients and mix thoroughly, but DO NOT beat. Spoon into greased 10" tube pan. Bake at 325° for 1 hour and 20-25 minutes. Remove from oven and let stand 15 minutes, then invert onto serving plate. Frost, if desired, and decorate with banana and pineapple slices and whole roasted almonds.

Frosting:
Beat cream cheese, butter and vanilla until smooth. Beat in remaining ingredients until frosting is smooth and of spreading consistency.

Preparation: 25 min.	Easy	Serves: 12-14
Cooking: 1 hr. 25 min.	Can do ahead	

Lynn Popovich

ORANGE CAKE
"Different with a pineapple icing"

Cake:
1 box yellow cake mix
¾ cup Crisco oil
4 eggs
1 11-oz. can mandarin
    oranges, undrained

Icing:
1 15-oz. can crushed pineapple
1 3½-oz. pkg. instant vanilla
    pudding
1 8-oz. container Cool Whip
    topping

Cake:
Mix all ingredients together. Blend for 2 minutes. Bake at 350° for 20-25 minutes in three greased and floured 8" pans.

Icing:
Mix crushed pineapple and instant vanilla pudding at medium speed for 2 minutes. Fold in Cool Whip. Spread on cake and in-between layers.

Preparation: 15 min.	Easy	Serves: 8-10
Cooking: 20-25 min.	Can do ahead	

Judie Vescio

195

PINEAPPLE SWIRL CAKE

1 8¾-oz. can crushed
   pineapple
⅓ cup shortening
½ cup granulated sugar
1 egg
1 tsp. vanilla
1¼ cups sifted all-purpose
   flour
1½ tsp. baking powder
¼ tsp. salt
⅓ cup brown sugar
3 Tbsp. butter or margarine,
   melted
½ cup flaked coconut
⅓ cup chopped walnuts

Drain pineapple well, reserving ½ cup syrup. Cream shortening and sugar. Add egg and vanilla; beat until light. Sift together flour, baking powder and salt; add to creamed mixture alternately with reserved syrup, beginning and ending with flour mixture. Spread half in a greased 8″ square baking dish; spread with pineapple. Top with remaining batter. Combine remaining ingredients; sprinkle over all. Bake in a preheated 350° oven for about 30-35 minutes.

Preparation: 30 min.   Easy   Yield: 1 8″ cake
Cooking: 35 min.   Can do ahead   Can freeze

Susan L. Nitzberg

KATE'S ALMOND CAKE

Cake:
2 eggs
1 cup sugar
1 cup flour
1 stick butter, melted
1 tsp. + almond extract

Topping:
1 stick butter
½ cup sugar
1 Tbsp. flour
1 Tbsp. milk
1 tsp. + almond extract
½ cup sliced almonds

Cake:
Preheat oven to 350°. Combine and beat cake ingredients until thick. Pour into greased and floured 10″ tart pan. Bake for 20-25 minutes.

Topping:
Melt butter and sugar in pan. Add flour, then milk, extract and almonds. Spread topping on cake. Broil 2-4 minutes until browned. WATCH IT CAREFULLY! Turn, if necessary, to brown evenly.

Preparation: 20 min.   Easy   Serves: 10-12
Cooking: 20-25 min.   Can do ahead   Can freeze

Judy Jones

TUNNEL OF FUDGE

1½ cups butter or margarine
6 eggs
1½ cups sugar
2 cups flour
1 pkg. double Dutch fudge
   butter cream frosting mix
2 cups chopped walnuts

Preheat oven to 350°. Cream butter, eggs and sugar by hand. Stir in flour, frosting and nuts. Bake for 60-65 minutes in greased and floured bundt or 10″ tube pan. Cool 2 hours, then remove from pan.

NOTE: Do not omit nuts!

Preparation: 10 min.   Easy   Serves: 12
Cooking: 60-65 min.   Can do ahead

Eve Rogers

ESTHER'S COCONUT CAKE

"A Cool Whip and coconut topping"

1 pkg. yellow cake mix
1 tsp. vanilla
7 oz. coconut (save a few
  sprinkles for topping)
1 small can (⅔ cup) evaporated
  milk
1 cup water
½ cup powdered sugar
1 8-oz. container Cool Whip
  topping

Follow package directions for yellow cake. Before mixing batter, add vanilla and coconut. Mix batter for a minute longer than the directions say on cake mix box. Batter will be fairly heavy. Pour batter into a greased 9x13" pan and bake about 5 minutes longer than package directions call for. While cake is still warm, punch holes with fork on top of cake.

Pour the mixture of evaporated milk, water and powdered sugar over holes on cake. When cake is cool, spread Cool Whip over entire top of cake. Sprinkle coconut over Cool Whip (slight amount).

Preparation:	15 min.	Easy	Serves: 10-12
Cooking:	45-50 min.	Can do ahead	Can freeze

Betsy Ellen Donehoo

VANILLA BUTTERNUT POUND CAKE

"Maraschino cherries add flavor and color"

2 sticks butter
½ cup Crisco shortening
3 cups sugar
¼ tsp. salt
5 large eggs
3 cups flour
1 5-oz. can evaporated milk
2 Tbsp. vanilla butternut
  flavoring
1 cup chopped walnuts
1 10-oz. jar maraschino
  cherries, drained

Cream together butter, Crisco, sugar and salt. Add eggs, one at a time. Add flour and milk, alternately, ending with flour. Add vanilla butternut flavoring, nuts and cherries. Bake in greased and floured tube pan (bundt pan is fine) for 1 hour and 45 minutes (for a firmer cake, add 10 minutes) at 350°. DO NOT PRE-HEAT OVEN. Start in a cold oven. DO NOT OPEN OVEN DOOR WHILE BAKING. Remove from pan immediately.

Preparation:	30 min.	Moderately difficult	Serves: 10-12
Cooking:	1 hr.45-55 min.	Can do ahead	

Margaret Sechler

DESSERTS & SAUCES

CHOCOLATE TRUFFLE LOAF WITH RASPBERRY SAUCE

Truffle loaf:
2 cups heavy cream, divided
3 egg yolks, slightly beaten
2 8-oz. bars semi-sweet baking
  chocolate (not chips)
½ cup light corn syrup
½ cup margarine
1 tsp. vanilla
¼ cup powdered sugar

Raspberry sauce:
3 10-oz. pkgs. frozen raspberries, thawed
1 cup light corn syrup
2 Tbsp. Chambord (optional)
fresh raspberries (optional)

Truffle loaf:
Mix ½ cup cream with egg yolks.
In saucepan, stir chocolate, corn
syrup and margarine over
medium heat until melted. Add
egg mixture. Stirring constantly,
cook gently for 3 minutes. Cool
to room temperature. Beat
remaining cream until soft peaks
form. Add vanilla. Add powdered
sugar, 1 Tbsp. at a time, until
beaten thoroughly. Fold into
chocolate until thoroughly
blended. Pour into an 8½x
4½x2½" loaf pan, which has
been lined with plastic wrap.
Refrigerate overnight.

Raspberry sauce:
In blender or food processor, purée thawed raspberries. Strain out
seeds. Stir in corn syrup and Chambord.

To serve:
Spoon some sauce into enough shallow bowls to serve your guests.
Place slice of truffle loaf on pool of sauce. Top with a few fresh
raspberries.

Preparation: 30 min.	Moderately difficult	Serves: 16
Cooking: 3 min.	Must do ahead	Can freeze

Catherine C. Johnson

PEAR TART

Pastry shell:
2 cups flour
1 Tbsp. sugar
⅓ cup butter and ½ cup Crisco
shortening
1 tsp. salt
4 Tbsp. milk

Filling:
4-5 ripe pears, peeled
3 Tbsp. sugar
2½ tsp. flour
½-¾ cup apricot preserves

whipping cream, whipped

Pastry shell:
Mix ingredients together well, as
you would for pie crust. Place
rolled out dough into a 10″ tart
pan. Prick with a fork and bake
at 400° for 7 minutes; cool.

Filling:
Slice pears and place in cooled
crust. Mix sugar and flour
together; sprinkle on top of
pears. Bake at 375° for 20
minutes. Heat apricot preserves
until liquid. Brush over tart and
bake for 20 minutes more.
Serve warm with whipped cream.

Preparation: 30 min.	**Moderately difficult**	**Serves: 8-10**
Cooking: 47 min.	**Can do ahead**	

Suzanne Blackburn

GREENBRIER BREADPUDDING AND DELUXE VANILLA SAUCE

Pudding:
5 slices plain, white bread
½ cup melted butter
6 whole eggs
1 quart milk
1 cup sugar
vanilla, to taste
1 cup raisins

Deluxe vanilla sauce:
2 cups heavy cream
½ cup sugar
4 egg yolks
1 Tbsp. flour
1 Tbsp. vanilla extract
¼ tsp. salt
2 scoops vanilla ice cream

Pudding:
Cut bread slices into 1″ squares
and toast in a hot oven. Place in
the bottom of a casserole and
drizzle with melted butter. Combine remaining ingredients and
pour over bread. Bake at 350°
until custard is firm, approximately 45 minutes. Serve topped
with Deluxe vanilla sauce.

Deluxe vanilla sauce:
Combine cream and sugar in a
2-quart saucepan and bring just
to a boil. Remove from heat.
Beat egg yolks, flour, vanilla
extract and salt together and stir
in a little of the hot cream. Add
this mixture to the rest of the hot cream. Cook, stirring constantly, (DO
NOT OVERCOOK) until just thickened. Remove from heat and add ice
cream, stirring until melted. Strain. This sauce may be served hot or
cold.

NOTE: Use ½ cup of sauce per bread pudding serving.

Preparation: 50-60 min.	**Easy**	**Serves: 8-10**
Cooking: 50-60 min.	**Can do ahead**	**Can freeze**

Sharon H. Rowe
The Greenbrier

LEMON TORTE
"Totally easy crust"

Crust:
1 5½-oz. pkg. lemon crunch
 cookies, finely crushed
6 Tbsp. butter, melted

Lemon filling:
4 eggs, separated
1 cup sugar
½ cup fresh lemon juice
1½ Tbsp. grated lemon peel
1½ cups whipping cream,
 whipped

Topping:
1 10-oz. pkg. frozen raspberries,
 thawed

Crust:
Blend crushed cookies and butter well. Pat into bottom and sides of an 8½" springform pan. Refrigerate.

Filling:
Beat egg whites until foamy, gradually add sugar, beating constantly until stiff peaks form. In separate bowl, beat egg yolks until thick and lemon-colored. Stir in lemon juice and lemon peel. Gently fold in egg whites, blending well. Gently fold in cream. Pour into crust and freeze.

Topping: Purée raspberries in processor or blender. Press through strainer into a serving bowl. Let torte stand at room temperature for 10 minutes before serving. Remove springform pan. Transfer to serving platter. Pour on raspberries as serving each piece.

Preparation: 30 min.   **Moderately difficult**   **Serves: 8**
                             Must do ahead   **Must freeze**

Jane Birnie

HUNGARIAN DESSERT
"Try your hand at a flaming dessert"

Palachinka or crepes:
4 eggs
4 Tbsp. sugar
2 cups milk
1 cup + 1 Tbsp. flour
¼ tsp. cinnamon, ground
margarine

Filling:
4 pints heavy cream
1 tsp. sugar
1½ cups finely ground nuts,
 hazelnuts or walnuts
1 Tbsp. sugar
½ tsp. cinnamon
3-4 Tbsp. Cognac, Brandy or
 Amaretto

Crepes:
Mix all ingredients in blender. Heat medium-sized skillet (medium to high temperature) and melt dab of margarine, tipping skillet to spread over bottom for each crepe. Place ½-¾ soup ladle full of mixture into pan. Tip to spread. Edges will crisp slightly - then turn over and cook (about 1 minute each in total cooking time). Turn out onto large platter. Fill and serve, or cool and heat in microwave for 2 minutes before using.

Filling:
Whip cream with sugar (add more sugar, to taste). Mix nuts, sugar, cinnamon and liqueur together. Fold in ¾ of the whipped cream mixture. Divide mixture among crepes, place on large serving dish seam-side down. Heat additional liqueur, pour over crepes and ignite at table. Serve individual crepes with remaining whipped cream on top.

Preparation: 30 min.   **Moderately difficult**   **Serves: 10**
Cooking: 30 min.   **Can do ahead**   **Can freeze**

Lynn Popovich

ECLAIR TORTE

"Layers of graham crackers and vanilla pudding - a happy blend"

Crust:
graham crackers (whole)

Filling:
2 3½-oz. instant vanilla or
  French vanilla pudding
3 cups milk
9 oz. whipped topping

Glaze:
2 1-oz. squares unsweetened
  chocolate
3 Tbsp. butter
2 Tbsp. light corn syrup
3 Tbsp. milk
1 tsp. vanilla
1½ cups powdered sugar, sifted
1 tsp. granulated sugar

Crust:
Line bottom of a 9x13" pan with whole graham crackers.

Filling:
Mix pudding and milk. Beat on low speed for 2 minutes. Fold in whipped topping. Spread one half of the filling over crackers. Then put another layer of crackers over filling. Add remaining filling. Top with one final layer of crackers.

Glaze:
Melt chocolate and butter over very low heat. Add corn syrup, milk and vanilla. Blend. Add sugars and mix, until spreading consistency. (If too thick, add a drop or two of hot water.) Pour glaze over top and spread evenly.

Refrigerate at least 6 hours. May be made a day ahead.

| Preparation: 20 min. | Easy | Serves: 8-12 |
| Cooking: 5 min. for glaze | Must do ahead | |

Karen G. Smith

"ORESTES" CHOCOLATE PARFAIT

"Tia Maria and Rum add special flavor"

4 eggs
½ cup sugar
2 oz. semi-sweet chocolate
1 lb. Marscapone cheese*
36 Amaretti cookies*
6 oz. Rum
6 oz. Tia Maria
¼ cup almonds, toasted and
  sliced

*Amaretti cookies and Marscapone cheese can be purchased at a specialty grocer.

In a non-reactive bowl, whip the eggs and sugar with an electric mixer until ribbons form. Melt the chocolate in a small bowl over double boiler. Slowly add the melted chocolate to the egg mixture, while whipping. Remove the egg mixture from the mixer and fold in Marscapone cheese. In 12 saucer champagne glasses, or small glass bowls, place 3 Amaretti cookies and drizzle with the liqueurs. Spoon the cheese mixture over the cookies and sprinkle with toasted almonds.

NOTE: This dessert is best if made 3-6 hours prior to serving, so the cookies get a bit soft.

| Preparation: 20 min. | Easy | Serves: 12 |
| | Should do ahead | |

Vince Sanzotti, Executive Chef
The Westin William Penn

INDIVIDUAL GRAND MARNIER SOUFFLÉS
"Worth the time"

7 Tbsp. butter
⅔ cup flour
2 cups milk
⅔ cup sugar
6 Tbsp. orange liqueur
8 egg yolks
8 egg whites
½ tsp. salt
½ tsp. cream of tartar

Sauce:
1 cup cream or Half & Half
1 whole egg
½ cup sugar
1 Tbsp. orange liqueur

Melt butter and stir in flour; blend thoroughly. Whip in milk. Add sugar to the flour mixture and stir. Add orange liqueur and stir. Blend in egg yolks and continue to cook mixture for about 1 minute on low heat. Cool. Put a piece of butter wrap on top. Beat egg whites until stiff, but not dry. As you beat, add salt and cream of tartar. Fold egg whites into cooled roux. Butter and sugar individual soufflé cups. Spoon mix into soufflé cups. (At this point, soufflés may be held, covered loosely, in a draft-free place for up to an hour. They may also be wrapped in aluminum foil at this point and frozen.) Bake in a bain marie (water bath) at 350° for 45-60 minutes.

NOTE: To bake after freezing, do not thaw; but unwrap before baking according to above directions.

Sauce: Combine ingredients in a double boiler, stirring continually until it coats back of spoon.

Preparation: 40 min.   Difficult   Serves: 8-10
Cooking: 45 min.   Can do ahead   Can freeze

Lorraine Trice

FRESH PEACH BUTTERMILK SHERBET
"Serve with fresh peaches and black raspberries"

3 medium peaches, pitted and
  sliced
1 cup sugar
1 egg
4½ tsp. lemon juice
1½ tsp. vanilla
dash salt
2 cups buttermilk

In blender, purée peach slices with all ingredients, except buttermilk. Stir in buttermilk. Pour into ice cream maker and freeze according to manufacturer's instructions. It will not be solid, but will just keep its shape. Pack into freezing containers. Freeze firm.

Preparation: 20-30 min.   Easy   Serves: 10
                           Must do ahead   Must freeze

Mary Martha Emmert

APPLE CHEESE TORTE

"Pretty with the apples on top"

Crust:
½ cup margarine
⅓ cup sugar
¼ tsp. vanilla
1 cup flour

Filling:
8 oz. cream cheese, softened
¼ cup sugar
1 egg
½ tsp. vanilla

Topping:
¼ cup sugar
½ tsp. cinnamon
4 cups apple slices
⅓ cup sliced almonds

Crust:
Cream together margarine, sugar and vanilla. Blend in flour and spread in the bottom of a 9" springform pan and 1¼"-1½" up the side.

Filling:
Combine all ingredients; mix well and pour into crust.

Topping:
Combine sugar and cinnamon. Toss with apple slices. Gently spoon over filling; sprinkle with almonds.

Bake at 450° for 10 minutes. Reduce heat to 400° and bake 25 minutes longer. Cool before removing from pan.

| Preparation: | 35 min. | Easy | Serves: 6 |
| Cooking: | 35 min. | Can do ahead | |

Marion F. Shaw

PUMPKIN CHEESE ROLL

"Can be a wonderful holiday gift"

3 eggs
⅔ cup pumpkin
1 cup sugar
1 tsp. lemon juice
¾ cup flour
1 tsp. baking powder
2 tsp. cinnamon
1 tsp. ginger
½ tsp. nutmeg
½ tsp. salt
1 cup chopped walnuts

Filling:
1 8-oz. pkg. cream cheese, softened
1 cup powdered sugar
4 Tbsp. margarine
½ tsp. vanilla

powdered sugar for rolling

Beat eggs for 5 minutes; then add next 3 ingredients. Fold in sifted dry ingredients. Add walnuts. Grease a jellyroll pan and line with waxed paper. Bake for 15 minutes at 350°. Remove from oven and turn over on powdered sugared tea towel while cake is still hot. Peel off waxed paper and roll like a jelly roll, still in towel. Cool 15 minutes. Refrigerate at least 2 hours. Remove from refrigerator and carefully unroll and spread with filling. Reroll. Divide roll into thirds, wrap and freeze.

| Preparation: | 35 min. | Moderately difficult | Serves: 15-20 |
| Cooking: | 15 min. | Must do ahead | Must freeze |

Mary W. Scott

STRAWBERRY CHANTILLY WITH RASPBERRY SAUCE
"A spectacular dessert"

4 large egg whites
1 cup sugar
½ tsp. vanilla
1 qt. raspberry sherbet OR ice
   cream OR strawberry ice
   cream
1 pt. heavy cream
2 Tbsp. Chambord
2 Tbsp. strawberry preserves

Sauce:
1 10-oz. pkg. frozen raspberries
1 pt. strawberries, sliced
2 Tbsp. Cassis or Chambord

Garnish:
Strawberries
Mint leaves

Preheat oven to 275°. Beat egg whites to soft peaks. Gradually add sugar and vanilla and beat until stiff. Spread meringue onto 3 (7") parchment or brown paper circles placed on cookie sheets. Bake for 50-55 minutes, or until dry. Turn off oven and leave meringues until cool. Line an 8" springform pan with foil and spread ice cream or sherbet evenly. Freeze. Beat cream to soft-peak stage. Add Chambord and preserves and beat until stiff.

Sauce:
Process raspberries in food processor. Strain. Gently stir in sliced berries and Cassis or Chambord. Refrigerate.

Assembly:
Place one meringue on plate. Invert ice cream on it; remove foil. Top with second meringue and spread with about 1 cup of cream mixture. Top with third meringue. Cover top and side with remaining cream. Freeze. Garnish and serve with the sauce.

NOTE: This could also be done in individual meringue shells without layering. Fill with ice cream, top with cream mixture. Garnish and serve with sauce.

Preparation: 35 min.	Moderately difficult	Serves: 6-8
Cooking: 50-55 min.	Must do ahead	Must freeze

Carolyn S. Hammer

UNFORGETTABLE CHOCOLATE MOUSSE
"So smooth and satisfying"

6 oz. semi-sweet chocolate
2 Tbsp. Kahlua
1 Tbsp. orange juice
2 egg yolks
2 whole eggs
1 tsp. vanilla
¼ cup sugar
1 cup whipping cream
whipped cream and chocolate
   shavings for garnish

Melt chocolate in Kahlua and orange juice over very low heat. Set aside. Put egg yolks and eggs in blender with vanilla and sugar. Blend 2 minutes at medium-high speed. Add cream and blend 30 seconds. Add chocolate mixture and blend until smooth. Pour into bowl or small individual cups. Chill for 1-2 hours. Garnish.

Preparation: 20 min.	Easy	Serves: 4-5
	Must do ahead	

Gretchen S. Hansen

POACHED PEARS AU CHOCOLAT WITH ORANGE CREME ANGLAISE

"Très fancy"

Sauce:
1¾ cups milk
½ cup sugar
4 egg yolks
1 Tbsp. Grand Marnier

Pears:
1 750-ml bottle inexpensive
  Champagne
½ cup sugar
zest of 1 orange
1 whole clove
4 d'Anjou pears with stems

12 oz. semi-sweet chocolate
4 oz. pistachio nuts, shelled,
  cleaned and coarsely chopped

Sauce:
Bring milk to a boil in saucepan. Remove from heat. In small bowl, gradually beat sugar into egg yolks at high speed of mixer until pale (about 6 minutes). Continue beating at medium speed while very slowly adding hot milk in thin stream. Pour mixture into heavy saucepan. Stir gently, but continuously, over medium heat until sauce coats spoon (sauce will be thin). Pour sauce into a bowl placed inside of another bowl filled with ice water. Stir in Grand Marnier. Cool 5 minutes; stir gently. Place clear plastic wrap directly on surface of sauce. Refrigerate at least 4 hours.

Pears:
In large saucepan, combine Champagne, sugar, orange zest and clove. Bring to a boil. Meanwhile, peel pears, leaving stems on. Place pears in boiling mixture. Reduce heat. Cover and simmer for 5 minutes. Remove from heat and let stand, covered, until tender, but firm (about 20 minutes). Remove pears and refrigerate for 30 minutes. Drain on paper towels.

Melt chocolate in double boiler. Stir until smooth. Holding pears by stem, spoon chocolate over pears, coating evenly. Sprinkle with nuts. Refrigerate until serving time. Spoon 2 Tbsp. of creme sauce on each plate and place pear in center.

NOTE: Sounds difficult; but it is really easy and looks smashing for a dinner party!

Preparation: 45 min.	Moderately difficult	Serves: 4
Cooking: 30 min.	Must do ahead	

Lynn Popovich

RASPBERRY-BANANA SORBET

"A very lo-cal dessert"

1 frozen banana
1 pt. fresh raspberries
mint sprig for garnish

Peel banana and clean berries. Put both in blender or food processor. Blend until whipped consistency. Garnish with mint sprig.

Preparation: 5 min	Easy	Serves: 2
	Serve immediately	Can freeze

Natasha S. Green

PENNY'S LEMON LUSH

"How about a garnish of twisted lemon slices"

1 cup flour
1 stick butter or margarine
½-1 cup crushed walnuts
1 8-oz. pkg. cream cheese
1 cup powdered sugar
1 + cup Cool Whip topping
2 3½-oz. pkgs. lemon instant
   pudding
3 cups cold milk
whipped topping

Mix the flour, butter and walnuts together. Spread on the bottom of two 9" pie plates or one 9x13" pan. Bake at 350° for 15-20 minutes until lightly browned. Let cool a bit. Beat together the cream cheese, sugar and whipped topping and put into crust. Mix together the pudding and milk and put on top of cream cheese mixture. Top with remaining whipped topping.

NOTE: Can cut recipe in half (keeps in refrigerator a day or two).

Preparation: 30 min.   Easy   Serves: 8-12
Cooking: 15-20 min.   Can do ahead

Gretchen R. Burnham

APRICOT SOUFFLÉS

"For apricot lovers only"

butter and sugar for cups
1 11-oz. box dried apricots
½ cup sugar
6 eggs, separated
⅛ tsp. salt
1 qt. milk
½ cup sugar
1 tsp. vanilla

Butter and sugar 8 large custard cups. Cook apricots - add water to cover and bring to a boil; simmer for 15 minutes. Drain. Purée apricots in food processor, adding ½ cup sugar. Beat egg whites stiffly. Fold purée into egg whites. Put mixture into cups. Set cups in pan of hot water. Bake in 275° oven until firm (about 40 minutes). Cool soufflés in water in which they are cooked. Cook egg yolks, salt, milk and sugar until custard coats spoon thoroughly. Custard will be thin. Add vanilla after custard is cooked. When serving, pour custard over soufflés. Serve extra custard in bowl.

Preparation: 30-45 min.   Easy   Serves: 8
Cooking: 40 min.   Can do ahead

Carol Regan Dickson

CANDIED VIOLETS

"Everyone will be SO impressed"

egg whites
violets (wild)
granulated sugar, extra fine

Beat an egg white until frothy, not stiff. Dip violets in egg white and lay out on waxed paper. Sift granulated sugar over violets, making sure to cover both sides. Dry completely (MAY TAKE TWO WEEKS). Pack in tight tin. Use as decorations on your fancy desserts!! MAY BE EATEN!!

Preparation: 20 min.   Easy
                     Must do ahead

Jane VanKirk

TRIPLE CHOCOLATE BROWNIE TART

"A terrific tart, sweet and rich"

Crust:
1 cup flour
¼ cup brown sugar
1 oz. unsweetened chocolate, shaved
1 stick butter
2 Tbsp. milk

Filling:
½ cup chocolate chips
3 oz. unsweetened chocolate
1 stick butter
1½ cups sugar
3 eggs
¾ cup flour
½ cup chocolate chips
½ cup chopped nuts
1 tsp. vanilla

Icing:
½ cup chocolate chips
4 Tbsp. butter
1 Tbsp. vegetable oil

Crust:
In bowl, mix flour, brown sugar and unsweetened chocolate. Cut in butter until it resembles coarse meal. Add milk and mix until dough gathers into ball. Press into bottom and up sides of a 9" tart pan.

Filling:
Melt ½ cup chocolate chips and unsweetened chocolate over a double boiler. Remove from heat. Stir in butter, one Tbsp. at a time, until melted. Stir in sugar, and eggs one at a time. Stir in flour, the other ½ cup of chocolate chips, nuts and vanilla. Pour into crust and bake at 350° for 45 minutes.

Icing:
While filling is baking, melt chocolate chips, butter and oil over double boiler. Stir until smooth. Remove from heat. After tart is baked, refrigerate for 1 hour. Take out and smooth icing over top. Refrigerate ½ hour more to set icing.

NOTE: Best served at room temperature.

Preparation:	30 min.	Easy	Serves: 10-12
Cooking:	45 min.	Must do ahead	Can freeze

Noreen G. Prokopovich
The Ultimate Pastry Shop

THREE BERRY COBBLER

"Summer or winter, this is a winner"

1½ cups sugar
5 cups blueberries, raspberries, strawberries (if frozen, and thawed, remove 1 cup liquid)
1 cup flour
1½ tsp. baking powder
1 tsp. cinnamon
¼ tsp. salt
1 cup warmed milk
½ tsp. vanilla
1 stick butter

Sprinkle ½ cup sugar over berries and let stand. Combine remaining sugar and dry ingredients, then add milk and vanilla. Stir to moisten. Melt butter and put in large oval dish. Add batter, then top with berries. Bake at 350° for 30 minutes. Increase heat to 400° and bake an additional 15 minutes.

Preparation:	20-25 min.	Easy	Serves: 10-12
Cooking:	45 min.	Can do ahead	

Mrs. John A. Lindquist

DATE AND NUT TORTE

"Even if you hate dates, you'll still love this"

1 cup boiling water
1 cup finely chopped dates
½ cup flour
1 tsp. baking soda
1 tsp. salt
1 cup nuts, chopped
1 egg, beaten
1 cup sugar
1 Tbsp. oil or melted butter
½ tsp. vanilla

Pour boiling water over dates. Sift flour, soda and salt together. Add nuts, egg, sugar, oil, and vanilla. Add to date mixture. Mix well. Pour into an 8x8" greased pan. Bake at 275° for 1½ hours. Serve with ice cream or whipped cream.

Preparation: 20 min.   Easy   Serves: 6-8
Cooking: 1½ hrs.   Can do ahead

Mrs. Allan W. Beatty

BARBARA'S BOMBE

"Whipped cream and ice cream - dieters beware!"

1 cup sugar
½ cup slivered almonds
2 cups heavy cream
1 cup chocolate syrup
1 qt. pink or green ice cream
   (any flavor)

Make praline by stirring sugar in saucepan over medium heat until liquified; add slivered almonds. Pour on greased cookie sheet quickly. Cool. Place hardened brittle into blender or food processor. Chop into crunchy

pieces. Whip heavy cream and add chocolate syrup. After cream and chocolate are whipped, add praline pieces. Pour into jello mold. Freeze overnight. Unmold by inverting onto plate and placing hot, wet towels over mold. Soften ice cream and cover frozen chocolate with ice cream using a spatula. Refreeze. Slice to serve. Serve immediately.

Preparation: 45 min.   Moderately difficult   Serves: 6-8
     Must do ahead   Must freeze

Barbara Laman Gaudio

FRIED APPLE SLICES OR FRITTERS

3 egg yolks
1 Tbsp. sugar
6-8 oz. white wine
1 cup milk
¼ tsp. salt
½ lb. flour, sifted
6 large apples, sliced (your
   favorite)
cinnamon and sugar to sprinkle
   on apple slices and on top

Mix first 6 ingredients together to make dough, remember to add wine slowly—you want the consistency of pie dough. Roll out and cut in thin squares. Place apple slices in center. Sprinkle with cinnamon and sugar. Bring the four corners to center and seal. Drop into hot grease and fry until golden brown. Remove and drain on paper. While warm, sprinkle with cinnamon and sugar.

Preparation: 30 min.   Easy   Yield: 24-30 fritters
Cooking: 2 min/fritter   Serve immediately

Jeanne L. Vanich

APRICOT AND NUT ROLL

"Even better when made the day before"

¾ cup dried apricots
½ cup apricot preserves
½ cup sugar
6 eggs, separated
1 cup firmly-packed dark brown
  sugar
8 oz. walnut or pecan halves,
  finely ground
1 tsp. baking powder
powdered sugar
1½ cups heavy cream, whipped

In small saucepan, simmer apricots in water to cover until tender. Drain; reserve juices. Place in blender, add preserves and granulated sugar. Whirl 2-3 minutes, adding juice if mixture seems too thick. Set aside. Beat egg yolks with brown sugar until double in volume. Beat in ground walnuts, reserving some for garnish, and the baking powder. Separately, beat egg whites until stiff. Spoon ⅓ of whites into nut batter and blend to lighten. Fold in remaining whites. Pour batter into a 10x15″ jelly roll pan that has been buttered, lined with wax paper, and buttered again. Bake 20 minutes at 350°. Remove from oven, cover with a damp dish towel and let cool for 15 minutes. Remove towel. Cut off piece of wax paper 20″ long. Sift a dusting of powdered sugar over wax paper. Turn cake out of pan, upside down, onto sugared paper. Carefully roll cake up lengthwise sandwiched between the two wax papers. Cover completely with damp towel. Set aside (not necessary to refrigerate) until ready to finish. Remove towel and unroll. Peel off top piece of wax paper. Spread with puréed apricots and top with ⅔ of whipped cream within 1″ of cake edges. Using bottom piece of wax paper, gently roll cake lengthwise. Transfer to serving dish, seam side down. Spread with remaining cream and sprinkle with reserved nuts. Refrigerate until ready to serve. (Will hold for 4 hours.)

Preparation: 1 hr.   Moderately difficult   Serves: 12
Cooking: 20 min.

Hannah Wedeen

BLUEBERRY TORTE

"Rather like a cheesecake"

Crust:
1 pkg. graham crackers
½ cup powdered sugar
¾ stick butter, melted

Crust:
Crush graham crackers. Add sugar and butter. Press in a 9-10″ round pan.

Filling:
1 8-oz. pkg. cream cheese,
  softened and well-beaten
2 eggs
½ cup sugar

Filling:
Blend all ingredients together. Pour into crust.

Bake in a 375° oven for 10 minutes. Let cool. Spread 1 can blueberry pie filling on top. Serve with whipped cream.

Topping:
1 can blueberry pie filling
whipped cream

Preparation: 20 min.   Easy   Serves: 6-8
Cooking: 10 min.   Can do ahead

Christina R. Bradley

CRUNCHY FRUIT TART

"Very easy, very colorful, very wonderful"

Base:
¾ cup soft brown sugar
12 Tbsp. butter
2½ cups quick oats

Middle:
½ pt. plain yogurt (1 cup)
¼ pt. sour cream (1/2 cup)
2 oz. extra fine sugar (1/4 cup)
lemon rind, grated (optional)

Topping:
Strawberries OR raspberries OR
  blueberries OR a mixture of all
  three
½ lb. red currant jelly OR clear
  red jam for glaze (in winter a
  good raspberry OR black
  cherry jam makes a good
  alternative)

whipped cream (optional)

Preheat oven to 350°. Place brown sugar and butter in a saucepan; let it melt, but do not let it boil. Remove from heat and stir in oats. Grease a 9-10" china or aluminum flan dish. Put mixture in the dish and spread evenly. Bake in top half of oven for 15-20 minutes. Cool slightly. Stir the yogurt, sour cream, sugar and lemon peel together and pour onto base. Put dish back in the oven for 8 minutes. Cool. Slice the strawberries in half and arrange on top. Melt the red currant jelly gently and glaze the fruit with it. (Either spoon it over or use a pastry brush — a Tbsp. of water added to the jelly makes it easier to pour.) Once you have glazed, keep it in a cool place (NOT THE REFRIGERATOR). You can make the first 2 layers the day before, but do not put the fruit on top sooner than 2-3 hours before eating it. Serve with whipped cream and use a sharp knife to cut into the crisp base.

NOTE: To make extra fine sugar, place granulated sugar in food processor for a few seconds.

Preparation: 20-25 min.	Easy	Serves: 6-8
Cooking: 25-30 min.	Can do ahead	

Vivian Brown

CHILLED LEMON FLAN

"A no-bake delight"

Filling:
½ pint heavy cream
12 oz. condensed milk (do not
  use the whole 14 oz. can)
juice of 4 lemons
grated rind of 4 lemons

Crust:
graham cracker ready-crust

Topping:
whipped cream
fresh or crystallized lemon
  slices

Mix together cream, condensed milk and finely grated lemon rind. Slowly beat in lemon juice. Pour mixture into the crust and chill overnight. Just before serving, decorate the flan with a whirl of cream and the lemon slices.
NOTE: Microwave lemons for 45 seconds to get more juice.

Preparation: 15 min.	Easy	Serves: 8
	Must do ahead	Can freeze

Jean I. MacMurray

HEAVENLY TORTE

"Attention, chocolate lovers"

Meringue:
3 egg whites
½ tsp. almond extract
¼ tsp. salt
¾ cup brown sugar

Filling-frosting:
1 6-oz. pkg. (1 cup) semi-sweet
  chocolate morsels
1 8-oz. pkg. cream cheese,
  softened
1 Tbsp. milk
¾ cup brown sugar
⅛ tsp. salt
1 cup heavy cream, whipped
1 tsp. vanilla

½ cup finely chopped nuts,
  optional

Meringue:
Preheat oven to 300°. Cut three 8" circles from brown paper. Beat egg whites, almond extract and salt until stiff peaks form. Add brown sugar gradually until peaks are stiff and glossy. Spread evenly among the three brown paper circles. Place in preheated oven for 35 minutes. Cool. Peel paper off gently.

Filling-frosting:
Melt chocolate (microwave or stove top). Cool approximately 10 minutes. Beat cream cheese and milk until creamy. Gradually add brown sugar and salt and beat. Fold into the semi-sweet chocolate, the cream cheese mixture, whipped cream, and vanilla. Spread evenly on the three meringue circles. Stack in layers. Chill for several hours or overnight. Cut in wedges to serve.

NOTE: Use filling-frosting as a frosting on angel food cake.

Preparation: 40 min.	**Moderately difficult**	**Serves: 12-16**
Cooking: 35 min.	**Must do ahead**	**Can freeze**

Maureen T. Senetra

APPLE DUMPLINGS AND SAUCE

Pastry:
2 cups flour
2 tsp. baking powder
1 tsp. salt
½ cup butter or margarine
⅔ cup cold milk
8 medium apples, peeled and
   cored
sugar and cinnamon

Sauce:
½ cup sugar
6 Tbsp. flour or cornstarch
pinch salt
½ cup water
1 qt. milk
1 tsp. vanilla

Pastry:
Mix dry ingredients; cut in short-ening and add milk a little at a time. Roll dough and cut into 8 squares. Place apple in center of each square. In center of apple, put a pat of butter and sprinkle with a little sugar and cinnamon. Wrap apple with dough and place on cookie sheet. Bake at 425° for 40 minutes or until crust is golden and apples are tender.

Sauce:
Blend sugar, flour, and salt in a 2-quart saucepan. Stir in water and milk. Cook over medium heat, stirring constantly, until mix-ture thickens and boils. Boil and stir for one minute. Remove from heat, add vanilla. Pour over warm apple dumplings in dessert dishes.

Preparation: 45 min.	Moderately difficult	Serves: 8
Cooking: 40 min.	Can do ahead	Can freeze

Joan M. Fitzpatrick

BANANA BUTTERSCOTCH RUM SAUCE WITH ICE CREAM
"A terrific taste treat"

½ cup (1 stick) butter
½ cup packed brown sugar
⅛ cup dark Rum
4 small, ripe (not over-ripe)
   bananas, cut into halves
   lengthwise
4 large scoops of banana (or
   vanilla) ice cream

Combine butter and sugar in a 2-cup glass measuring cup. Microwave on High for 1½ minutes, stirring after 45 seconds. Stir in Rum. Pour mix-ture into a shallow glass baking dish, large enough to hold bananas in single layer. Place bananas in sauce. Cook in micro-wave on High, uncovered, for 45 seconds. Turn bananas over and cook an additional 45 seconds. Place ice cream on dessert plates. Spoon sauce over and arrange banana half on each side.

Preparation: 3 min.	Easy	Serves: 4
Cooking: 3 min.	Serve immediately	

Tina Morrison

FROZEN LEMON CREAM

"For a pretty presentation - serve in half orange shell"

3 cups whipping cream
  (1½ pints)
½ cup lemon juice
1¼ cups sugar
3 Tbsp. grated lemon peel
whipped cream and mint leaves
  for garnish

In a large bowl, mix cream, juice, sugar and lemon peel until blended. Pour into 8 small serving dishes or orange shells. Cover with foil. Freeze overnight. DO NOT THAW! Garnish with whipped cream and mint leaves, if desired.

Preparation: 15 min.   Easy   Serves: 8
                              Must do ahead   Must freeze

Gae C. Bradley

ROSE RASPBERRY SAUCE

"Lovely to look at, so easy to make"

1 10-oz. pkg. sweetened frozen
  raspberries, thawed
¼ cup sugar
2 Tbsp. cornstarch
½ cup rose wine

Combine berries, sugar and cornstarch in a 4-cup glass measuring cup, blending well. Cook in microwave for 3-3½ minutes*, stirring once or twice, until mixture thickens and clears. Add wine and cook 1½ minutes* longer, stirring once. Serve hot or chilled.

*Time may vary with different microwaves.

Preparation: 2 min.   Easy   Yield: 2 cups
Cooking: 8 min.   Can do ahead

Tina Morrison

CHOCOLATE SAUCE

"Has a slight hint of caramel"

1 13-oz. can evaporated milk
1 lb. caramels
1 cup butter
12 oz. semi-sweet chocolate
  chips OR 1 12-oz. chocolate
  bar

In top of double boiler, combine milk, caramels, butter and chocolate. Stir until smooth and cook for 30 minutes, stirring frequently. Remove from heat and beat 3 minutes with electric mixer. Serve warm or refrigerate.

Preparation: 10 min.   Easy   Serves: 20
Cooking: 30-40 min.   Can do ahead

Marilyn Linford

PIES

NANA'S PLUM PIE
"Try your local farmers market for plums"

Filling:
26-30 prune plums*
½ cup sugar
2 Tbsp. flour
1 Tbsp. lemon juice

Crust:
3 cups flour
**1 cup shortening (Crisco - not
  butter-flavored)**
pinch of salt
½ cup ice water
butter

***NOTE: Prune plums are only
available in late summer, early
fall.**

Filling:
Wash plums. Cut plums in half
and remove pits. Place plums in
a large mixing bowl and add
sugar, flour and lemon juice. Mix.

Crust:
In large mixing bowl, place flour,
shortening and salt. Cut shortening into the flour and salt by
briskly rubbing it between your
hands. Pastry dough is ready
when mixture is thoroughly
blended and resembles coarse
meal. Add ice water and mix
together quickly by squeezing
with your hands and forming into
a large ball. Divide ball into two
parts. Roll each part between two sheets of wax paper. Place first crust
in one 10″ pie plate. Add plum mixture. Dot with butter. Before placing
top crust on pie, puncture crust with fork 6-8 times, then place on pie.
Fold sides of bottom crust over top and crimp. Remove excess with
knife. Brown in hot oven - 450° for 10 minutes, then lower to 350° and
bake for 1 hour. Cool. Best served warm!

Preparation: 30 min.	Easy	Serves: 8
Cooking: 1 hr. 10 min.	Can do ahead	Can freeze

Pam Gregg

214

TRIPLE BROWNIE PIE

"A triple threat chocolate treat"

Crust:
1 cup flour
¼ cup packed brown sugar
1 oz. Hershey's baking chocolate, grated
1 stick butter
2 Tbsp. milk
1 tsp. vanilla

Filling:
3 oz. Hershey's baking chocolate
1 oz. Hershey's semi-sweet chocolate chips
1 stick butter
1½ cups sugar
3 large eggs, beaten
2 tsp. vanilla
¾ cup chopped walnuts
¾ cup flour

Glaze:
4 oz. Hershey's semi-sweet chocolate chips
½ stick butter
2 tsp. honey

Crust:
Combine flour, brown sugar and grated chocolate. Cut in butter until mixture resembles coarse meal. Lightly blend in milk and vanilla. Press into a 10″ tart pan.

Filling:
Preheat oven to 350°. Melt chocolate in top of a double-boiler over simmering water.* Remove from heat and add butter which has been cut into 6 pieces. After butter has melted, pour mixture into a large bowl. Add sugar and beat well. Slowly add beaten eggs and mix thoroughly. Mix in vanilla and stir in walnuts. Carefully blend in flour. Pour into prepared shell. Bake until a knife inserted into center comes out clean. Do not overbake, should take 20-25 minutes. Let cool on rack.

Glaze:
Melt chocolate chips in top of double-boiler over gently simmering water.* Remove from heat and add butter, stir until melted. Add honey. Pour over cooled tart, spreading glaze to within 1″ of edge. Let stand until set and cut into wedges to serve.

*May microwave in glass bowl until melted, approximately 1 minute.

Preparation: 30 min.	Moderately difficult	Serves: 8
Cooking: 20-25 min.	Can do ahead	

Susan Mottern

CANDY BAR PIE

"Almonds are a nice surprise"

1 tsp. instant coffee
2 Tbsp. hot water
7½ oz. Hershey's chocolate bar with almonds
4 cups Cool Whip
1 graham cracker crust

In medium saucepan, dissolve instant coffee in hot water. Add candy bar. Stir over low heat until melted. Remove from heat. Fold into Cool Whip. Fill pie crust and freeze. Serve with Cool Whip garnish.

Preparation: 7 min.	Easy	Serves: 6-8
	Must do ahead	Must freeze

Robyn Johnson

PUMPKIN-PRALINE CHIFFON PIE

"Be sure you can buy eggnog"

1 10" pie crust, unbaked
5 Tbsp. unsalted butter
½ cup packed light brown sugar
¾ cup chopped walnuts
¾ cup granulated sugar
1½ envelopes unflavored
  gelatin
1 tsp. cinnamon
¼ tsp. nutmeg
½ tsp. ginger
1½ cups eggnog
3 egg yolks
1 16-oz. can pumpkin
3 egg whites
¼ tsp. cream of tartar
1 cup heavy cream

Bake pie crust in preheated 450° oven for 10 minutes. Beat butter and brown sugar in small bowl until blended. Stir in nuts. Spread over bottom of pastry shell. Bake 5 minutes longer until sugar is bubbly. Cool. Combine ½ cup granulated sugar, gelatin, cinnamon, nutmeg and ginger in saucepan. Mix in eggnog and egg yolks. Cook over medium heat, stirring until mixture is very hot and thick enough to leave a path on spoon when finger is drawn across; DO NOT BOIL. Remove from heat. Stir in pumpkin. Cook until thick enough to mound. Beat whites of eggs in large bowl until foamy. Beat in cream of tartar until soft peaks form. Gradually beat in remaining sugar until stiff. Spoon over pumpkin mixture. Beat cream until stiff in large bowl. Fold pumpkin with egg whites into whipped cream and spoon into pastry shell. Refrigerate for 4 hours.

Preparation:	1 hr.	Easy	Serves: 10
Cooking:	10 min.	Must do ahead	

Jean C. Kestner

SPANISH GOLDEN APPLE PIE

"Don't know why this is Spanish"

1 9" pastry shell, unbaked
1 egg white
½ cup sugar
2 Tbsp. flour
⅛ tsp. salt
1 cup sour cream
1 egg yolk
1 tsp. vanilla
4 cups pared, cored and
  chopped Golden Delicious
  apples (about 3 large)

Brush pastry shell with beaten egg white. Bake at 375° for 7 minutes. Combine sugar, flour, and salt. Stir in sour cream, remainder of egg white, yolk, and vanilla; beat until smooth. Stir in apples. Pour into partially-baked pastry shell. Bake at 375° for 45 minutes. Spread Streusel topping over apples. Bake 20 minutes longer, or until knife inserted near center comes out clean. Serve warm or chilled.

Streusel topping:

⅓ cup sugar
⅓ cup flour
1 tsp. cinnamon
¼ cup butter or margarine

Streusel topping:

Combine sugar, flour and cinnamon. Cut in butter or margarine until crumbly. (Makes 1 cup)

Preparation:	15 min.	Easy	Serves: 8
Cooking:	1 - 1½ hrs.	Can do ahead	

Phyllis Strauss

STRAWBERRIES & CREAM CRUMB PIE

"A no-bake summertime treat"

Crust:
1½ cups fine vanilla wafer
   crumbs
⅓ cup butter or margarine,
   melted

Cream layer:
½ cup butter
1½ cups powdered sugar
2 eggs, beaten

Fruit layer:
½ pint whipping cream
2 10-oz. pkgs. frozen strawberries or raspberries*,
   well-drained
4 Tbsp. fine vanilla wafer
   crumbs

*Alternate Fruit Layer:
1 can (small) crushed pineapple,
   well-drained
½ cup maraschino cherries
½ cup chopped nuts

Crust:
Combine crumbs and butter.
Press into an 8″ or 9″ pie plate.
Chill until firm (about 45
minutes).

Cream layer:
Cream butter, stir in sugar. Add
eggs and beat until fluffy. Spoon
into crust. Smooth top and
refrigerate until topping is firm.

Fruit layer:
Whip cream and fold in the
strawberries or raspberries.*
Pour over cream layer and chill
for 24 hours, after covering lightly
with crumbs.

Preparation: 25 min.   **Easy**   **Serves: 6-8**
                        Must do ahead

Phyllis Waits

GRAPE PIE
"Something new and different"

4 cups Concord grapes
½ - 1 cup sugar
3 Tbsp. all-purpose flour
1 Tbsp. lemon juice
1 Tbsp. melted butter
Pastry for 9" double crust pie

Wash and remove grapes from stem. Remove skins by gently squeezing and reserve skins. In a heavy saucepan, heat grape pulp to boiling. DO NOT ADD WATER TO PULP. Reduce heat; simmer 5 minutes, stirring to loosen seeds. While hot, press pulp through sieve and remove seeds. Discard seeds. Mix reserved skins with pulp.

NOTE: Grapes may be frozen at this point for future use. To use: thaw and continue with recipe.

Combine sugar and flour; add to grapes along with lemon juice and melted butter. Pour mixture into unbaked pie crust. Add top crust, seal and flute edges. Make slits in top crust to release steam. Bake at 425° for 10 minutes, then reduce heat to 350° and bake for 30 minutes or until pastry is golden brown and filling bubbles. Remove from oven and cool. Serve with vanilla ice cream, optional.

Preparation: 1 hr.	**Moderately difficult**	**Serves: 8**
Cooking: 40 min.	**Can do ahead**	**Can freeze**

Chris A. Luffy

MOTHER'S STRAWBERRY PIE
"Mother knew best - it's terrific"

1 baked pie crust
1 cup sugar
3 Tbsp. strawberry Jello
  (undissolved)
3 Tbsp. cornstarch
¼ cup cold water
1 cup boiling water
red food coloring
1 Tbsp. butter or margarine
1 tsp. lemon juice
1 qt. washed and freshly
  prepared strawberries
whipped cream (optional)

Mix sugar, Jello, cornstarch and cold water in a saucepan forming a paste. Add 1 cup boiling water and a dash of food coloring. Cook over medium heat until it lightly thickens. Remove from heat; add margarine and lemon juice. Allow mixture to cool. Add strawberries. Pour into prepared pie shell. Do not refrigerate. Top with whipped cream just before serving.

Preparation: 30 min.	**Easy**	**Serves: 6-8**
Cooking: 5 min.	**Must do ahead**	

Dee Ann Sisak

SHAKER LEMON PIE

4 large lemons, thinly sliced
  (leave rind on)
14 oz. sugar
8 eggs
28 oz. pie crust (4 crusts)

Sprinkle the lemon slices with sugar and let marinate for 24 hours. Beat the eggs until foamy and carefully blend with the marinated lemon slices. Line two 9" pie pans with pie crust and ladle the mixture into the pie shells. Cover with remaining pie crusts. Sprinkle with 1 tsp. of granulated sugar. Bake in preheated oven of 450° for 15 minutes, then reduce heat to 375° and bake for about 20 minutes.

Preparation: 15 min.   Easy   Yield: 2 9" pies
Cooking: 30-35 min. Must do ahead   Can freeze

Norbert Bomm, Ex. Chef
Orchard Cafe
Vista International Hotel

ICE CREAM PIE

1 can Pet evaporated milk
6 oz. pkg. semi-sweet chocolate pieces
1 cup miniature marshmallows
¼ tsp. salt
vanilla wafers
1 qt. vanilla ice cream
pecan halves

Stir evaporated milk, chocolate pieces, marshmallows, and salt over medium heat until thick. Cool at room temperature. Line bottom and sides of 9" pie pan with wafers. Spoon ½ of ice cream over wafers. Cover with ½ chocolate mixture. Repeat with ice cream and chocolate. Place pecan halves on top. Freeze until frozen.

Preparation: 30-45 min.   Easy   Serves: 8
                          Must do ahead   Must freeze

Sandy Seymour

LEMONADE PIE

"Give this pie a try in a graham cracker crust"

1 qt. vanilla ice cream,
  softened
1 6-oz. can frozen lemonade
  concentrate, thawed
1 9" pie shell, baked
sliced lemon twists

Combine ice cream and lemonade in blender or food processor until smooth. Pour into pie shell. Freeze until firm (about 1½ hours). Let stand 10 minutes before serving. Garnish with lemon twists.

Preparation: 10 min.   Easy   Serves: 6-8
Cooking: 20 min. - crust   Must do ahead   Must freeze

Tina Morrison

219

RHUBARB CUSTARD PIE

"The first pie of spring"

2 eggs
1½ cups sugar
3 Tbsp. flour
3 Tbsp. milk
dash of salt
3 cups fresh rhubarb, cut up
1 8" or 9" unbaked pastry shell
  (homemade pie crust
  preferably)
butter

Beat first 5 ingredients together. Add rhubarb and pour into pastry shell. Dot the top of pie with butter. Bake at 400° for 40-50 minutes.

Preparation: 15 min.   Easy   Serves: 6-8
Cooking: 40-50 min. Can do ahead

Mary Cronrath

MACADAMIA NUT PIE

"Has a chocolate surprise"

3 eggs
⅔ cup sugar
1 cup light corn syrup
3 Tbsp. melted butter
1 tsp. vanilla
1½ cups chopped macadamia
  nuts
½ cup chocolate chips
1 pie shell, unbaked

Combine eggs, sugar, corn syrup, butter, and vanilla and beat until blended. Stir in nuts. Spread chocolate chips over pie crust in single layer. Turn filling into pie shell and bake at 350° for 45 minutes or until filling is set. Place on wire rack to cool.

Preparation: 20 min.   Easy   Serves: 6-8
Cooking: 45 min.   Can do ahead   Can freeze

Kate Sawyer

"PEACHY" COCONUT PIE

"A cool summery pie"

Filling:
1 3-oz. pkg. peach gelatin
¾ cup boiling water
1 cup peach ice cream
1 cup cold milk
1 3½-oz. pkg. instant coconut
  pudding and pie filling
1 9" pie shell, baked

Glaze:
¼ cup peach Schnapps
  (optional)
¼ cup water
1 Tbsp. lemon juice
1 Tbsp. cornstarch
2 Tbsp. sugar
1 cup fresh sliced peaches

Garnish:
red jelly OR
fresh blueberries or
strawberries

Filling:
Dissolve gelatin in water; add ice cream and stir until melted. Combine milk and pudding mix in small bowl. Beat at low speed for 2 minutes. Add the gelatin mixture. Whip until thick and fluffy. Turn into prepared shell. Chill for 2 hours.

Glaze:
Combine Schnapps, water, sugar, lemon juice, cornstarch and bring to a boil. Continue cooking until thickened, stirring occasionally.* Add peaches and chill. Garnish with jelly or fruit.

*NOTE: This can be done in the microwave - Combine ingredients for glaze in a microwave dish and cook for 3 minutes on HIGH, stirring after 1½ minutes.

Preparation: 20 min.	**Easy**	**Serves: 8**
Cooking: 6 min.	**Must do ahead**	**Can freeze**

Nancy S. Bush

ICE CREAM FRUIT PIE

¼ cup graham cracker crumbs
1 quart vanilla ice cream,
  softened
½ pint pineapple sherbet,
  softened
3 cups assorted fresh fruit

Raspberry Sauce:
2 10-oz. pkgs. frozen
  raspberries, thawed
⅓ cup powdered sugar
2 Tbsp. lemon juice
2 Tbsp. black raspberry liqueur

Lightly grease a 9½" or 10" pie plate. Sprinkle with crumbs; refrigerate to set. Spread vanilla ice cream evenly inside plate to form pie shell. Freeze until firm. Spread sherbet over ice cream. Cover and freeze. Fill with fruit when ready to serve.

Raspberry Sauce:
In processor or blender, combine raspberries and sugar and purée. Strain to remove seeds. Stir in lemon juice and liqueur. Serve over pie.

Preparation: 20 min.	**Easy**	**Serves: 6-8**
	Must do ahead	**Must freeze**

Wendie Riordan

PUMPKIN MERINGUE PIE

"Nice to serve to goblins and witches"

1 9" pie crust
1 Tbsp. unflavored gelatin
⅔ cup brown sugar
½ tsp. salt
1 tsp. cinnamon
½ tsp. nutmeg
½ tsp. ginger
1¼ cups pumpkin
3 eggs, separated
½ cup milk
¼ tsp. cream of tartar
½ cup sugar
whipped cream

Blend gelatin, brown sugar, salt, spices, pumpkin, egg yolks and milk in saucepan. Cook over medium heat, stirring constantly until it boils. Place pan in cold water until mixture mounds slightly when dropped from a spoon. Beat egg whites, then gradually add the cream of tartar and sugar until stiff peaks form. Fold pumpkin mixture into the meringue. Pour into cooled crust, chill at least 2 hours. Garnish with whipped cream.

Preparation: 30 min.   Moderately difficult   Serves: 8-10
Cooking: 20 min.   Must do ahead

Jamie H. Magovern

PUMPKIN ICE CREAM PIE

"Syrup enhances this pie"

Pie:
1 baked 9" pie shell
1 qt. vanilla ice cream
1 cup pumpkin
¾ cup sugar
¼ tsp. salt
¾ tsp. pumpkin pie spice
1 cup whipping cream

Syrup: (optional)
½ cup brown sugar
¼ cup dark corn syrup
¼ cup hot water
½ tsp. vanilla

Pie:
Spread ice cream in cooled pie shell. Freeze until hardened. Blend pumpkin, sugar, salt and spice. Whip cream until stiff and fold into pumpkin mixture. Spoon into frozen pie shell over ice cream. Freeze. When serving, top with additional whipped cream. Drizzle syrup over top, if desired.

Syrup:
Boil brown sugar, corn syrup, and hot water until thickened. Add vanilla when mixture cools.

Preparation: 30 min.   Easy   Serves: 6-8
Cooking: 30 min.   Must do ahead   Must freeze

Lucille Cardone

COOKIES

THIRD GENERATION APRICOT AND DATE BARS
"Certain to get raves"

Mixture one:
1 lb. dried apricots
½ pkg. pitted dates
1 cup water
1 cup sugar
juice of one fresh lemon

Mixture two:
1½ cups all-purpose flour
½ tsp. salt
½ tsp. baking soda
1 cup brown sugar, packed
1½ cups uncooked rolled oats
  (do not use quick oats)
1 cup melted butter
1 cup coarsely chopped walnuts

Mixture one: Cut dried apricots and dates into small pieces and place in top of double boiler. Add remaining ingredients and cook until mixture has consistency of marmalade (may take 15-30 minutes).

Mixture two: Mix all ingredients together. Press three-fourths of this mixture into a greased 9 x 11" glass baking dish. Spread the apricot/date mixture on top. Top with the remaining one-fourth of mixture two. Bake for 25-30 minutes at 350°.

Preparation: 55 min.	Easy	Yield: 24 bars
Cooking: 25-30 min.	Can do ahead	Can freeze

Mim Dyhouse

HIP HUGGERS

1 12-oz. pkg. semi-sweet
  chocolate chips
1 12-oz. pkg. butterscotch chips
1½ cups peanut butter
1 oz. unsweetened chocolate
  (bar, not powder)
1 cup margarine
⅓ cup evaporated milk
5 Tbsp. vanilla pudding mix
1 tsp. vanilla
3 cups powdered sugar
2 cups chopped peanuts

Melt the chocolate chips, butterscotch chips, peanut butter and unsweetened chocolate together. Pour half of mixture into an ungreased 10 x 15" jelly roll pan. Chill. Keep remaining half at room temperature. Melt margarine. Add evaporated milk. Heat. Remove from heat and stir in pudding mix. Do not cook. Add the vanilla. Beat in the powdered sugar. Pour this mixture over the chilled chocolate in pan. Sprinkle the chopped peanuts over the top of this. Then top with the remaining chocolate mixture (remelted if necessary). Chill several hours before serving.

Preparation: 30 min.   Easy   Yield: 48 bars
                        Must do ahead

Pat Morrison

SOUR CREAM CHOCOLATE DROPS

"Chocolate cookies with chocolate frosting"

2 cups brown sugar
½ cup margarine
2 eggs
1 cup sour cream (can use
  imitation)
3 cups flour
½ tsp. baking powder
½ tsp. salt
½ tsp. baking soda
4 oz. Nestle's Choco-Bake,
  unsweetened, pre-melted
  baking chocolate
1 tsp. vanilla
1 cup chopped nuts

Cream together sugar and margarine. Beat in eggs. Stir in sour cream. Sift dry ingredients together and stir into sugar mixture. Add chocolate, vanilla, and nuts. Drop by teaspoonsful onto a greased cookie sheet. Bake at 350° for 10-12 minutes. Cool and frost.

Frosting: Stir all ingredients with mixer or fork. Spread on cooled cookies.

Frosting:

1 tsp. margarine
2 oz. Nestle's Choco-Bake,
  unsweetened, pre-melted
  baking chocolate
6 Tbsp. boiling water
powdered sugar to stiffen

Preparation: 1 hr.   Easy   Yield: 3 doz.
Cooking: 10-12 min.   Can do ahead

Catherine C. Johnson

BANBURY TARTS

¾ lb. butter or margarine
1 cup sugar
2 egg yolks
1 tsp. vanilla
3 cups flour
⅛ tsp. salt
pecan halves OR preserves

Cream butter and sugar together. Beat in egg yolks and vanilla. Add flour and salt and mix well. Form dough into walnut-sized balls. Place 2" apart on an ungreased cookie sheet. Dent each cookie in the center with finger and fill with preserves or a pecan. Bake at 325° for 20-25 minutes or until golden brown around edges.

Preparation: 15 min.   Easy   Yield: 5 dozen
Cooking: 20-25 min.   Can do ahead   Can freeze

Jane Birnie

CHOCOLATE CHIP COOKIES

½ cup Crisco
1 cup brown sugar (do not pack)
1 egg
1 cup flour
½ tsp. salt
½ tsp. baking soda
¼ tsp. hot water
1 cup oatmeal (regular)
½ tsp. vanilla
1 6-oz. pkg. semi-sweet
  chocolate chips
1 cup nut meats, cut up

Mix the Crisco, sugar, and egg together. Sift flour, salt, and soda together; add to first mixture. Add hot water, oatmeal and vanilla. Add chocolate chips and nut meats (batter will be very stiff). Place cookies on greased double pan or insulated cookie pan. Bake at 350° for 10-12 minutes.

Preparation: 15 min.   Easy   Yield: 3½ doz.
Cooking: 10-12 min.   Can do ahead   Can freeze

Mrs. H. R. Wright

DANISH OATMEAL COOKIES
"Excellent delicate flavor"

1 stick margarine
1 stick butter
1 cup powdered sugar
2 tsp. vanilla
1 cup flour
½ tsp. salt
1 cup oatmeal
1 cup chopped nuts
powdered sugar for top

Mix butters and powdered sugar until fluffy. Add remaining ingredients. Mix. Drop on ungreased cookie sheet (should be about the size of a walnut). Bake at 325° for 20 minutes. After cookies have cooled, sprinkle with powdered sugar.

NOTE: Let cookies cool on cookie sheet for a few minutes before serving.

Preparation: 15-20 min.   Easy   Yield: 2 dozen
Cooking: 18-20 min.   Can do ahead   Can freeze

Joy Ann Hughes

OAT BRAN BROWNIES

1 stick margarine
2 oz. unsweetened chocolate
1 cup sugar
½ cup egg beaters (equivalent of 2 eggs)
1 tsp. vanilla or almond extract
¼ cup oat bran
1 cup walnuts or pecans, omit nuts if using the almond extract

Melt margarine and chocolate in microwave or on stove top. Add sugar and mix well. Add egg beaters, mixing well with spoon for about 1 minute. Add extract; then add oat bran and mix. Add nuts only if vanilla extract is used, and stir well. Spray an 8 x 8″ pan with vegetable spray. Pour batter into pan and bake for 45-50 minutes at 325°.

| Preparation: | 15 min. | Easy | Yield: 16 brownies |
| Cooking: | 45 min. | Can do ahead | Can freeze |

Sharon Novak

IONE'S SWEDISH COOKIES

1 cup butter or margarine
1 cup sugar
1 egg
1 tsp. vanilla or almond extract
2½ cups flour
1 tsp. baking powder
powdered sugar

Cream butter, sugar, egg and vanilla. Sift flour; measure 2½ cups. Add baking powder. Mix together. For flat cookies, drop teaspoonsful on a greased cookie sheet and press with glass covered with damp cloth (or roll thin and cut in rounds). Bake at 350° for 8-10 minutes. Sprinkle with powdered sugar when baked.

| Preparation: | 25 min. | Easy | Yield: 2 doz. |
| Cooking: | 8-10 min. | Can do ahead | Can freeze |

Judy Scioscia

LEMON SNOW DROPS

"These are fabulous and well worth the effort"

1 cup butter
½ cup powdered sugar
1 tsp. lemon extract
2 cups flour
¼ tsp. salt
granulated sugar
powdered sugar

Lemon Butter Filling:

1 egg, slightly beaten
1 tsp. lemon rind
⅔ cup sugar
1 tsp. cornstarch
3 Tbsp. lemon juice
1½ Tbsp. butter, softened

Cream butter; add ½ cup powdered sugar and gradually blend in extract, flour and salt. Shape teaspoonsful of dough into balls. Place on ungreased cookie sheet. Flatten with bottom of drinking glass dipped in granulated sugar to ¼″ thickness. Bake at 375° for 12 minutes. Cool. Put together, sandwich fashion, with lemon butter filling. Then roll in powdered sugar.

Lemon Butter Filling: Combine all ingredients. Cook at low heat until thickened, stirring constantly. Chill until thick.

| Preparation: | 20 min. | Moderately difficult | Yield: 4 doz. |
| Cooking: | 10-12 min. | Can do ahead | Can freeze |

Holly B. Worth

BITTERSWEETS
"Very sweet and rich"

Cookie:
1 cup butter
1 cup powdered sugar
½ tsp. salt
2 tsp. vanilla
2¼ cups sifted flour

Filling:
6 oz. cream cheese, softened
2 cups powdered sugar
4 Tbsp. flour
2 tsp. vanilla
1 cup chopped nuts
1 cup coconut

Frosting:
1 cup semi-sweet chocolate
   chips
4 Tbsp. butter
4 Tbsp. water
1 cup sifted powdered sugar

Cookie: Cream butter. Add sugar, salt and vanilla. Cream together well. Gradually add flour. Shape into balls. Place on ungreased cookie sheets. Press thumb in center of each, making a deep well. Bake at 350° for 12-14 minutes.

Filling: Cream all ingredients together well. Place a small amount in the well of each baked cookie.

Frosting: Melt chocolate chips, butter and water over very low heat, stirring occasionally. Add powdered sugar. Beat until smooth. Drizzle on each cookie.

Preparation: 45 min.	Moderately difficult	Yield: 34 cookies
Cooking: 14-20 min.	Can do ahead	Can freeze

Norma Linfors

RUTH'S NEAPOLITAN COOKIES
"A pretty cookie that stands out in the cookie crowd"

1 cup butter or margarine
1½ cups sugar
1 egg
1 tsp. vanilla
2½ cups flour
1½ tsp. baking powder
½ tsp. salt

Additions:
½ tsp. almond extract
5 drops red food coloring
½ cup chopped walnuts
1 oz. unsweetened chocolate,
   melted

Cream together butter or margarine and sugar. Beat in egg and vanilla. Slowly add dry ingredients and beat mixture for 3 minutes. Divide dough into three parts. To one third of the batter, stir in almond extract and the red food coloring. Line a 9 x 5″ loaf pan with waxed paper. Pat the first prepared third of dough into pan. To another third, add chopped nuts and stir. Spread evenly over pink dough in pan. To remaining dough, add melted chocolate. Spread evenly on top.

Cover. Refrigerate for at least 4 hours. Preheat oven to 350°. Remove dough from pan. Cut in half lengthwise; slice each half into ⅛″ slices. Place on cookie sheet and bake for 10-12 minutes.

Preparation: 40 min.	Moderately difficult	Yield: 5 doz.
Cooking: 10-12 min.	Must do ahead	Can freeze

Eve Rogers

FROSTED BROWNIES
"Rich and tempting"

1 cup butter
4 oz. unsweetened chocolate
2 cups sugar
4 eggs, well beaten
1 tsp. vanilla
1½ cups sifted flour
½ tsp. salt

Mocha Frosting:
1 lb. powdered sugar
½ cup butter, melted
⅓ cup cocoa
3 Tbsp. brewed coffee, cooled
2 tsp. vanilla

In the top of a double boiler, melt butter and chocolate over hot water.* Add sugar and mix well. Transfer chocolate mixture to the bowl of an electric mixer and, while beating slowly, add eggs, vanilla, then flour and salt, mixing thoroughly after each addition. Spread mixture in a well-greased 9 x 13" baking dish and bake in a preheated 400° oven for 20 minutes. Cool.

Mocha Frosting: Combine all ingredients in a bowl and with an electric mixer, beat until completely smooth. If too thick, add a little more coffee. Spread with frosting and let frosting set before cutting.

*Can also microwave butter and chocolate for about 1-2 minutes, stirring after 1 minute.

Preparation: 30 min.	Easy	Yield: 2½-3 doz.
Cooking: 20 min.	Can do ahead	Can freeze

Missy Zimmerman

LAYERED PEPPERMINT BROWNIES

First layer:
2 oz. unsweetened chocolate
½ cup butter
2 eggs
1 cup sugar
½ cup flour
½ tsp. mint extract
dash salt

Second layer:
3 Tbsp. butter, softened
1 cup powdered sugar
2 Tbsp. cream
1 tsp. mint extract
green food coloring

Third layer:
1½ oz. unsweetened chocolate
2 Tbsp. butter

Preheat oven to 350°.

First layer: Melt chocolate and butter. Beat eggs and add sugar. Add to chocolate mixture. Add flour, extract and salt. Mix well. Spread in a 9 x 9" pan. Bake at 350° for 20-25 minutes. (Don't overcook.) Cool to room temperature.

Second layer: Mix the butter, powdered sugar, cream, mint extract and green food coloring until a frosting-like consistency. Spread over brownie mixture which has already cooled.

Third layer: Melt chocolate and butter together. Cool. Spread on top.

Preparation: 30 min.	Easy	Yield: 16 brownies
Cooking: 20-25 min.	Can do ahead	

Francye Kinney

PECAN PIE BARS

"Better than pecan pie"

2 cups unsifted flour
½ cup powdered sugar
2 sticks butter
1 14-oz. can Eagle Brand
   sweetened condensed milk
1 egg
1 tsp. vanilla extract
1 6-oz. pkg. almond brickle
   chips
1 cup chopped pecans

Preheat oven to 350° (325° if using a glass dish). In medium mixing bowl, combine flour and sugar; cut in butter until mixture resembles coarse meal. Press firmly on bottom of an ungreased 9 x 13" baking pan. Bake 15 minutes. Meanwhile, in medium mixing bowl, beat milk, egg and vanilla. Stir in chips and pecans. Spread evenly over prepared crust. Bake 25 minutes or until golden brown. Cool. Chill thoroughly. Cut into bars. Store covered in the refrigerator.

Preparation:	30 min.	Easy	Yield: 36 bars
Cooking:	40 min.	Can do ahead	Can freeze

Teresa A. Surgeon

COOKIE BRITTLE

"Get out your jelly roll pan"

1 cup unsalted butter, softened
1½ tsp. vanilla
1 tsp. salt
2 cups sifted unbleached flour
1 cup sugar
1 7.8-oz. pkg. Heath Bits
   O'Brickle candy
6 Hershey bars, optional

Preheat oven to 375°. Combine butter, vanilla, and salt in medium bowl and beat with electric mixer until fluffy. Add flour, sugar and candy and blend well. Press mixture into a 15 x 11" jelly roll pan sprayed with PAM. Cover with waxed paper and flatten with a rolling pin. Discard paper. Bake for about 20 minutes or until golden brown.

VARIATION: Upon removal from oven, lay chocolate bars over cookies and spread when melted.

Preparation:	15 min.	Easy	Yield: 48 cookies
Cooking:	20 min.	Can do ahead	Can freeze

Linda D. Orsini

MOM'S APRICOT BARS

"Tangy and not too sweet"

½ cup Crisco shortening
½ cup granulated sugar
1 tsp. grated lemon rind
2 eggs, separated
1 cup sifted all-purpose flour
½ tsp. salt
¼ tsp. baking soda
1½ cups apricot jam
¼ cup granulated sugar
½ cup chopped walnuts or
  pecans
powdered sugar

Cream together shortening, ½ cup sugar and lemon rind thoroughly. Add egg yolks, one at a time. Beat after each addition. Add flour, salt and soda to creamed mixture. Spread the dough, with floured fingers, into a greased 9 x 13" pan. Cover with apricot jam. Beat egg whites until stiff, but not dry. Gradually add ¼ cup sugar and continue beating. Fold in the nuts. Spread meringue over apricot jam layer.

Bake at 350° for 35-40 minutes, depending on the heat of your oven. Do not let it get too brown. Sprinkle with powdered sugar after cooling and cut into bars.

Preparation: 20 min.   Easy   Yield: 24 bars
Cooking: 35-40 min. Can do ahead   Can freeze

Mrs. Wesley E. Smith, Sr.

FILLED COOKIES - RAISINS OR DATES

"Like Grandma's old-fashioned cookies"

1 cup Crisco shortening
3 eggs
2 cups brown sugar
4 cups flour
1 tsp. soda
2 Tbsp. cold water

Raisin Filling:

1 box raisins
1 cup sugar
1 Tbsp. cornstarch
1 cup water

Date Filling:

1½ lb. dates, chopped
1 cup sugar
1 cup water

Cream Crisco, eggs, and brown sugar. Add flour with soda; then add cold water and stir. Chill dough for 1 hour or overnight. When ready to use, take it out in sections, so it will be easier to work with. Roll out to ¼" thickness and cut into circles with round cookie cutter or doughnut cutter. Place one circle on greased cookie sheet, put filling on this layer; then top with another circle and press around circle with fork or fingers. Cut a small "x" in the center of the top circle or you can make the top circle with a round hole (like a doughnut). Bake at 350° for 10-12 minutes.

Fillings: Cook ingredients until thick. Cool prior to putting on dough.

Preparation: 30 min.   Moderately difficult   Yield: 4 doz.
Cooking: 25-30 min. Must do ahead

Ti DiGiorno

GRANDMA'S FROSTED COOKIES

3 cups pre-sifted flour
½ tsp. soda
½ tsp. baking powder
¼ tsp. salt
1 cup butter, at room
  temperature
2 eggs
1 cup sugar

Frosting:

2 cups powdered sugar
½ stick butter, melted
½ tsp. vanilla
cream or milk (to blend in for
  right consistency)

Sift together flour, soda, baking powder and salt. Add butter. Mix as for pie crust. In separate bowl, beat eggs and sugar. Mix and add to first mixture. Refrigerate for at least 3 hours. Roll thin on lightly floured board. Cut into desired shapes. Bake at 375° for 6 minutes. Check often to make sure they do not burn.

Frosting: Mix all ingredients together, adding the cream or milk a little at a time until the right consistency is reached.

Preparation: 40 min.   Moderately difficult   Yield: 3 doz.
Cooking: 6 min.   Must do ahead   Can freeze

Mary Murphy

MA'S BROWNIES

"Added attractions are mini-marshmallows and walnuts"

2 oz. unsweetened chocolate
1 cup semi-sweet chocolate
  chips
2 sticks butter or margarine
4 eggs
1½ cups sugar
2 tsp. vanilla
1 cup pre-sifted flour
2 cups miniature marshmallows
1 cup coarsely chopped
  walnuts (optional)

Grease and flour a 9 x 13″ pan. Preheat oven to 350°. Melt chocolate squares, chocolate chips, and butter or margarine together. Allow to cool. Cream together the eggs and sugar. Add vanilla. Gradually add cooled chocolate mixture to creamed mixture. Fold in flour, marshmallows and walnuts. Pour mixture into prepared pan. Bake at 350° for 30-35 minutes. Cool.

NOTE: To prevent from crumbling, refrigerate several hours before cutting into squares.

Preparation: 30 min.   Easy   Yield: 24 brownies
Cooking: 35 min.   Can do ahead   Can freeze

Denise Schiller

LACE COOKIES

"Oatmeal makes these good for you"

1 cup quick-cooking oatmeal
1 cup sugar
¼ lb. butter, melted
3 Tbsp. flour
¼ tsp. salt
1 tsp. vanilla
1 egg
¼ tsp. baking powder

Mix all ingredients together well. Drop by ½ tsp. (be exact) onto foil-lined sheet, 2″ apart. Bake at 350° for 6-8 minutes. Allow to cool thoroughly on foil. When cool, peel off of foil.

Preparation: 10 min.   Easy   Yield: 3 dozen
Cooking: 6-8 min.   Can do ahead

Gwen H. Willard

231

SWISS ALMOND HEARTS

1 cup + 2 Tbsp. butter, softened
1 cup powdered sugar, sifted
2 egg yolks
1 cup ground almonds
3 cups all-purpose flour, sifted
80 whole almonds

Beat butter, powdered sugar and 1 egg yolk in large bowl until pale and creamy. Add ground almonds and flour. Knead quickly to a firm dough. Press into a ball and wrap in foil or plastic wrap. Refrigerate for 2 hours. Preheat oven to 400°. On floured surface, roll dough to ¼" thickness. Cut into 40 small heart shapes and place on a large cookie sheet sprayed with PAM. Beat second egg yolk; brush over cookies. Place 2 almonds on each cookie. Bake 10-12 minutes until golden. Cool and remove from rack.

Preparation: 20 min.   Easy   Yield: 40 cookies
Cooking: 10-12 min.   Must do ahead   Can freeze

Lynn Popovich

CHESS PIE COOKIES

Crust:
1 box yellow cake mix
1 stick butter or margarine, melted
1 egg, beaten

Filling:
1 8-oz. pkg. cream cheese, softened
3 eggs
1 box powdered sugar
1 Tbsp. vanilla

Crust: Mix all ingredients together. Pat into an ungreased 9 x 13" pan. (Mixture will be "doughy".)

Filling: Beat the cream cheese and eggs together well. Add the powdered sugar and vanilla gradually. Pour over crust and bake at 350° for 40 minutes.

Preparation: 15 min.   Easy   Yield: 24 squares
Cooking: 40 min.   Can do ahead

Betsy Maloney

DATE NUT MERINGUE SQUARES

4 egg whites
⅛ tsp. salt
1 cup sugar
1 cup chopped dates
1 cup chopped pecans
½ tsp. vanilla
½ tsp. almond extract
1 cup heavy cream, whipped

Beat egg whites with salt until stiff, gradually adding sugar after eggs are frothy. When sugar seems completely absorbed, fold in dates, nuts and flavorings. Turn into well-greased 8" square pan. Bake at 350° for 45 minutes. Let cool and cut into squares. Serve topped with whipped cream.

Preparation: 20 min.   Easy   Serves: 6-8
Cooking: 35-40 min.   Can do ahead

Diane White

FROSTED SCOTCH SHORTBREAD
"Good even without frosting"

1 cup salted butter
½ tsp. salt
¾ cup powdered sugar
1 tsp. vanilla
2 cups flour

Frosting:
2 Tbsp. butter
2 oz. baking chocolate
½ cup sugar
⅓ cup evaporated milk or
 heavy cream

Cream butter, salt and sugar together. Mix in vanilla. Add flour and mix well. Mixture will be dry. Roll into small balls the size of a walnut. Place on an ungreased cookie sheet. Bake at 300° for 25 minutes. Do not brown. Cool completely before frosting.

Frosting: Melt butter and chocolate in a saucepan. Add sugar and cream. Boil for 1 minute. Remove from heat. Beat until thick enough to stick to cookie. Dip the top of each cookie into frosting and return to cookie sheet or wire rack to set until frosting is firm. If frosting gets too hard to dip into, add a few drops of cream.

Preparation: 20-25 min.   Easy   Yield: 2 dozen
Cooking: 25 min.   Can do ahead Can freeze

Emilie Szakach

CHOCOLATE YUM-YUM BARS
"A three layer cookie"

First layer:
1 egg, slightly beaten
1 stick butter, melted
⅓ cup cocoa
⅓ cup sugar
1 tsp. vanilla
2 cups graham cracker crumbs
 (⅓ box + 4 squares)
½ cup chopped walnuts or
 pecans
1 cup coconut

Second layer:
½ stick butter, melted
3 Tbsp. milk
2 Tbsp. instant vanilla pudding
 powder
2 cups sifted powdered sugar

Third layer:
4 oz. unsweetened chocolate,
 melted
1 Tbsp. butter

First layer: Mix egg, butter, cocoa, sugar and vanilla over low heat until custard consistency. Remove from heat and add graham crackers, nuts and coconut. Pack into an ungreased 9 x 9" pan. Refrigerate.

Second layer: Add milk to melted butter. Stir in pudding powder and beat. Add powdered sugar and beat until well blended. Spread over first layer after it is firm and cool. Refrigerate.

Third layer: Melt chocolate, then add butter. Drizzle over second layer and spread. Allow to harden outside refrigerator unless a warm kitchen or hot weather makes it necessary to refrigerate. When top is firm, cut into squares.

Preparation: 1 hr.   Easy   Yield: 16 2" squares
                     Must do ahead

Marilyn J. Sittig

TOFFEE BARS

"Cookies from crackers"

40-45 saltine crackers
1 cup butter or margarine
1 cup brown sugar, not packed
¼ tsp. baking soda
1 12-oz. pkg. semi-sweet
  chocolate chips
1 cup chopped nuts

Line a large cookie sheet or jelly roll pan with foil. Spray foil with PAM. Arrange as many saltines as you can on the cookie sheet until all space is covered. In medium saucepan, melt butter and brown sugar together, stirring occasionally, until it comes to a boil. Boil 1 minute only. Remove from heat and add baking soda. Stir. Pour over saltines and spread around until all are covered. Bake at 350° for 10 minutes only. Remove from oven. Immediately sprinkle chocolate chips on top of crackers. Let set for 2 minutes (approximately) until melted, then carefully spread on top of all crackers. Sprinkle with nuts. Cut into squares at this time, but leave in pan for 8 hours before removing. (You may want to put in refrigerator for a while to help harden the chocolate.)

Preparation: 15 min.   Easy   Yield: 36 bars
Cooking: 10 min.   Must do ahead   Can freeze

Marcia J. Titus

GOBLIN BARS

"Think pumpkins and autumn"

1 16-oz. pkg. yellow cake mix
1 egg
2 Tbsp. margarine or butter
2 tsp. pumpkin pie spice
6 oz. cream cheese*, softened
1 14-oz. can sweetened
  condensed milk*
1 16-oz. can pumpkin
½ tsp. ginger
½ tsp. salt
1½ tsp. pumpkin pie spice
2 eggs
¾ cup chopped nuts
*lo-cal substitutes:
  8 oz. vanilla yogurt
  4 pkgs. Equal or Twin
    sweetener (not Sweet'n
    Low) + 4 oz. skim or
    2% milk

Preheat oven to 350°. Combine cake mix, egg, margarine and pumpkin pie spice until crumbly. Press into bottom of a greased 14 x 10″ pan (or a 15 x 10″ jelly roll pan). Using hand or electric mixer, beat cream cheese until fluffy. Add remaining ingredients, except for nuts, one at a time. Pour mixture over crust. Sprinkle nuts on top and press into topping, if not submerged. Bake 30-35 minutes, until firm. Chill and serve. Store in refrigerator for best results.

NOTE: Good served with cinnamon ice cream.

Preparation: 20 min.   Easy   Yield: 48 bars
Cooking: 35 min.   Can do ahead

Susan D. Craig

CANDIES

MICROWAVE PEANUT BRITTLE
"A Halloween-Fall favorite"

1 cup sugar
½ cup light corn syrup
dash of salt
1 cup raw peanuts
1 tsp. butter
1 tsp. vanilla
1 tsp. baking soda

In a 4-cup glass measuring cup, stir sugar, corn syrup and salt together. Microwave on High for 4 minutes. Add raw peanuts; stir and microwave on High for 3½ minutes. Add butter and vanilla; stir and microwave for 1½ minutes. Add baking soda (it will fizz and froth); stir and pour into lightly buttered jelly roll pan. Cool. Break into pieces.

NOTE: DO NOT MAKE ON DAMP, HUMID DAYS!

Preparation: 10 min.   Easy   Serves: 8-12
Cooking: 9 min.   Can do ahead

Karol Creech

SWEDISH CHRISTMAS PECANS
"Great any time of the year"

4 cups pecan halves
1 cup sugar
2 egg whites, stiffly beaten
½ cup butter

Toast pecans at 325° for about 20 minutes, until light brown. Fold sugar into beaten egg whites. Beat again to blend sugar (meringue). Fold cooled nuts into meringue. Melt butter in large baking pan (or melt butter in microwave and pour in). Spread nut mixture over butter. Bake at 325° for about 50-60 minutes, "lifting" nuts up and turning over (with spatula) every 10 minutes. Cool on brown paper bags or on "lintless" paper towels.

Preparation: 30 min.   Easy   Serves: A crowd
Cooking: 40-50 min.   Can do ahead

Clee McBee

235

MOM'S BEST ENGLISH TOFFEE

"A holiday treat for one and all"

½ lb. butter (no substitutions)
1 cup sugar
3 Tbsp. water
½ tsp. vanilla
4 Hershey bars
1½ cups sliced almonds

Cook butter, sugar and water slowly over medium heat until brownish—about 20 minutes (300° crack stage). Add vanilla and quickly pour onto a greased cookie sheet, spread very thin. Spread broken Hershey bars on top, then sprinkle with almonds. Put in refrigerator to cool. Break in pieces.

Preparation: 40 min.   Moderately difficult   Serves: A crowd
Cooking: 20-30 min.   Must do ahead

Arlene Wilgus

PEANUT BUTTER FUDGE

2 sticks butter
1 cup peanut butter
4 Tbsp. cocoa
2 Tbsp. vanilla
1 1-lb. box powdered sugar

Melt butter and peanut butter in a 2-qt. pan. Remove from heat. Add remaining ingredients and beat with hand mixer until mixed together. Transfer to an 8x8" ungreased pan and cool.

Preparation: 5 min.   Easy   Serves: 12
                             Can do ahead   Can freeze

Crystal Marmarella

5-MINUTE MICROWAVE FUDGE

"An old-fashioned favorite done in a modern manner"

1 12-oz. pkg. (2 cups) semi-sweet chocolate morsels
1 14-oz. can sweetened condensed milk
1¼ cups chopped walnuts (or favorite nut)
1 tsp. vanilla extract

In a 4-cup glass measuring cup, combine chocolate morsels and sweetened condensed milk.* Microwave on High for 3 minutes (watch to make sure it does not burn in your microwave). Stir until chocolate melts and mixture is smooth. Stir in nuts and vanilla. Spread evenly into foil-lined 8" square pan. Chill until firm, about 2 hours. Cut into squares.

*If you have an old can of evaporated milk that has carmelized, it will work fine in this recipe.

NOTE: Can be made in a double-boiler instead of microwave and glass measuring cup.

Preparation: 2 min.   Easy   Yield: 1¼ lbs.
Cooking: 3 min.   Must do ahead

Karen Eileen Lindeman

JUST FOR KIDS

PITTSBURGH'S CHILDREN'S MUSEUM AND FESTIVAL

The Old Post Office Museum, North Side, is the home of the Children's Museum and site for the annual Children's Festival. It contains hands-on exhibits, crafts, and a TV studio and puppets from Mister Rogers' Neighborhood.

Additional illustrations in this section:

PPG's Wintergarden Hall furnishes visitors with an oasis of green while providing a dramatic gathering place for all seasons.

MR. MCFEELY'S SHAKE AWAKE
"Refreshing breakfast treat"

1 cup milk
1 scoop ice cream
1 egg
½ cup berries, fresh or frozen,
  peaches, plums, apricots or
  bananas

Mix all ingredients in blender for no more than 5 seconds, until creamy. Pour into a large glass and enjoy!

Mr. Fred Rogers
Family Communications, Inc.

ABC PRETZELS
"For birthday party activity"

16 oz. frozen bread dough,
  thawed
½ cup flour
1 egg white, beaten
1 tsp. water
coarse salt

Preheat oven to 350°. Cut dough into 24 pieces. Flour your hands and roll each piece of dough into a long "worm" and shape into a letter. Place on cookie sheet. Beat egg white with water and brush each pretzel with egg white mixture. Sprinkle with salt. Bake for 12 minutes or until brown.

Preparation: 10 min.   Easy   Yield: 24 pretzels
Cooking: 12 min.   Can do ahead

PACE School
HOT classes

CANDY BAR BUTTERSCOTCH BROWNIES

"Tastes like a Snickers candy bar"

¼ cup margarine, softened
1 cup light brown sugar, packed
1 egg
1 cup flour
1 tsp. baking powder, rounded
½ tsp. vanilla
½ cup chocolate chips
½ cup butterscotch morsels
½ cup peanuts, coarsely chopped

Blend together the margarine, sugar and egg. Add all other ingredients and stir. Spread in well-greased 8″ square pan. Bake at 350° until a slight imprint remains when touched, approximately 25 minutes. Cut into bars while warm.

Preparation: 10 min.   Easy   Yield: 18 brownies
Cooking: 25 min.   Can do ahead   Can freeze

Josie Carey
Josie's Storyland KDKA-TV

DR. BILL'S GINGER SPICED APPLES

4 baking apples
1 cup cinnamon red hot candies
½ cup brown sugar
1 7-oz. bottle ginger ale

Preheat oven to 350°. Core the apples and peel them about a third of the way down. Arrange them in a baking dish and fill cavities with candies and brown sugar. Pour ginger ale into the dish and bake, uncovered, for 40 minutes. Baste apples with the liquid every 10-12 minutes.

Preparation: 5 min.   Easy   Serves: 4
Cooking: 40 min.   Serve immediately

Mr. Fred Rogers
Family Communications, Inc.

OLD FASHIONED WHOOPIE PIES

Cookie:
½ cup shortening
1 cup sugar
½ cup buttermilk
1 tsp. baking soda
1 egg
1½ cups flour
½ cup cocoa
⅓ cup liquid coffee
1 tsp. vanilla
pinch of salt
Filling:
½ cup milk
2 Tbsp. flour
½ cup sugar
½ cup shortening
1 tsp. vanilla
pinch of salt

Cookie:
Mix all ingredients together and drop by teaspoonsful onto a greased cookie sheet. Bake for 10 minutes at 350°.
Filling:
Cook milk and flour until a smooth paste consistency, stirring constantly. Cool. Cream sugar and shortening; add to paste. Add vanilla and salt. Beat about 10 minutes with electric mixer. Spread filling on one cookie and top with another one.

Preparation: 30-40 min.   Easy   Yield: 12-18
Cooking: 10 min.   Can do ahead

Linda D. Orsini

FUNNEL CAKES

"Have Mom or Dad help with this recipe"

2 beaten eggs
1½ cups milk
1 tsp. vanilla
2 cups flour
1 tsp. baking powder
½ tsp. salt
2 cups oil
powdered sugar
honey or syrup

In bowl, or pitcher, combine eggs, milk and vanilla. Add flour, baking powder and salt; beat smooth. In a deep fry pan, heat oil to 360°. Covering bottom opening of funnel with finger, pour ½ cup of batter into funnel. Remove finger and release batter into hot oil (hold funnel close to surface of oil) in a spiral shape.

Fry until golden, turn carefully, and cook other side. Drain on paper towel on cookie sheet. Keep warm in oven until all funnel cakes are fried. Sprinkle with powdered sugar and serve with honey or syrup.

Preparation: 30 min.   Moderately difficult   Serves: 4
                         Serve immediately
                                                     Emilie Szakach

CHOCOLATE PEANUT BUTTER BARS

"Always a favorite"

1 1-lb. box powdered sugar
1 cup margarine or butter
1 cup crunchy peanut butter
1½ cups graham cracker
  crumbs
1 8-oz. pkg. milk chocolate
  bits, melted

Cream sugar and margarine together. Add peanut butter and cracker crumbs. Press firmly into a lightly greased 9x13" pan. Pour melted chocolate over mixture and spread with a knife. Cut into squares and refrigerate.

Preparation: 20 min.   Easy   Yield: 24 bars
                         Must do ahead   Can freeze
                                                     Christina Bagwell

HEAVENLY DIRT

"Great party attraction"

2 8-oz. pkgs. cream cheese,
  softened
2 cups powdered sugar
2 3½-oz. boxes vanilla instant
  pudding
3 cups cold milk
16 oz. Cool Whip topping,
  softened in refrigerator
2 tsp. vanilla
1 20-oz. pkg. Oreo cookies
8" flower pot
silk flowers
gummy worms

Beat cream cheese and powdered sugar until creamy and set aside. Mix pudding and milk until thick. Combine with cheese mixture, using a wire whisk. Add Cool Whip topping and vanilla to pudding-cheese mixture. Crush Oreo cookies, including filling. Using an 8" flower pot, put a layer of cookie crumbs, then a layer of cream mixture. Continue layering, ending with a layer of crumbs (to look like dirt)! Add silk flowers and decorate with gummy worms.

HINT: Use half recipe of cream and less than a 16 oz. pkg. of Oreos when using a 6" flower pot.

Preparation: 25 min.   Easy   Serves: A crowd
                         Can do ahead
                                                     Ede Finnegan

CINNAMON TOAST ROLLS
"Good slumber party breakfast"

¼ cup sugar
2 tsp. cinnamon
12 ⅜" thick slices of very fresh homemade-type white bread, crust removed (Do not use Pepperidge Farm)
½ stick unsalted butter, melted

In bowl, stir the sugar and cinnamon together. Roll the bread ¼" thick between pieces of waxed paper. Brush both sides of each slice with melted butter. Spread 1 tsp. cinnamon sugar mixture on one side of each slice. Roll the bread tightly, jelly roll fashion, starting with long side and cinnamon sugar on outside. Trim ends on diagonal.* Transfer rolls to baking sheet, seam-side down. Bake in a preheated 350° oven for 15 minutes or until lightly browned.

*Rolls may be made up to 1 week ahead - tightly wrapped and frozen to this point.

Preparation: 15 min.	Easy	Serves: 4-6
Cooking: 15 min.	Can do ahead	Can freeze

Mary Lee Parrington

SPAGHETTI CASSEROLE
"Makes great leftovers"

1 8-oz. pkg. vermicelli
1½ lbs. ground beef
1 chopped onion
1 28-oz. can whole tomatoes
1 tsp. garlic salt
1 lb. grated Cheddar cheese
tomato juice

Cook noodles according to package directions and drain. While noodles are cooking, brown onion and ground beef. Drain. Chop tomatoes and add to beef (including juice). Mix in noodles and garlic salt. Place in a 9x13" glass casserole. Sprinkle cheese over mixture and pour tomato juice over casserole. Bake at 350° for 45 minutes.

Preparation: 25 min.	Easy	Serves: 8-10
Cooking: 45 min.	Can do ahead	Can freeze

Nancy Coyle

NO-BAKE CHOCOLATE COOKIES
"Good school snack"

6 Tbsp. cocoa
1½ cups sugar
1 stick margarine
½ cup milk
¾ cup peanut butter
1 tsp. vanilla
3 cups quick-cooking oats

In a saucepan over medium heat, mix together cocoa and sugar; add margarine and milk. Bring to a boil for 1 minute. Remove from heat. Add peanut butter, vanilla and oats. Stir. Drop by teaspoonsful onto waxed paper. Let harden.

VARIATIONS: Can substitute ½ cup raisins or Cheerios for the ½ cup of oats.

Preparation: 6-8 min.	Easy	Yield: 2½ dozen
	Must do ahead	Can freeze

Kathleen L. Sheehan

INDEX

244

245

MEASUREMENTS AND EQUIVALENTS

MEASUREMENTS

dash	= less than 1/8 tsp.
1 tbsp.	= 3 tsp.
2 tbsp.	= 1 oz.
4 tbsp.	= ¼ cup
5⅓ tbsp.	= ⅓ cup
8 tbsp.	= ½ cup
16 tbsp.	= 1 cup
8 oz.	= 1 cup
16 oz.	= 1 lb.
2 cups	= 1 lb./1 pt.
2 pints	= 1 qt./4 cups
4 quarts	= 1 gallon
8 quarts	= 1 peck
4 pecks	= 1 bushel

METRIC CONVERSION

VOLUME		
1 tsp.	=	5 ml.
1 tbsp.	=	15 ml.
2 tbsp.	=	30 ml.
1 cup.	=	240 ml.
1 pint	=	480 ml.
1 quart	=	960 ml.
WEIGHT		
1 oz.	=	28 gm.
1 lb.	=	454 gm.
2.2 lbs.	=	(1 Kg.) 1,000 gm.
LENGTH		
1 in.	=	2.54 cm.
39.37 in.	=	1 meter

EQUIVALENTS

Apples	4 oz.	=	1 cup sliced
Bread	1 slice	=	⅓ cup dry crumbs
Butter	1 oz.	=	2 tbsp.
	¼ lb. = ½ cup	=	1 stick
	1 lb.	=	2 cups
Cheese, dry	1 lb.	=	4 cups
grated	1 lb.	=	4-5 cups
cottage	½ lb.	=	1 cup
cream	3 oz.	=	6 tbsp.
Chicken	3½ lbs. drawn	=	2 cups cooked, diced
Coconut, flaked	3½ oz.	=	1⅓ cups
Cream, heavy	1 cup	=	2 cups whipped
Eggs, whole	5	=	1 cup
whites	8-10	=	1 cup
yolks	10-12	=	1 cup
Flour,	1 lb.	=	4 cups
for thickening	5 tsp.	=	2 tsp. arrowroot
	2 tbsp.	=	1 tbsp. cornstarch
	1 tbsp.	=	2 tsp. quick-cooking tapioca
Gelatin	¼ oz. env.	=	1 tbsp. (gels 2 cups)
Herbs	⅓-½ tsp. dried	=	1 tbsp. fresh
Lemon	1	=	2-3 tbsp. juice
		=	2 tsp. rind
Meat, cooked	1 lb.	=	3 cups minced
Mushrooms	1 lb. fresh = 5 cups sliced	=	6 oz. canned
Nuts	1 lb. in shell = ½ lb. kernels	=	3-4 cups
Orange	1 med.	=	6-8 tbsp. juice
			1-2 tbsp. rind
Potatoes	1 lb. raw	=	2 cups mashed
Raisins, seedless	1 lb.	=	2 cups
Rice	2-2½ cups (1 lb.)	=	8 cups cooked
Sugars, brown	1 lb.	=	2¼ cups packed
confectioners'	1 lb.	=	4 cups
white	1 lb.	=	2 cups

CONTRIBUTORS

"Chappy", our Child Health puppet, visits with the younger children served by our dental care program. Dental hygiene was one of the earliest projects funded by the Child Health Association around 1930 and continues today. "Chappy" has come to symbolize the history of giving of time and funds to the total welfare of children.

We wish to thank the following people for their financial contributions toward the production expenses of THREE RIVERS COOKBOOK III.

CHAppy's BENEFACTORS

Mr. and Mrs. Donald S. Birnie
Barbara B. Burton
Nancy B. Cogswell
Mr. and Mrs. George H. Craig, Jr.
Mr. and Mrs. Walter E. Gregg, Jr.
Mr. and Mrs. Paul Hammer
Mr. and Mrs. Wm. Gregg Hansen
Mr. and Mrs. William S. Hansen
Dr. and Mrs. Jonathan E. Hottenstein
Mr. and Mrs. Thomas R. Johnson
Dr. and Mrs. Robert P. Mantica

Mr. and Mrs. William Metcalf, III
Mr. and Mrs. Peter Henkels Moriarty
Elizabeth L. Palmer
Mr. and Mrs. W. Thomas Parrington, Jr.
Mary Jane and Joseph Platt
Mrs. C. Snowdon Richards
Mr. and Mrs. Robert W. Riordan
Dr. and Mrs. Benjamin V. Smith, Jr.
Mr. and Mrs. Bruce E. G. Smith
Mrs. Edward I. Sproull, Jr.
Mr. and Mrs. George Szakach

CHAppy's SUPPORTERS

Jack and Gerry Armstrong
Judson Brooks
Mrs. David Brown
Mr. and Mrs. Robert C. Burnham
Mr. and Mrs. Edward L. Campbell
Mrs. Henry Chalfant
Mr. and Mrs. Joseph S. D. Christof, II
Mrs. Wm. Howard Colbert
Dr. and Mrs. James D'Antonio
Mr. and Mrs. Clayton Deutsch
Anne Fulton Dithrich
Eleanor H. Friedman
Mr. and Mrs. Giles Gaca
Mrs. William A. Galbraith
Dr. and Mrs. Harlan Giles
Mr. and Mrs. Clete O. Gilson
Mrs. Henry L. Hillman
Mrs. Josephine S. Houston
Philip and Susan Jones
Mr. and Mrs. Robert Y. Kopf, Jr.
Dr. and Mrs. Christopher Modic
Mr. and Mrs. Don Morrison

Mr. and Mrs. David A. Murdock
Mr. and Mrs. Hugh W. Nevin, Jr.
Mr. and Mrs. William R. Newlin
Dr. and Mrs. Robert S. Nitzberg
Constance H. Oliver
Laura Liggett Oliver
Lisa A. Pegden
Mr. and Mrs. Robert L. Popovich
Mr. and Mrs. C. J. Ramsburg
Mr. and Mrs. Philip S. Rossin
Dr. and Mrs. Anthony R. Scalercio
Mrs. A. Reed Schroeder
Mark O. and Judith B. Scioscia
Peggy Shoener
Mr. and Mrs. Robert W. Sittig
Mr. and Mrs. Thomas J. Smith
Mr. and Mrs. Peter M. Standish
Mr. and Mrs. Daniel J. Sullivan
Mr. and Mrs. Steven C. Thomas
Mrs. LeRoy Thompson
Carolyn Whyman
Pamela E. Wright

Diane and Christopher Abell
Mr. and Mrs. Walter R. Abell
Betsy Allyn
Arch Interiors
Mr. and Mrs. Kelso Baker
Kiles and Vern Baker
Lee W. Bass, M.D., Jerome H. Wolfson,
    M.D. and Jane M. Breck, M.D.
Mr. and Mrs. George Bayly
Mr. and Mrs. Frank Bennett
Judi A. Bishop
Mrs. Alexander Black
Ann Willets Boyd
Dick and Marilyn Brink
Dr. and Mrs. Timothy A. Brown
Mr. and Mrs. James Browne
Mr. and Mrs. James D. Buescher
Mr. and Mrs. Anthony Buzzelli
Dr. and Mrs. William Castle
Mr. and Mrs. Dennis Ciccone
Dr. and Mrs. Robert Cincala
Dr. and Mrs. Ira Cohen
Mr. and Mrs. William C. Coyle
Mr. and Mrs. George Davidson
Mr. and Mrs. Louis J. Dell Aquila
Mr. and Mrs. Mark De Simone
Dr. and Mrs. Stanley Denver
Mr. and Mrs. Henry F. Devens
Dr. and Mrs. Robert W. Doebler
Mr. and Mrs. John W. Eichleay, Jr.
Mr. and Mrs. Richard Elste
Mr. Daniel J. Evans
Mrs. Peter M. Feltwell, Jr.
Frances Fetterolf
Mrs. W. Michael Fitzgerald
Mr. and Mrs. Peter Friday
Mr. and Mrs. Robert L. Froman
Dr. and Mrs. S. Froman and Family
Dr. and Mrs. Robert Fusco
Dr. and Mrs. Robert Galey
Dr. and Mrs. Ralph Gaudio
Mr. and Mrs. Klaus Gensheimer
Mr. and Mrs. Gere E. Grimm
Mr. and Mrs. David Gordon
Mrs. J. Barr Haines
Mr. and Mrs. Dennis Hamill
Mrs. Jackie Hamilton
Mr. and Mrs. Peter J. Hannaway
Mr. John Hartnett
Mr. and Mrs. Thomas Hay
Dr. and Mrs. A. F. Hetherington
Mrs. K. Alan Himes
Mr. and Mrs. Sam W. Indingaro
Mr. and Mrs. John Isherwood
Mr. and Mrs. Charles H. Juliusburg
Dr. and Mrs. William G. Kaliden, Jr.
Mr. and Mrs. Charles Kelly

Mr. and Mrs. R. Craig Kirsch
Kidding Around - Specialty Toys
Mr. and Mrs. Edward J. Klein
Dr. and Mrs. Milton J. Klein
Mrs. Byron J. Korb
Mr. and Mrs. Charles T. Koval
Dr. and Mrs. Douglas M. Landwehr
Mr. Robert J. Lanza - Geyer Printing
Mr. and Mrs. Samuel Larson
Mr. and Mrs. John Lindquist
Mr. and Mrs. W. H. Logsdon
Mrs. Ronald E. Long
Edward Lutz - Cold Comp
Mr. and Mrs. J. Jerome Mansmann
Mr. and Mrs. John T. McKnight
Mr. and Mrs. John K. Means
Mr. and Mrs. Richard K. Means, Jr.
Ed and Becky Miller
Joy Palm Miller
Dr. and Mrs. Chris W. Modic
Mrs. James H. Morgens
Dr. and Mrs. John F. Moyer
Mr. and Mrs. Juergen Mross
Mr. and Mrs. Gary Murphy
Mary and Wayne Murphy
Mr. and Mrs. Ralbern Murray
Dr. and Mrs. Daniel J. Nadler
Linda M. Nave
Mr. Charles S. Nimick
Miss Eleanor H. Nimick
Mr. and Mrs. Francis B. Nimick, Jr.
Mr. and Mrs. Malcolm G. Nimick
Mrs. Frederick W. Okie, Jr.
Mrs. Henry Oliver, Jr.
Mrs. George P. O'Neil
Dr. and Mrs. Michael A. Orsini
Mr. and Mrs. Nathan W. Pearson
Mr. and Mrs. Gary Pell
Dr. and Mrs. John Paul Piccolo
Dr. and Mrs. James G. Pitcavage
Jebby Potter
Mr. and Mrs. Robert Purvis
Dr. and Mrs. David Rafalko
Mr. and Mrs. C. J. Ramsburg
Mr. and Mrs. Rick Rawe
Mr. and Mrs. Charles H. Reed
Mr. and Mrs. Ben B. Richardson
Mr. and Mrs. John Robb, Jr.
Mr. and Mrs. Albert C. Roemhild
Mr. and Mrs. Bernard S. Rubb
Mr. and Mrs. Duane Russell
Mary Louise Scholl
Mr. and Mrs. H. Donald Scott
Mrs. Harton S. Semple
Mr. and Mrs. Donald Seymour
Mrs. Edward Sherry

Ms. Christine Siegel
  -Associated Graphics
Revs. Marnie and John Silbert
Mr. Charles Smith
Dr. and Mrs. Gary Smith
Mr. and Mrs. Gregory Smith
Mr. and Mrs. Steven J. Smith
Mr. and Mrs. Edward Smyth
Mr. and Mrs. Robert H. Snow
Mrs. J. Brandon Snyder
Mr. and Mrs. Furman South, III
Mr. and Mrs. Douglas G. Sparks
Mr. and Mrs. Charles Spencer
Dr. and Mrs. John Straka
Dr. and Mrs. Robert Stiegel
Mr. and Mrs. Louis Tarasi, Jr.
Mr. and Mrs. David Thomas
Tris Anne Thorne

Dr. and Mrs. Stewart Urban
Mr. and Mrs. J. Robert VanKirk
Mr. and Mrs. John Vorberger
Mr. and Mrs. Hay Walker
Mr. and Mrs. Christopher Wallace
Mr. and Mrs. Donald Weil
Mrs. Jeffrey S. Wells
Mr. and Mrs. Daniel L. Wessels
Mr. and Mrs. Paul Whitehead
Mr. and Mrs. Daniel P. Wilhelm
Gwen Willard
Betsey Wilson
Drs. Bruce and Barbara Wilson
Mr. and Mrs. Joseph D. Wilson, III
Mr. and Mrs. John Wittekamp
Mr. and Mrs. Michael Zamagias
Mr. and Mrs. John G. Zimmerman, Jr.

HOSTS FOR FUNDRAISING DINNER

Mr. and Mrs. Hiram Ball
Mr. and Mrs. John Benz
Mr. and Mrs. Robert Berini
Mr. and Mrs. Thomas Brandt
Mr. and Mrs. Peter W. Casella
Dr. and Mrs. Robert Doebler
Mr. and Mrs. Holland Donaldson
Mr. and Mrs. Peter Friday
Mr. and Mrs. Paul Hammer
Mr. and Mrs. Philip L. Jones

Mr. and Mrs. Samuel Larson
Mr. and Mrs. Kennedy Linge
Mr. and Mrs. Hugh Nevin
Mr. and Mrs. Malcolm Nimick
Mr. and Mrs. William Paul
Mr. and Mrs. Larry Pryor
Mr. and Mrs. William Riley
Mr. and Mrs. George Scott
Mr. and Mrs. Allen Williamson

IN-KIND DONATIONS

Christopher Gronta - Atrium Flowers
Horne's Department Stores

Karen Smith Ombres - Grape Harvest
  Wine Services
USAir

Call 1-800-624-8753 for current prices, phone orders, rush orders, and quantity discounts.

allow 4-6 weeks for regular delivery

_____ copies of THREE RIVERS COOKBOOK, **Volume I** - Postpaid @$14.95 ea. _____
(Red Cover)

_____ copies of THREE RIVERS COOKBOOK, **Volume II** - Postpaid @$14.95 ea. _____
(Green Cover)

_____ copies of THREE RIVERS COOKBOOK, **Volume III** - Postpaid @$14.95 ea. _____
(Blue Cover)   Tax per book (PA residents only)   .91 ea. _____

Make Checks Payable to: THREE RIVERS COOKBOOKS 1108 Ohio River Blvd., Sewickley, PA 15143

Charge to VISA ☐ MasterCard ☐ Exp. Date _____   TOTAL ENCLOSED _____

CARD NO: _____ DAYTIME PHONE: _____

BILL AND SHIP TO: _____ SHIP TO (IF DIFFERENT): _____

ADDRESS: _____ ADDRESS: _____

CITY/STATE: _____ ZIP _____ CITY/STATE: _____ ZIP _____

- -

Call 1-800-624-8753 for current prices, phone orders, rush orders, and quantity discounts.

allow 4-6 weeks for regular delivery

_____ copies of THREE RIVERS COOKBOOK, **Volume I** - Postpaid @$14.95 ea. _____
(Red Cover)

_____ copies of THREE RIVERS COOKBOOK, **Volume II** - Postpaid @$14.95 ea. _____
(Green Cover)

_____ copies of THREE RIVERS COOKBOOK, **Volume III** - Postpaid @$14.95 ea. _____
(Blue Cover)   Tax per book (PA residents only)   .91 ea. _____

Make Checks Payable to: THREE RIVERS COOKBOOKS 1108 Ohio River Blvd., Sewickley, PA 15143

Charge to VISA ☐ MasterCard ☐ Exp. Date _____   TOTAL ENCLOSED _____

CARD NO: _____ DAYTIME PHONE: _____

BILL AND SHIP TO: _____ SHIP TO (IF DIFFERENT): _____

ADDRESS: _____ ADDRESS: _____

CITY/STATE: _____ ZIP _____ CITY/STATE: _____ ZIP _____

- -

Call 1-800-624-8753 for current prices, phone orders, rush orders, and quantity discounts.

allow 4-6 weeks for regular delivery

_____ copies of THREE RIVERS COOKBOOK, **Volume I** - Postpaid @$14.95 ea. _____
(Red Cover)

_____ copies of THREE RIVERS COOKBOOK, **Volume II** - Postpaid @$14.95 ea. _____
(Green Cover)

_____ copies of THREE RIVERS COOKBOOK, **Volume III** - Postpaid @$14.95 ea. _____
(Blue Cover)   Tax per book (PA residents only)   .91 ea. _____

Make Checks Payable to: THREE RIVERS COOKBOOKS 1108 Ohio River Blvd., Sewickley, PA 15143

Charge to VISA ☐ MasterCard ☐ Exp. Date _____   TOTAL ENCLOSED _____

CARD NO: _____ DAYTIME PHONE: _____

BILL AND SHIP TO: _____ SHIP TO (IF DIFFERENT): _____

ADDRESS: _____ ADDRESS: _____

CITY/STATE: _____ ZIP _____ CITY/STATE: _____ ZIP _____

Call 1-800-624-8753 for current prices, phone orders, rush orders, and quantity discounts.

allow 4-6 weeks for regular delivery

_____ copies of THREE RIVERS COOKBOOK, **Volume I** - Postpaid @$14.95 ea. _____
(Red Cover)

_____ copies of THREE RIVERS COOKBOOK, **Volume II** - Postpaid @$14.95 ea. _____
(Green Cover)

_____ copies of THREE RIVERS COOKBOOK, **Volume III** - Postpaid @$14.95 ea. _____
(Blue Cover)   Tax per book (PA residents only)   .91 ea. _____

Make Checks Payable to: THREE RIVERS COOKBOOKS 1108 Ohio River Blvd., Sewickley, PA 15143

Charge to VISA ☐ MasterCard ☐ Exp. Date _____   TOTAL ENCLOSED _____

CARD NO: _____   DAYTIME PHONE: _____

BILL AND SHIP TO: _____   SHIP TO (IF DIFFERENT): _____

ADDRESS: _____   ADDRESS: _____

CITY/STATE: _____ ZIP _____   CITY/STATE: _____ ZIP _____

- -

Call 1-800-624-8753 for current prices, phone orders, rush orders, and quantity discounts.

allow 4-6 weeks for regular delivery

_____ copies of THREE RIVERS COOKBOOK, **Volume I** - Postpaid @$14.95 ea. _____
(Red Cover)

_____ copies of THREE RIVERS COOKBOOK, **Volume II** - Postpaid @$14.95 ea. _____
(Green Cover)

_____ copies of THREE RIVERS COOKBOOK, **Volume III** - Postpaid @$14.95 ea. _____
(Blue Cover)   Tax per book (PA residents only)   .91 ea. _____

Make Checks Payable to: THREE RIVERS COOKBOOKS 1108 Ohio River Blvd., Sewickley, PA 15143

Charge to VISA ☐ MasterCard ☐ Exp. Date _____   TOTAL ENCLOSED _____

CARD NO: _____   DAYTIME PHONE: _____

BILL AND SHIP TO: _____   SHIP TO (IF DIFFERENT): _____

ADDRESS: _____   ADDRESS: _____

CITY/STATE: _____ ZIP _____   CITY/STATE: _____ ZIP _____

- -

Call 1-800-624-8753 for current prices, phone orders, rush orders, and quantity discounts.

allow 4-6 weeks for regular delivery

_____ copies of THREE RIVERS COOKBOOK, **Volume I** - Postpaid @$14.95 ea. _____
(Red Cover)

_____ copies of THREE RIVERS COOKBOOK, **Volume II** - Postpaid @$14.95 ea. _____
(Green Cover)

_____ copies of THREE RIVERS COOKBOOK, **Volume III** - Postpaid @$14.95 ea. _____
(Blue Cover)   Tax per book (PA residents only)   .91 ea. _____

Make Checks Payable to: THREE RIVERS COOKBOOKS 1108 Ohio River Blvd., Sewickley, PA 15143

Charge to VISA ☐ MasterCard ☐ Exp. Date _____   TOTAL ENCLOSED _____

CARD NO: _____   DAYTIME PHONE: _____

BILL AND SHIP TO: _____   SHIP TO (IF DIFFERENT): _____

ADDRESS: _____   ADDRESS: _____

CITY/STATE: _____ ZIP _____   CITY/STATE: _____ _____ ZIP _____